共建亚太安全家园

Make Concerted Efforts toward a Secure Homeland in Asia-Pacific

——首届万寿国际安全研讨会论文集

——Anthology of the First Wanshou Dialogue on Global Security

王亚军/主编
安月军　陶涛/执行主编

Wang Yajun: Chief Editor
An Yuejun, Tao Tao: Executive Editor

图书在版编目（CIP）数据

共建亚太安全家园：首届万寿国际安全研讨会论文集 / 王亚军主编 . -- 北京：当代世界出版社，2018.12
ISBN 978-7-5090-1299-4

Ⅰ . ①共… Ⅱ . ①王… Ⅲ . ①国家安全－世界－学术会议－文集 Ⅳ . ① D815.5-53

中国版本图书馆 CIP 数据核字 (2018) 第 270327 号

书　　名：共建亚太安全家园——首届万寿国际安全研讨会论文集
出版发行：当代世界出版社
地　　址：北京市复兴路4号（100860）
网　　址：http://www.worldpress.org.cn
编务电话：(010) 83907332
发行电话：(010) 83908409
(010) 83908455
(010) 83908377
(010) 83908423（邮购）
(010) 83908410（传真）
经　　销：新华书店
印　　刷：北京毅峰迅捷印刷有限公司
开　　本：710毫米×1000毫米　1/16
印　　张：14
字　　数：191千字
版　　次：2019年5月第1版
印　　次：2019年5月第1次
书　　号：ISBN 978-7-5090-1299-4
定　　价：88.00元

凝聚时代共识 共建亚太安全家园

——中共中央对外联络部部长宋涛主旨讲话

2018 年 6 月 21 日

尊敬的各位来宾，

女士们、先生们、朋友们：

大家上午好！非常高兴出席首届万寿国际安全研讨会，并愿借此机会就国际和亚太安全形势与大家交流。

当今世界正处于百年未有之大变局。世界多极化、经济全球化、社会信息化、文化多样化深入发展，全球治理体系和国际秩序变革加速推进，各国相互联系和依存日益加深，国际力量对比更趋平衡，和平发展大势不可逆转。与此同时，世界面临的不稳定性不确定性突出，人类面临许多共同挑战。对此，中共中央总书记习近平在十九大上明确提出，中国将坚持走和平发展道路，推动构建新型国际关系，推动构建人类命运共同体。构建新型国际关系，就是要在相互尊重、公平正义、合作共赢基础上开创国与国关系的新前景。构建人类命运共同体，就是每个民族、每个国家都坚持风雨同舟、荣辱与共，同心协力建设持久和平、普遍安全、共同繁荣、开放包容、清洁美丽的世界，把各国人民对美好生活的向往变成现实。

“两个构建”高瞻远瞩、内涵丰富，不仅成为中国外交的努力方向和目标，也提供了解决当今世界性难题的中国智慧和中国方案。目前，“两个构建”正在从理念转化为实实在在的行动。特别是“一带一路”倡议以人类命运共同体为旗帜，已经成为迄今最受欢迎的国际公共产品，成为世界各国实现共同发展的最大合作平台。只要我们顺应时代潮流、合力应对挑战、抓住变革机遇，人类将第一次真正实现全球大协作，前所未有地具备构建人类命运共同体的能力和环境。

首届万寿国际安全研讨会主题聚焦亚太安全，具有重要意义。亚太是世界经济最大的板块。亚太要实现发展和繁荣，离不开一个和平稳定的地区环境。亚太安全不仅攸关本地区各国人民的幸福安康，也关系到整个世界的和平、稳定和发展。

当前，亚太地区形势总体稳定，通过对话协商处理分歧和争端成为各国重要政策取向。亚太经济保持平稳增长，仍然是拉动全球经济复苏的"火车头"。但也要看到，老的安全问题没有解决，新的安全挑战又快速出现，给地区和平与发展增添了新的复杂因素。

面向未来，亚太国家要与时俱进，摒弃你赢我输、你兴我衰的旧思维，抛弃弱肉强食、损人利己的老做法，创新安全理念、拓展安全合作、打造安全机制，坚持以构建新型国际关系和构建人类命运共同体为引领，努力走出一条共建共享共赢的亚太安全之路。我愿就此谈几点看法与大家分享。

第一，坚持合作共赢、促进共同发展，夯实亚太安全的经济基础。安全是发展的前提，发展是安全的基础。亚太地区的很多安全问题，根源在发展，出路也在发展。实现共同发展是维护和平稳定的根本保障，是解决各类安全问题的"总钥匙"。亚太国家要聚焦发展主题、拓展合作空间、加强互联互通、深化利益融合，让各国和人民共享发展成果，通过可持续发展实现可持续安全。

中国将继续奉行互利共赢的开放战略，将自身发展机遇同世界各国分享，欢迎亚太各国搭乘中国发展的"快车"，做大合作的蛋糕，实现共同繁荣和安全。我们欢迎地区国家积极参与"一带一路"建设，对接发展战略、描绘发展蓝图、共享发展成果，推动"一带一路"成为亚太合作的新平台和增长极。

第二，坚持相互尊重、促进平等互信，筑牢亚太安全的政治基础。政治互信是安全互信的根本。经过多年实践，亚太国家形成了一些行之有效的合作模式和做法，如平等相待、尊重主权、协商一致、循序渐进、照顾各方舒适度等，这为各方深化政治互信、加强安全合作提供了重要前提。亚太国家要坚持这些好的经验和做法，率先走出一条“对话而不对抗、结伴而不结盟”的国与国交往新路，在此基础上开创地区安全新局。

中国坚持与邻为善、以邻为伴，秉持亲诚惠容周边外交理念，积极发展同周边国家的睦邻友好合作关系。这些年来，我们在周边的“朋友圈”越来越大，同周边国家的互信合作越来越深，为推进亚太安全合作增添了正能量。我们愿继续同地区国家和有关大国开展政治对话、加强战略沟通、增进相互理解，尊重相互核心利益和底线，正确认知彼此发展走向，进一步建立和积累政治互信。

第三，坚持文明互鉴、促进心灵相通，营造亚太安全的社会基础。亚太地区民族、宗教、文化多样，社会制度、发展道路、经济发展水平各异。差异不是冲突的根源，多样应成为进步的动力。亚太国家应更加自觉地反对文明对抗与冲突，倡导文明对话与互动，致力于超越社会制度和意识形态的差异和偏见，增进各国人民的相互理解和信任，将多样性和差异性转化为地区安全合作的动力和活力。

中国始终坚持以文明交流超越文明隔阂、文明互鉴超越文明冲突、文明共存超越文明优越，推动各国相互理解、相互尊重、相互信任。我们愿继续以开放的眼光、开阔的胸襟，积极开展同地区各国的人文对话、交流与合作，以人民之间的友谊为种子，结出各国共同发展、共享安全的果实。未来5年，中国共产党将向世界各国政党提供1.5万名人员来华交流的机会，我们期待亚太国家在其中占有重要份额。

第四，坚持对话协商、促进理念创新，凝聚亚太安全的更大共识。面对安全挑战日益复杂严峻的新现实，以不变应万变不行，穿新鞋走老路更不行。地区国家要坚持多管齐下、综合施策，妥善管控矛盾分歧，协调推进安全治理，既着力解决当前突出的地区安全问题，也统筹谋划应对各类潜在安全威胁，携手维护地区安全稳定大局。

中国始终是维护地区和平稳定的重要力量。在中国与东盟共同努力下，南海形势明显降温趋稳并呈现积极发展态势。中国积极推动朝鲜半岛有关方通过和平方式解决问题，为半岛问题重回对话谈判轨道发挥了重要作用。中国积极参与阿富汗、叙利亚、伊朗核等问题的解决进程，同各国合力应对恐怖主义、海洋安全等挑战，为维护亚太安全作出了积极贡献。面向未来，中国将继续大力践行共同、综合、合作、可持续的新安全观，为推动地区和平稳定发挥积极的建设性作用。

第五，坚持共商共建、促进安全合作，探索亚太安全的有效架构。亚太国家应坚持平等参与、开放包容、循序渐进的原则，逐步积累互信、扩大共识、拓展合作，朝着构建亚太一体化安全架构的大方向不懈努力。

中国是地区多边安全机制的倡导者和推动者，坚定支持东盟在东亚区域合作中的中心地位，大力推动上海合作组织、亚信会议等相关机制发展。中国是现有地区安全架构的支持者和维护者，中国不会对这些机制推倒重来、另起炉灶，而是本着共建共享共赢原则对现有机制进行补充和完善。我们愿同各方一道，携手推动地区安全机制实现更大发展，促进亚太共同安全和普遍安全。

女士们，先生们，朋友们：

亚太发展需要我们共同促进，亚太安全需要我们共同维护。中国将一如既往做亚太和平的建设者、亚太发展的贡献者、亚太安全的维护者，愿同亚太各国一道共商共建亚太安全家园，共创共享亚太繁荣安宁的明天！

谢谢大家。

目录
CONTENTS

凝聚时代共识　共建亚太安全家园 …………………………………… 1

——中共中央对外联络部部长宋涛主旨讲话

第一篇 中美关系与亚太安全 ………………………………………… 1

中美安全战略博弈 …………………………………………………… 3

中国人民争取和平与裁军协会常务理事
中国人民大学国际关系学院副院长、教授
金灿荣

中美大国竞争是否进入"新冷战"？ ……………………………… 20

日本中曾根康弘世界和平研究所高级研究员
大泽淳

中美关系的重大变化及对亚太安全的影响 ……………………… 24

中国人民争取和平与裁军协会常务理事
国防大学国家安全学院教授
孟祥青

亚太地区形势演变中的中美关系发展动态 …………………… 29

越南外交学院战略研究所高级研究员

丁氏贤良

中美战略认知与东亚地区安全 ………………………………… 33

中国人民争取和平与裁军协会常务理事

中国社会科学院台湾研究所所长、研究员

杨明杰

中美南海冲突的未来轮廓：地区冲突向全球冲突过渡 ………… 36

俄罗斯科学院东方学研究所东南亚研究中心主任

德米特里·莫夏科夫

印度视角下的中美关系 ……………………………………… 38

印度辨喜基金会副研究员

特舒·辛格

中美关系恶化的结构性原因 ………………………………… 40

中国人民争取和平与裁军协会常务理事

中国现代国际关系研究院院长、研究员

袁鹏

● **第二篇 东北亚安全形势及前景** ………………………… 43

特朗普对朝政策的变化与选择 ……………………………… 45

中国人民争取和平与裁军协会常务理事

中国国际问题研究院美国研究所所长、研究员

滕建群

朝鲜迈入后核武时代的战略影响 …………………………………… 50

菲律宾外交关系委员会研究员

亚伦·雷宾纳

东北亚需要谋求可持续安全 …………………………………………… 52

——基于朝美领导人首次会晤后的思考

中国人民争取和平与裁军协会常务理事

清华大学国际关系研究院教授

刘江永

建立朝鲜半岛和平机制面临的问题与挑战 ……………………… 60

韩国世宗研究所研究企划本部长、韩国核政策研究会会长

李相铉

东北亚地区安全治理：重大机遇及其把握 ……………………… 63

国际关系学院校长、教授

陶坚

东北亚需建立地区安全机制 ………………………………………… 68

瑞典斯德哥尔摩国际和平研究所研究员

蒂蒂·埃拉斯托

蒙古视角下的东北亚安全合作 ……………………………………… 71

蒙古地缘政治研究所教授

噶尔山加姆茨·瑟利特

● **第三篇 亚太安全机制建设** …………………………… 75

构建亚太地区全面合作安全伙伴关系 …………………………… 77

巴基斯坦伊斯兰堡战略研究所研究员

马利克·穆斯塔法

亚太秩序重构中的日本与中国 …………………………… 79

日本庆应义塾大学教授

细谷雄一

南亚和印度洋对亚太安全的影响：机遇与挑战 ………………… 83

英国伦敦国际战略研究所南亚及核安全问题研究员

安托万·莱维斯克

“无冲突”应成为印太战略的底线 …………………………… 85

印度和平与冲突研究所所长、退役中将

阿尔文德·辛格·兰巴

后 记 …………………………………………………………… 87

Contents

Build Consensus and Make Concerted Efforts toward a Secure Homeland in Asia-Pacific 91

Keynote Address by Mr. Song Tao
Minister of the International Department of the
Central Committee of the Communist Party of China

Session I: China-U.S. Relations and Asia-Pacific Security Situation 97

China-U.S. Security Strategic Game: Common Evolution or Doomed to War 98

Jin Canrong, Council Member, CPAPD
Vice Dean of the School of International Relations, Professor, Renmin University of China

U.S.-China Great Power Rivalry: Turning Back to a Future Cold War Situation? 120

Jun OSAWA Senior Research Fellow, Nakasone Yasuhiro Peace Institute (NPI), Japan

Major Changes of China-U.S. Relations and their Impacts on the Asia-Pacific Security 124

Meng Xiangqing, Council member, CPAPD
Professor, Institute of Strategic Studies, PLA National Defense University

Sino-US Developments amidst the Evolving Strategic Dynamics of an Extended Asia-Pacific (Indo-Pacific) 130

Julia Luong Dinh, Senior Research Fellow,
Institute for Foreign Policy and Strategic Studies, Diplomatic Academy of Vietnam.

Sino-US Strategic Cognition and East Asian Regional Security 136
Yang Mingjie, Council Member, CPAPD
Director of Institute of Taiwan Studies, Research Fellow, CASS

Contours of the Future in the Conflict between the US and China in the South China Sea: the Transition of the Regional Conflict to the Global Conflict 140
Dmitrii Mosyakov
Head of the Centre for Southeast Asia, Australia and Oceania
Institute of Oriental Studies at RAS, Russia

Locked in a Spiral? Sino-US Relations in the Asia-Pacific Region: An Indian Perspective 143
Dr.Teshu Singh
Associate Fellow, Vivekananda International Foundation, India

The Structural Factors for the Deteriorating China-U.S. Relations 146
Yuan Peng, Council Member, CPAPD
President of China Institute of Contemporary International Relations, Research Fellow

Session II: Security Situation in Northeast Asia and Its Prospect 151

The Changes and Options of Trump's Policy toward the DPRK 152
Teng Jianqun, Council Member, CPAPD
Director of Institute of American Studies, China Institute of International Studies. Research Fellow

Strategic Implications of a Post-Nuclear North Korea 158
Aaron Jed Rabena, Senior Consultant, Warwick & Roger
Program Convenor, Asia-Pacific Pathways to Progress,
Associate Fellow, Philippine Council for Foreign Relations

Northeast Asia Needs Pursuit of Sustainable Security: Thinking Based on the First DPRK-U.S. Summit 161
Liu Jiangyong, Council Member, CPAPD
Professor, Department of International Relations, Tsinghua University

The Security Situation in Northeast Asia and its Prospect 171
Sang Hyun Lee, Senior Research Fellow, the Sejong Institute, KOREA

Regional Security Governance in Northeast Asia: Major Opportunities and their Command 174
Tao Jian, President of University of International Relations, Professor

The Need for a Regional Security Regime in Northeast Asia 180
Dr. Tytti Erästö, Stockholm International Peace Research Institute, Sweden

Security Cooperation in North East Asia: Mongolian Perspective 184
Galsanjamts Sereeter, Professor, the Mongolian Institute for Geopolitical Studies

Session III: Security Mechanism Building in the Asia Pacific Region 189

Building a Comprehensive Cooperative Security Partnership in Asia Pacific Region 190
Malik Qasim Mustafa
Senior Research Fellow, Institute of Strategic Studies, Islamabad.

Two Initiatives and One Regional Order: The Integration of Japan's FOIP and China's BRI 195
Yuichi Hosoya, Professor of International Politics, Keio University, Japan

South Asia & the Indian Ocean's Contribution to Asia-Pacific Security: Opportunities and Challenges 200
Antoine Levesques, Research Fellow for South Asia
The International Institute for Strategic Studies (IISS)

No Conflict: the Bottom Line of the Indo-Pacific Strategy.................. 203
Lamba Arvinder, President, Institute of Peace and Conflict Studies,
Retired Lieutenant General, India

Epilogue 205

Session III: Security Mechanism Building in the Asia-Pacific Region

第一篇

中美关系与亚太安全

中美安全战略博弈

中国人民争取和平与裁军协会常务理事
中国人民大学国际关系学院副院长、教授
金灿荣

2016年11月，美国共和党总统候选人唐纳德·特朗普击败民主党候选人希拉里·克林顿，出乎意料赢得大选。考虑到特朗普竞选期间在对华政策上的强硬立场，一些人认为未来几年中美关系将充满变数。但看待中美关系，不仅要看到领导人执政理念和风格对两国关系的影响，还要看到两国关系正常化以来中美关系的总体特征，更要看到国际发展的潮流趋势。作为世界上最重要的一对双边关系，中美两国未来将保持竞争与合作并存的态势，这不是任何一个领导人所能改变的。中美关系只能顺势而为，走共同演进、合作共赢之路。

一、中美关系的总体特征

（一）中美关系在当今中国外交中具有特殊重要地位

1. 从国家层面上讲，中美关系是中国外交最大的议题

回顾中美关系的发展历史，我们会发现，中美两国是一对不对称的关系，中国对美国对外政策的影响十分有限，而美国是近代以来对中国影响最大的国家。在一定程度上，中国近现代史与中美关系史的发展轨迹是几近平行的。这使得美国因素对中国的国内外决策产生重要影响。就国内而言，维护和扩展国家利益是中国对外政策和外交工作的重要准则，中国尤为关注美国因素对中国政府维护政权的合法性和国内秩序的影响，而美国因素对中国外交的

影响几乎无处不在。在一些情况下，中美关系处理得好，中国就有安全感，就放松、宽容，一旦宽容，政策自由度就比较大。反之，中美关系处理不好，中国的国内国际政策就比较紧。就国外而言，美国因素是中国外交布局上的重要考量。大国外交、周边外交、发展中国家外交和多边外交共同构成了中国外交的四根支柱。大国是关键，周边是首要，发展中国家是基础，多边是重要舞台。还有一句话，叫“中美关系是整个中国外交的重中之重”。这是因为中美关系的好坏在很大程度上取决于美国，中国发展中美关系的诚意不容置疑，而美国掌握中美关系更多的主动权，美国对中国的外交关系施加更大的影响，具体表现在：大国关系的关键是中美关系；中国周边外交中，美国常以弱小国家庇护者或平衡者身份对中国形成掣肘，美国的态度和行为影响中国周边国家的对华政策；中美在非洲、南美等发展中国家的博弈影响到中国在当地的经济利益和软实力；当前国际组织主要的活跃对象也是美国。

2. 从体系层面上讲，美国是中国外交最大的外部因素

国际政治格局对大国关系产生深刻影响。冷战结束后，美国一超独大的国际格局凸显。但进入 21 世纪以来，世界多极化加速发展，从综合实力结构的角度看，世界正迈向两超多强，形成了包括中国、美国、欧洲、日本、俄罗斯、印度等国家和地区的以经济实力为特征的权力格局。从经济总量来看，中美经济领跑全球，中美两国与欧、日、俄、印等国家地区的经济差距日益增大。从发展前景来看，尽管中国面临产能过剩、有效供给不足、区域发展不平衡、经济下行压力加大等挑战，但总体来说，中国经济仍然保持健康稳定发展。

与之相比，日本虽然从经济实力上来讲仍然是多强中的一强，但体量更大的中国很容易发挥后发优势超越日本。从根本上说，日本与英、德等国都属于保罗·肯尼迪所说的“中等强国”，无法与中美相提并论。2009 年日本畅销书《做十分之一的国家》告诫日本人：过去 5000 年大部分时间中国都是东亚的中心，这是常态，过去 100 年日本成为东亚的中心是非正常现象。其原因在于，日本充分学习借鉴了西方的工业文明，不仅成为亚洲第一，而且是全世界非西方第一。日本因此拥有了工业国对农业国的优势，成为了东亚的地缘政治中心。而中国有一段时间拒绝学习工业化，特别是晚清 70 年。该书作者提醒日本人：日本所获得的优势，本质上讲是知识的优势，因为日本学习态度好，所以它知识掌握得好，但知识优势是一种脆弱的优势，通过学习完全可以弥补。日本能保持知识优势的前提是中国人曾经拒绝学习。自邓小平提出改革开放的政策以来，中国正在技术上追赶日本，超越日本只是时间问题。一旦中国的技术和日本拉平，中日之间的力量将由规模决定。最终日本的地位会回到常态，那就是日本的 GDP 是中国的 1/10。作者告诫日本做好准备，那一天会来，到时日本将是中国的 1/10。

欧洲国家近些年来同样面临多重挑战：一是欧洲一体化带来负面效应，欧洲缺乏竞争优势的劳动者在外部竞争加强的压力下面临困境；二是金融危机和债务危机恶化了经济形势；三是来自北非和东南欧的“难民潮”激化了社会矛盾。未来欧洲发展的首要任务是聚焦社会治理，中欧关系将面临深化合作和构建全新双边关系的机遇，中国可以通过投资和金融合作“锁定”中欧战略关系、增强中欧之间要素流动的广度和深度，为建立亚欧大市场奠定坚实基础。

俄罗斯的问题则在于，国内市场经济发展不完善，经济结构不合理，经济增长过度依赖能源，是一个“单一作物经济体”。从社会结构来讲，俄罗斯面临的最大问题是人口出生率过低，2016 年人口增长率是 –0.06%。目前中俄建立了全面战略协作伙伴关系,中俄经济的互补性有利于提高双方的务实合作，发展稳定的双边关系。

从以上情况可以看出，当前国际政治格局中的主要强国或面临国内危机自顾不暇，或发展前景与潜力与中国不可同日而语，从长期来看，中国将在未来的安全战略博弈中具有更大优势。而中美关系则与此不同。作为世界上最大的两个经济体，中美两国的综合实力差距正在逐年缩小。据世界银行测算，2015 年美国 GDP 总量为 17.9 万亿美元，中国则达到 10.8 万亿美元，中国的经济增长不仅在量上增长迅速，质上也有了很大提高。世界知识产权组织发布报告称 2015 年中国专利申请总数首次在单一年度内超过 100 万件，这一数量几乎是排名第二、三、四位的美国、日本、韩国的总和。随着两国实力水平的接近，互相冲突的利益增加，两国间的竞争程度也将进一步深化。在进攻性现实主义者看来，大国权势的增长必然导致国际权力再分配的事实，作为后发国家的新兴大国为在国际体系内争夺于己有利的发展空间，将会试图挑战现存国际体系，从而引发新兴大国与守成大国的冲突与战争。因而，作为新兴大国的中国如何实现与守成大国的和平相处成为中国外交的最大考量因素。

总之，中美关系是 21 世纪国际关系的决定性因素，中美两国将主导未来几十年的国际体系，但如何定位中美关系则是 21 世纪国际关系的最大难题。中美和则两利，斗则两伤。如果中美两国陷入地缘斗争、军备竞赛或零和对抗，那么全球体系的和平与稳定将岌岌可危。中美若能求同存异，并在经济、政治和安全合作领域找到更广泛的共同语言，那么亚洲乃至全球和平与稳定的前景都将得到增强。

（二）中美关系竞争又合作，重要且复杂，风险挑战多元，影响因素多种多样

1. 中美两国是一对竞争又合作的关系

中美关系不同于过去美国与其他强国关系。冷战时期，美苏两国以竞争为主，除了在军控方面保持脆弱的平衡之外，合作很少；现在的日美两国尽管在贸易、防务等领域存在分歧与矛盾，但两国之间是牢固的盟友关系，双方仍以合作为主。中美关系介于两者之间，既竞争又合作，美国学者沈大伟将其称为“竞合关系”，但最近合作与竞争的平衡正在从前者向后者倾斜。

鉴于中美关系有很大的反复性，同时又有很强的韧性，所以以前我们经常说“中美关系好不到哪里去，也坏不到哪里去”。但现在有学者提出，从现在到中国超过美国成为世界第一大经济体的几年间，中美间会存在一个相互适应期，中美关系要么好起来，要么坏下去；要么深入开展合作，要么走向战略竞争。中美之间存在冲突性因素，甚至有学者将中美这种既非冷战也非“热战”的关系称为“凉战”。

2. 中美关系是一对重要且复杂的双边关系

就其重要性而言，中美关系决定整个 21 世纪人类的命运，是中国外交的重中之重，所谓牵一发而动全身，不可不谨慎。就其复杂性而言，一方面，中美之间经济上高度相互依存，2015 年中国对美国进出口总额超过加拿大，成为美国最大的贸易伙伴国。但另一方面，中美两国在军事上、战略上互相视对

方为竞争对手，在人类近代史上很少有这么复杂的关系。

从结构性特征来看，中美两国目前似已陷入了“修昔底德陷阱”，两国的战略利益具有对抗性和冲突性。所谓“修昔底德陷阱”，是指一个新兴大国必然挑战守成大国，守成大国必然应对新兴大国的挑战，从而使得战争不可避免。冷战结束以后，美国成为世界上唯一的超级大国，拥有无可挑战的霸主地位，属于守成大国。而中国在改革开放和“入世”推动下，国内经济迅速发展，国际影响力不断提高，GDP 总量 2010 年超过日本，成为世界第二大经济体，属于异军突起的新兴国家。中美这种新兴国家和守成国家的关系决定了双方的战略利益在很大程度上是冲突性的。除了地缘政治与经济冲突，中美两国还存在政治制度与意识形态冲突，中国是世界上最大的社会主义国家，美国是世界上最大的资本主义国家；从文明形态上讲，美国是西方基督教文明，中国是儒家文明，两国在文明方面存在冲突的因素。与历史上的“修昔底德陷阱”相比，中美两国间的“修昔底德陷阱”更加复杂。

（三）中美一面结构对抗，一面利益捆绑

中美之间的结构对抗来自中美两国实力变化所带来的客观结果，结构性矛盾具体表现在四个方面：新兴大国与守成大国之间的矛盾、地缘政治矛盾、政治制度和意识形态矛盾以及台湾问题。与此同时，中美之间存在共同利益和全球利益，经济上相互依存，社会上相互联系，国际上面临共同威胁。中美两国开展了很多合作，取得了很有意义的成果，例如，共同打击恐怖主义、预防世界经济问题、维护全球金融秩序稳定、防止埃博拉病毒扩散、应对全球气候变化等。《赫芬顿邮报》曾将中美这种复杂关系比作 19 世纪时期的“权宜婚姻”：双方基于共同的利益而有必要结合在一起，即便互不喜欢，也不得不维持双方关系。

（四）中美关系受很多第三方因素干扰

回顾中美关系的发展历程，不难看出，中美关系在结构上是一种“外力推动型”关系，两国关系的起伏经常取决于有什么样的“第三者”存在，双边关系一直在这种变化中相互调适。从抗战时期到冷战时期，再到冷战结束后，两国都因为第三方因素进行了不同程度的合作。第三方因素可以成为两国建立密切关系的"粘合剂"，也会对双边关系产生干扰。朝鲜战争的爆发使得中美两国陷入近二十年的敌对，而近年来中美之间的战略博弈，很大程度上受到日本、菲律宾、越南、朝鲜、伊朗、缅甸等国的影响，中美两国与这些国家的关系经常引发双方的互相猜疑，有时甚至产生摩擦。可见，中美关系如何发展，有时候并不完全取决于中美自身。

近年来影响中美关系的新变量是伴随中国和平崛起，美国对中国未来发展意图愈发担忧。当前，美国国内掀起一场自 1989 年以来规模最大、程度最激烈的对华政策辩论。一些美国学者与政府官员认为，过去美国一厢情愿地认为中国经济发展会带动城市化，而城市化会带来中产阶级队伍的壮大，壮大的中产阶级会要求相应的政治权利，到那时中国就会从一党执政变成美国式民主社会。换言之，经济和社会发展会水到渠成地促成中国的政治自由化，使得中国变成一个没有区域或全球霸权野心的西方式民主和平国家，这也是一直以来美国欢迎中国成为一个"繁荣、和平、稳定"的国家的前提。但现在越来越多的美国精英认为，中国的崛起为美国带来了一个强大的竞争者和美国主导的国际体系的破坏者，中国日渐成为一个"通过削弱美国安全保障的可信度、破坏美国的联盟、最终把美国逐步赶出亚洲，并将自身打造成在亚洲占主导地位的大国"，美国过去几十年奉行的对话接触政策基本失败，未来美国需要大幅改变或调整对华政策。甚至有一些极端的观点主张美国应明确抛弃对华接触，在各个领域反击或制衡中国。在有关对华政策辩论中，美国对华遏制和敌对的思维有所上升。

二、中美关系面临巨大发展机遇

进入 21 世纪第二个十年，中国的快速崛起给中美两国同时带来了挑战，美国显然还没有做好准备应对中国实力不断增强的影响，而中国也面临如何向世界说明自身的强大不会使美国受到威胁，两国间战略信任下降，双边关系面临多重挑战，除了两国关于贸易、西藏、台湾、人权等领域老生常谈的"老"问题，双方还在亚太地区领导权、中国军事现代化、新疆域、海洋问题、中国发展模式等领域出现新的摩擦。尽管中美两国之间依旧问题重重，但两国自身的内在特性和在双边交往过程中积累的历史遗产，为双方把控分歧、避免冲突提供了重要条件，中美之间还是能够建立一种有别于以“对抗和冲突”为主要特征的传统大国关系模式的新型关系。

（一）第一类机遇：老游戏新选手

第一，中美两国都是具有洲际规模的超大型国家，这意味着双方都不可能压倒性地征服对方。美国学者米尔斯海默在《大国政治的悲剧》中指出，国际政治是大国政治，权力分配决定了大国政治模式，“一国要具备大国资格，它必须拥有在一场全面的常规战争中同世界上最强大的国家进行一次正规战斗的军事实力。”就规模而言，两国无论人口面积、领土数量、自然资源、生产能力、经济规模、军事实力等硬实力因素，还是文化、艺术、社会吸引力等软实力因素都在国际社会中首屈一指，相比历史上美国的主要竞争对手英国、德国、日本，中国和美国都是“全能型冠军”，谁也不能确保摧毁对方，这构成了双方竞争与合作的基础。尤其是近代以来，伴随着国际政治的进化，国家的数量逐渐减少，国家的平均规模普遍上升，征服变得愈加困难，“共同生存”成为当今世界大国政治的主要特征，对大国来说尤其如此。中美两国政府与精英都认识到，两个超大型国家爆发大规模冲突或战争对于世界来说是一场灾难，因此，即便双方出现摩擦或矛盾，双方都会尽量保持克制，避免冲突升级。

第二，不同于历史上的民族国家，中美双方都是文明型国家，更具有包容性特征。与历史上由单一民族构成的德国、日本相比，中国是一个建立在儒家文明基础上的多民族国家，数千年来拥有多民族和平相处的悠久历史与丰富经验，中华文明海纳百川，讲求包容性；美国则是一个建立在基督新教文明基础上的由多种族组成的多元文化国家。中美双方都是在文化交流与融合过程中发展壮大起来的，都对自己的文化充满自信，两国都不具备狭隘的民族利己主义和大国沙文主义，也缺乏亨廷顿所说的爆发“文明的冲突”的客观条件和主观动机。尽管不排除中美两国在特定阶段出现一定程度的民族主义情绪，但这与极端民族主义有着天壤之别。

第三，中美两国都是世俗国家，尽管两国政治制度、意识形态大为不同，但都讲求实用主义、物质主义和个人主义。19 世纪法国贵族托克维尔在《美国的民主》一书中就观察到美国人不关心理论而偏重实践、普遍爱好物质福利、坚定捍卫个人自由和民主权利的文化特性，正是这些特性成就了美国的强大与繁荣，并成就了美国人引以为傲的国家自豪感和优越感。同样，中国信奉的凡事可通融可变通的处事哲学就是一种实用主义观，中国人更加重视现世生活而非将希望寄托来世，这种物质主义观使得人们对世俗生活更加积极。传统上认为中国崇尚集体主义精神，但自明朝晚期以来，个人主义思想逐渐传播，李贽“人必有私”论开启了中国个人主义“思想启蒙运动”的先河。因此，中美两国虽然宗教伦理不同，但内在特性却极为相似，那就是强调艰苦劳动、积极奋斗、不断追求财富，并由此衍生出时间信誉观念、效率节俭观念、平等竞争观念、诚实谨慎观念以及计划收支观念等。

第四，中美两国都讲求软实力，重视文化认同，强调完善自身、增强吸引力和影响力。美国自诩为“山巅之城”，强调自身的道德制高点。中国则崇尚儒家的“以德服人”和道家的“无为而治”，依靠以身作则和循循善诱来影响世界，在遇到挑衅时能够保持克制，始终将发展和国内建设放在首位，这与霸权国家喜欢四处秀肌肉、依赖强制与恐吓对待弱小国家、遇到冲突时往往反应过度的行为截然不同。值得一提的是，中国在战术上保持有所作为的同时，还坚持在战略上保持克制。在应对美国挑衅时，除了被中国视作核心利益的台湾、海洋领土以及可能影响到中国政治制度合法性的问题，中国在应对国际安全挑战、全球治理等问题上总体上还是一种刺激—回应式反应，尽量避免刺激美国。

总之，这是第一类机遇，美国将中国视为现实社会的权力竞争者，却没有像过去的英国、日本和德国那样陷入冲突或战争，双方的游戏手法不一样，两国的竞争与过去的列强争霸迥然不同。

（二）第二类机遇：老游戏新背景

第一个新背景是核时代条件下“核恐怖平衡”。自人类进入核武器时代以来，核武器所具有的巨大杀伤力和破坏力，将人类战争的残酷性和毁灭性推向极致。人类对有核国家“确保相互摧毁”能力的恐惧对于制约有核国家爆发战争起到重要作用。冷战时期，美苏两国正是出于对对方核能力的恐惧而在处理双方矛盾和冲突时表现得格外谨慎。同样，中美都是核大国，虽然在核威慑方面是一对非对称关系，但双方都拥有足以彻底摧毁对方的核武库，同时两国都是理性的负责任的行为体，任何一方都不会利用核武器来打破平衡或双方的“战略稳定”。

第二个背景是自冷战结束以来，全球化在广度和深度上均达到前所未有的程度，并对国际体系产生了深远影响。首先，全球化时代，各国经济活动超越国界在全球范围内形成错综复杂的网络关系，全球化增强了中美两国的相互依存程度，各种利益交织，出现你中有我、我中有你的局面，双方形成一种天然的约束关系，任何针对对方的遏制或者孤立政策都会危害自己的利益。其次，伴随经济全球化而来的是治理问题的全球化，单一国家无力独自面对气候、资源、恐怖主义、疾病控制等全球挑战，必须携手合作。

第三个背景是两国民间社会正发挥日渐增长的影响力。中美两国都拥有强大的民间社会，随着信息化和全球化的推进，普通民众政治参与意识和发言权逐步增强，对政府决策过程的影响越来越大。两国民众都关注政府对于权利、义务、利益的分配。对战争的厌恶和对个人利益的关注是民间社会的普遍特征。在美国，大量的社团和积极的社区活动对美国政治实践产生重要影响，美国民众对小布什期间发动的伊拉克战争和阿富汗战争行为的不满和反战情绪使得奥巴马政府改变进攻性政策并减少对外直接军事干预。中国近几十年来城市化迅猛发展，民间社会发展迅速，媒体、意见领袖甚至普通民众对政策的影响日增。社会公众天然地要求个人自由、幸福生活以及和平稳定的发展环境，尤其是中国的独生子女政策使得民众更加反对伤亡与战争。

第四个背景是联合国和国际法的刚性化对大国冲突起到重要的约束作用。首先，二战结束以来，国际社会的制度化进程加快，国家行为日益受到联合国等国际组织和国际法的约束，越来越多的国际组织和法律法规对国家的行为具有强制性特征，国家出于对违规成本、国际信誉等的顾虑，经常会自愿加入某些具有强制性或约束力的国际组织。其次，在以和平发展为主题的时代，世界各国都倾向于用公开、公平、公正和更具权威的方法解决国际争端，国际组织和国际法的存在为此提供了有益的平台。对于中美两国间的某些矛盾、摩擦，各种国际法和国际仲裁机构为双方的仲裁或谈判提供了解决机制与途径。例如，世贸组织的争端解决机制为两国的贸易反倾销诉讼、知识产权纠纷等提供了重要平台。

第五个背景是国际政治“无政府文化”的进化有利于两国间的和平发展。在美国学者亚历山大·温特看来，无政府状态下有霍布斯式、洛克式、康德式三种不同的无政府文化，与之相对应的是体系中大国间的相互关系分别为“敌人”、“竞争对手”和朋友。从国际关系发展史来看，美国自一战开始后介入国际事务，倡导去殖民地化和法治，说服各国通过和平方式抢占世界市场份额，通过技术创新扩大市场，实现繁荣，这无疑对于国际政治从霍布斯式无政府文化逐步转变为洛克式无政府文化起到了重要的推动作用。二战结束时，美国的国内生产总值（GDP）占世界 GDP 总量的一半，但它依然建立起开放的经济秩序，让其他国家得以繁荣发展并参与竞争。战后，美国主导与推动了欧洲复兴和繁荣，同时在全球范围内推动了一系列有利于维持和平与发展的国际组织和国际制度。正是在洛克式无政府文化下，世界各国越来越将重心转移到经济发展和社会进步上而非领土争夺上，总体和平的国际环境为全球经济繁荣创造了前提条件。这一过程中的典型案例是日本在明治维新后的两次崛起。第一次是二战之前，日本学习西方列强抢占周边地盘，侵略中国、朝鲜等国，掠夺台湾，还伺机征服亚洲大陆建立“大东亚共荣圈”，但最终在二战中被打败。日本的第二次崛起则发生在洛克式无政府文化下，通过市场经济和法治力量，日本不断扩大在亚洲和全球的市场份额，实现了从“士兵”到“优秀工程师”的转变。因此，美国倡导建立的国际社会总体来说是和平、开放和公平的，同样，中国的改革开放实质上也受益于洛克式无政府文化下的这一和平的国际环境。毋庸置疑的是，中国的未来发展也必然以支持并维护这一环境为目的的，中国没有理由去破坏或改变这一环境。

（三）第三类机遇：中美关系中的历史遗产

自1972年尼克松访华到现在，中美两国共同经历了冷战的结束和双边关系的突破，并逐渐发展成为世界上最重要且最具复合性的一对双边关系，40多年来，中美两国关系为双方进一步开展合作提供了五个历史遗产。

第一，中美两国经济上相互依存。据美国商务部统计，中国是美国的第一大商品进口国和第三大商品出口国，2015年，美国与中国双边货物进出口额为5980.7亿美元，中国对美出口额度占美国进口总额的21.5%，2007年到2015年，美国的对华直接投资（FDI）年均增长12.2%，2015年达到1117亿美元。中国对美直接投资虽然数量上低于美国对华直接投资，但是近些年增长迅速。2015年中国对美FDI从2014年的119亿美元增加到150亿美元，增幅达25.8%。美国也是中国第一大贸易伙伴，截至2016年9月，中国持有美国1.15万亿美元国债，是美国国债最大持有者。甚至有人将中美两国间的资金相互依赖现象称作“金融恐怖平衡”。在某种程度上，经济上的相互依赖已经使中美两国发展成一对“命运共同体”。因此，美国总统特朗普将中国列为“贸易操纵国”，并大幅提高关税，对中国进行惩罚，不但会使美国国内物价大幅提高，民众生活恶化，而且在中国的美国跨国公司也无法找到能够取代中国的生产基地，美国经济也将会面临更多的不确定性。这说明，双边密切的经济交往已成为中美关系的“压舱石”。尽管学术界也有人质疑贸易并不必然带来和平，甚至可能会成为冲突的根源，但相互依赖至少使得双方在战争中都要付出巨大代价，从而缓解了任何一方制造冲突的冲动，成为促进和平的主要力量。

第二，中国和美国存在广泛的社会和人际联系。“国之交在于民相亲”，文化与人员交流可以缓解国家间的紧张关系并促进互信。目前在美国的华人华侨大概有600多万，与在美的犹太人数量相当，是中美之间特殊的粘合剂。中美两国间大量的次国家行为体还结成200多对姐妹省（州）和姐妹城市关系，这在一般国家是少见的，中美直接接触非常深入。中美两国人员往来密切，2015年达到475万人次，2016年突破500万人次。双方在对方国家的留学生总数也已经突破50万人。中美两国还互相举办中（美）国年、旅游年等活动。在一定程度上，人员往来与交流已经独立于两国间政治经济关系，并成为制约政治经济摩擦的“稳压器”。中美人文交流已经与政治互信、经贸合作共同构成了中美新型大国关系的三大支柱，这为两国关系的长期可持续发展提供了重要的民心保障。

第三，在全球治理问题上，中美两国共同应对了很多挑战，形成了良好的合作机制。近些年来，中美两国在全球范围内开展合作的范围、领域进一步扩大。除了在反恐问题上开展合作之外，中美两国在伊朗核问题谈判、朝鲜半岛无核化问题等国际合作中取得成效。2014 年，中美两国签署《中美气候变化联合声明》，这一声明打破了几十年来各国为应对气候变化努力达成有效的全球协议上所面临的僵局，两国还主导起草了气候变化《巴黎协定》，为应对气候变化作出重要贡献。总体来说，中美双方在参与全球治理过程中“积累了一定的共识、深厚的合作基础以及彼此打交道的丰富经验”，这意味着中美“确立一个更加稳定、可靠的良性互动架构，开创一种新型大国关系模式，是可能的和可行的”。

第四，邓小平做出的正确战略选择。回顾中美两国和解之初，不难发现，中美关系正常化是与中国确定改革开放联系在一起的。邓小平将处理对美关系与中国的现代化进程结合在一起，将建立稳定和平的中美关系视为中国实现富强的首要外部条件。基于这一判断，自邓小平时代开始，历届领导人关于中国发展的战略选择都是一脉相承的，那就是不另起炉灶，不试图挑战现行国际秩序的权威，选择在现行国际体系内发展，这一决策为中美双赢与合作创造了前提。

中国的崛起正是在现行国际体系内实现的，因此中国是现行国际体系的参与者、建设者和贡献者。中国的崛起对于亚洲地区的国际秩序是一个新的变量，但这并不是说中国就是一个革命者，要主导建立一个以中国为中心的亚洲秩序。实际上，中国是在维护联合国安理会权威、国际法和自由开放的国际贸易体系。正如美国国家安全委员会亚洲事务前主任杰弗里·贝德所述，中国国家主席习近平的对外政策和前几任领导人大为不同，其主要原因在于，中国无论是能力和实力都与过去截然不同，但总体上依然延续了过去尤其是

1978 年后中国的发展路线。

第五，中美建立了很好的对话机制。过去 10 年，中美间已建立起非常成熟有效的对话机制。据外交部统计，中美之间有 98 个副部长及以上级别的对话机制，两国高级官员之间保持了密切的沟通，彼此之间的联系甚至超过了美国与其盟友的联系。特朗普总统上任以来，中美高层保持频繁沟通互动，双方并建立了外交安全对话、全面经济对话、执法及网络安全对话、社会和人文对话四个高级别对话机制。这些对话机制为双方提供了交流的平台，有利于双方加深了解，减少信息不对称、管控分歧，控制冲突。

总之，中美两国近些年的双边关系出现复杂化的特征，双方竞争加剧，在一些方面甚至出现了矛盾和分歧的螺旋式上升，而且不按常理出牌的特朗普总统很可能会给中美关系增加变数。但是因为上述机遇的存在，中美关系的总体框架不会发生大的变化，合作依然是中美关系的主流。如果能够充分利用机遇，深化合作，中美关系总体上能够超越分歧，确保双边关系保持正确的发展方向。

三、中国的长期安全战略将会保持一贯性、连续性和持续性

特朗普就任美国总统前没有任何从政经验，更无有关国际治理的政策阐述，未来美国的长期战略是不确定的。但也应该看到，美国政治体制中蕴含一种源于改革传统的强大内在韧性，特朗普势必会对美国的政策进行调整。对中国而言，中国外交的长期安全战略在不断创新的同时也会保持一贯性、连续性和持续性，这一战略大概体现在如下几点。

（一）积极应对内部挑战

外交是内政的延续，中国的外交政策一直具有“内向性”特征。具体表现在推动经济发展、实现现代化，维护多民族国家的统一，维护政权合法性等几个方面。对中国来说，尽管改革开放以来中国经济大幅增长，但长期以来经济发展不平衡，仍然面临结构性矛盾和周期性问题相互交织、需求不振和产能过剩相互并存、经济持续发展的基础尚不牢固等挑战。国内问题解决不好，

就会影响到中国的软硬实力发展并拖累对外影响力量。届时就如美国学者约瑟夫·奈所说，唯一能遏制中国的国家是中国自己。未来，中国能否掌握中美关系的主动权，最终取决于中国的国内发展，只有国内社会矛盾缓解、民众生活质量改善、政府廉洁高效，实现中华民族伟大复兴的中国才能在亚太以及全球格局中发挥更大作用，承担更多责任并获得更深远的影响力。

（二）在不与美国直接冲突的情况下，积极扩大外交布局

中国外交的核心议题是争取和平的国际环境以实现自身发展，同时以自身发展促进世界和平。从根本上说，中国的外交战略体现并契合了和平与发展这一时代主题。面对新环境新挑战，中国不再仅仅是国际秩序的参与者，而努力成为国际秩序与国际治理体系的建构者与国际规则的制定者。一方面，中国的外交政策布局更加注重自主性与独立性。在 2014 年中央外事工作会议上，习近平强调，外交工作“要坚持独立自主的和平外交方针，坚持把国家和民族发展放在自己力量的基点上，坚定不移走自己的路，走和平发展道路，同时决不能放弃我们的正当权益，决不能牺牲国家核心利益。”在这一思想指导下，中国在坚定维护自身正当权益的同时，积极推出“一带一路”倡议、“金砖国家发展银行”、亚投行、东海防空识别区等一系列新概念新举措。另一方面，外交政策布局体现对美国利益尊重。“新型大国关系”的提出，就将“相互尊重”——尊重各自选择的社会制度和发展道路，尊重彼此核心利益和重大关切，求同存异，包容互鉴，共同进步——作为这一新型关系的重要内涵。不仅如此，中国反复强调对以美国为主导的现存国际体系的尊重，强调中美两国具有广泛的共同利益和合作空间，强调世界的和平与繁荣尤其是亚太地区的和平发展离不开中美两国间的深入沟通与坦诚合作，并欢迎美国在亚太地区发挥建设性作用。

（三）扩大合作面，以合作的增量淡化存量

邓小平说，改革是中国的第二次革命。改革开放 40 年来，中国之所以在短期内实现社会巨变而没有出现大的社会和经济动荡，最重要的原因就在于中国的改革是增量改革，而同期苏联的改革是存量改革。以 20 世纪国营企业改革为例，邓小平提出通过鼓励民营经济发展、搞多种经营，最终产生的示范效应和竞争压力促进国企改革，同时由于民营企业占GDP的比例逐步上升，使国企改革进程中的社会不安定因素被控制在一定范围和程度内，不至于造成大的社会动荡。

增量改革为处理中美关系提供了有益借鉴，现在中美关系的竞争性因素非常广泛，有些问题短期内无法解决，中国正试图建立一种基于共同利益的伙伴关系，在可能的情况下尽量减少影响双边关系的竞争性因素，把中美两国的合作面做大做强，中美关系稳定下来，再去解决竞争性分歧，就不会动摇双边合作的基础并引发关系恶化或动荡。

（四）积极承担国际责任

中美两国内部对于中国是否应该积极承担国际责任的看法是一致的，但是对于中国应该承担什么样的国际责任或者承担多大程度的国际责任，则存在较大分歧。美国方面，近年来越来越多的声音要求中国履行更多义务，承担更多责任。2005年，时任美国常务副国务卿佐利克在美中关系全国委员会上发表题为“中国向何处去——从正式成员到承担责任”的演讲，正式提出了促使中国成为国际体系中负责任的利益攸关方。2008年美国彼得森国际经济研究所所长弗雷德伯格斯登提出“G2”概念遭到中国政府拒绝后，美国相当一部分人批评中国履行的国际责任不足，而且存在“选择性”，只履行那些对中国有利的责任。中国方面，一种普遍性的观点认为中国依然是一个发展中国家，能力有限，无法承担超越自身实力的责任。

近些年来中国积极参与全球治理，在环境、气候、核安全、重大疾病、反恐、网络安全等方面加强与美国的合作，其中，中国在核安全工作中与美国合作，承担了保证地区核安全工作的责任，中美核安全合作也因此被视作中美双方在双边、地区和全球领域最为成功的合作领域。同样，在马拉喀什气候变化大会上，中国与美国等国就落实气候变化《巴黎协议》达成一致，这些合作有利于同美国“分担责任”，从而减轻美国对与中国“分享权力”的不满。与此同时，中国在承担责任的过程中也坚持透明公正，这对于坚持法治和程序透明的美国来说有利于增进彼此认知，减少对彼此意图的误解。

（五）坚持互利共赢，积极促进中美关系发展

搞好中美关系，重要的是拒绝零和思维，坚持互利共赢。尽管近些年来随着中国实力增长、产业升级以及美国的制造业回流，中美经济合作出现一些新变化，但总体来说，中美两国在经济上互补性大于竞争性。尤其是美国的经济增长需要大量的投资，而中国则拥有最多的外汇储备，未来中美双边投资协定（BIT）的达成更将有利于中国企业进入美国市场，带动美国国内的就业和经济增长。

随着中国对美投资稳步上升，美国公众、企业及利益集团对中国的看法将逐步改观。如果中国在美国每个国会众议员选区都有投资，同时这些投资都能发挥良好经济效益，为美国社会带来就业和经济增长，居民生活能够改善，普通美国民众能够分享中国经济发展的红利，那么美国民众也会欢迎中国投资，而不是将其视为洪水猛兽，从而在经济文化上形成你中有我、我中有你的“中美国”局面，就像20世纪80年代日本在美国俄亥俄州、肯塔基州大量投资汽车工业一样，丰沛的就业机会能使双边紧张关系降温并有利于改善和促进两国关系的健康积极发展。

总之，中国对美国的长期安全战略是“两条腿走路”：积极的一面是倡导发展“中美新型大国关系”，努力扩大两国的合作面，促进共同利益的实现；消极的一面是管控危机，消除战略互疑，避免冲突与对抗。

四、中美关系新前景是建立功能性伙伴关系或者实现两国协调

中美关系的复杂性决定了中美关系的前景没有现成答案，既不能说中美必有一战，也不能说中美必定不会跌入“修昔底德陷阱”。中美关系最终取决于双方的共同努力，也取决于双方领导人能否抓住当前的机遇。目前双方精英层有一些共识，要在一些方向上共同努力，合作共赢。

在美国，以基辛格为代表的一些学者精英提出，美国应与中国共同演进。基辛格认为中国的发展潜力不可限量，美国必须做出改变适应中国的崛起，同时中国也应该做出一些改变，具体做法是中美需要发挥磋商传统和双边信任，共同处理好三个层面的关系：通过磋商维护两国共同利益、消除紧张，全

面提升双方合作框架、共建太平洋共同体。这一思路在一部分美国精英层中很有市场。值得一提的是，“共同演进”思想虽然还未在战略层面上实施，但已经在中美两国民间有越来越多的体现。2013年中美两国关于“虎妈现象”的讨论就是例证之一。在教育上，中美两国都在向对方学习，取长补短，这就是共同演进。在文化、饮食、流行音乐上，中美两国都在共同演进。

未来中美两国关系最有可能的前景是建立功能性伙伴关系，或者是实现两国协调。两国协调源于19世纪初的欧洲协调，当时崛起的法国在拿破仑的率领下横扫欧陆，建立了庞大的帝国，欧洲国家在英国的领导下击败了拿破仑军队。战争结束后，列强在维也纳召开会议，决定以协商的方式处理欧洲重大问题。欧洲人认为，大国之间需要确立底线，也就是控制矛盾，避免兵戎相见，同时在重要问题上选择合作，实现共赢。欧洲协调体制使欧洲维持了从1815年到1914年近百年的和平。

中美功能性伙伴关系与此类似。具体而言，就是说中美两国不以建立同盟关系为目的，但在所有具有共同利益的领域加强合作，具体包括：双方共同维持地区的实力均衡、共同应对威胁人类生存的跨国问题和全球问题、通过协商方式承担关系人类可持续发展的共同责任，同时在有竞争的领域控制分歧，无论是合作还是竞争，都保持机制性的沟通，避免出现误判，增强战略互信。在此基础上，双方通过合作建立起互信，逐步扩大合作面，并最终解决两国间的深层次矛盾和争议。在这一点上，“功能性伙伴关系”与澳大利亚前总理陆克文关于中美“同梦想共使命的建设性现实主义”建议有异曲同工之妙，要实现这一关系到两国人民未来的历史使命，需要中美两国领导人拥有宽广的眼界和非凡的智慧，认识到两国友好的必要，并拿出20世纪70年代初中美两国领导人那样的巨大魄力，携手合作，克服不断上升的互疑螺旋，并引领中美两国共同走向繁荣与和平。

中美大国竞争是否进入“新冷战”？

日本中曾根康弘世界和平研究所高级研究员
大泽淳

一个具有挑战性大国的崛起和一个霸权国家的衰落引发国际秩序强烈震动，破坏国际政治力量平衡。主张“霸权稳定论”的罗伯特·吉尔平认为，纵观历史，解决国际体系结构与权力分配之间不平衡的主要手段是霸权战争。约翰·米尔斯海默说，“中国是理解未来权力分配的关键”，“它可能比美国在20世纪面临的任何潜在霸权都强大和危险。”另有现实主义学者认为，中国愿意继续遵守现存地区和国际秩序，还是成为一个挑战美国霸权的修正主义大国，是事关地区稳定的重要因素。

一、美中是否在“修昔底德陷阱”中越陷越深

修昔底德在他著作中指出，伯罗奔尼撒战争的起因是“雅典（海洋）力量的增长使斯巴达人陷入了恐惧，因此战争成为必要。”格雷厄姆·艾利森描述了16个新兴大国崛起的案例，其中有12个案例都在新兴国家和老牌大国之间爆发了对抗和战争。他还在新书中提出了一个问题：“美国和中国能逃脱修昔底德陷阱吗？”从修昔底德时代到今天的21世纪，海洋力量为一个国家的繁荣和安全提供了基础，因此，一个国家迅速崛起为海洋强国，会让邻国和在世界上具有统治地位的大国产生警惕。于是许多人都在思考，美中是否正在“修昔底德陷阱”中越陷越深。

二、中国推行“海洋强国”战略

中国曾长期坚持邓小平提出的“韬光养晦”的外交战略。2009 年 7 月 17 日，时任中国国家主席胡锦涛在北京举行的第 11 次驻外使节会议上提出“坚持韬光养晦，积极有所作为”的新外交战略。日本专家认为这是中国走向世界的转折点，即从“隐藏自己的实力或保持低调”转向“寻求具体的成就”。

从 2009 年到 2012 年，中国官员和学者不断强调“核心利益”和建设“海洋强国”。中国的海上强国愿景需要强大的海军和先进的海上执法力量。确保海上通道 (SLOC) 安全是中国人民解放军的当务之急。在 2015 年中国官方发布的军事战略中，海洋被称为是关键的安全领域。习近平主席也提到海上力量是中国梦的重要组成部分，并在 2017 年 5 月指出海军应该力争世界一流。

三、中国在空中和海上的“防御性”行动可能与美国发生冲突

东亚未来的地缘政治格局将由中国和美国决定。许多现实主义学者认为，随着中国成为一个强国，中国将利用自己的力量为国家利益服务，邻国则逐渐担心中国日益上升的影响力成为一种安全威胁。

随着经济和军事实力的增强，中国开始将影响力向周边海洋延伸，随着旨在确保国家安全的“海洋强国战略”的出现，中国正在东海和南海的海岸线建立缓冲区。中国于 2013 年 11 月设立的防空识别区就是建立这类缓冲区的努力之一，我们可将其视为中国的“空中万里长城”。

如果中国为了能在美军入侵等紧急情况下保护台湾、东海和南海，而采取缓冲区战略或“反干预作战”战略（也就是广为西方专家所知的“区域拒止 / 反介入”战略），与美国倡导的“航行自由”或“航空自由”唱对台戏。那么在中国沿海地区，中国陆上力量和美国海上力量的争斗将不可避免。

四、美中两国在网络领域的斗争具有长期性

在最近五年里，美中两国为保护各自的网络安全进行了斗争，这一斗争涵盖了数字、外交、司法、国际关系等诸多领域。美国怀疑中国政府和军方支持中国网络间谍组织刺探美国公司的知识产权和商业秘密。在斯诺登泄密之后，中国也怀疑美国军事情报机构——美国国家安全局（NSA）一直从网上入侵中国。

2015年9月，习近平主席和时任美国总统奥巴马在元首会晤上达成共识，宣布不实施或有意支持通过网络渠道窃取知识产权的行为，包括商业秘密或其他机密商业信息。即便如此，美中两国为在未来的物联网时代占据技术优势仍然会在这方面持续角力。

五、“一带一路”倡议仍可能被视为地缘政治风险

地缘政治学的开创者麦金德把历史描绘成陆地力量和海洋力量之间的较量。美国著名地缘政治学家尼古拉斯·斯皮克曼将他的“边缘地带理论”描述为：第一，“谁控制了边缘地带就统治了欧亚大陆；谁统治了欧亚大陆，就控制了世界的命运。”第二，“美国安全的最大风险就是让任何国家控制欧亚大陆的边缘地带。”第三，美国“有义务保护自身地位，确保在这些地区没有任何其他强权。”尽管习近平主席在2018年4月博鳌论坛的主旨演讲中称“一带一路”“不打地缘博弈小算盘”，中国政府也表示愿在“一带一路”倡议框架下，加强与欧亚国家的互联互通与合作，但“一带一路”倡议仍有被视为地缘政治风险的可能性。尤其在美国人看来，“一带一路”倡议中的“带”和“路”已完全跨越了尼古拉斯·斯皮克曼所说的“边缘地带”。

在历史上，有时一方对另一方意图的误解会让事态恶化，甚至导致战争，就像1938年的慕尼黑协定。对抗不仅来自于国际关系理论层面的现实主义观点或结构现实主义理论；美中两国从海洋到网络的广大领域都在相互影响，两国以及两国盟友之间发生的意外事件和反制措施，也可能使美中对对方意

图产生误解，从而导致双边关系恶化。哪些事件或因素会引起这些误解，从而产生反制性战略或政策？怎样才能避免误解升级？这些都是美中两国面临的严肃问题。

六、结论与建议

（一）大国竞争的升级在很大程度上是由于对对方意图的误解而产生的，在双边关系的不同领域，即使是很小的事件以及由此产生的反应也容易造成这种误解。由于互不信任而产生毫无根据的恐惧，很容易导致错估对方的意图，将有可能把美中两国推向冲突甚至战争。

（二）为了避免陷入误解和错估对手的恶性循环，美中两国及其盟友必须采取以下措施：

1、细心处理每一次摩擦，即使是微小的个案；

2、避免过于自信地实施某些行为，比如在其他国家附近开展军事演习；

3、要客观而不是戴着“有色眼镜”评估对方的能力和意图；

4、加强各层次、各领域的沟通与交流，比如高层领导、海军，以及民众和社会组织。

中美关系的重大变化及对亚太安全的影响

中国人民争取和平与裁军协会常务理事
国防大学国家安全学院教授
孟祥青

特朗普上台执政近一年半时间，美国先后出台了《国家安全战略报告》《国防战略报告》《核态势评估报告》等多份文件，对美国安全威胁等做出新的判断，对对外战略进行新的调整。在对华关系上，特朗普政府频频出招，从多领域多角度向中国持续施压，屡屡挑起争端，甚至挑战“一中”原则底线，使中美管控分歧、化解危机的难度越来越大。目前两国学术界和国际舆论界普遍对中美关系持悲观看法。

一、亚太安全很大程度上取决于中美关系好坏

回顾 70 年来的亚太安全形势，其发展变化取决于很多因素，但中美关系因素占的分量不轻。大致可分为两个阶段，第一阶段是从 1949 年新中国成立到 1979 年中美建交。这一阶段亚太安全形势的基本特征是对抗性的，标志性事件是 1950 年 2 月缔结的中苏同盟和 1951 年 4 月缔结的美日军事同盟。之后，两个对抗的集团分别以不同方式、在不同程度上向亚太地区扩展，到 20 世纪 60 年代中期，美国建立起一个军事同盟体系，而中苏同盟已名存实亡，中美随后不久走上了和解之路。第二阶段是从 1979 年中美建交至今。这一阶段亚太安全形势呈现出由对抗走向合作，合作成为主流，为亚太地区带来了近 40 年的基本稳定与和平，也是地区保持发展与繁荣局面的基本背景。亚太地区的持续发展与繁荣是历史性的，并对全球产生影响。未来亚太地区的稳

定与和平能否持续成为全球关注的焦点，也是今天的中美关系越来越受到关注的重要原因之一。

不可否认，在近 40 年中，中美两国不是盟友但曾建立过特殊且很密切的战略合作关系。这种在冷战中后期形成的战略合作关系，在中美两国学术界有不少系统性论述，也为不断公布的档案所证明。美国与中国开展战略合作的某些领域质量甚至超过了美国的欧洲盟友，所以也曾被定义为“准同盟”。冷战结束引发的国际形势和地缘政治的大变局，导致中美战略关系一度出现消极倾向，两国关系成为亚太地区一个不确定因素。这个地区美日之间不可能发生大的战略矛盾，但中美却有可能。中国与日本、越南、菲律宾等因为领土争端发生的矛盾甚至冲突都不会完全改变亚太安全形势的本质特征和安全秩序，但如果中美关系发生根本改变甚至逆转，亚太安全秩序就可能颠覆，对抗式安全格局的形成就会成为大概率事件。

冷战结束后，中美在冷战中后期形成的特殊战略合作关系随之结束，但双方很快开始寻求在战略安全领域维持合作的途径和办法，互相都在努力了解对方的意图。两国都曾提出过几种重新定义中美关系的建议，如美方提出的“建设性合作伙伴关系”“利益攸关方”“建设性的合作关系”，再到后来中方提出的“新型大国关系”等等。比较这些概念，以及观察双方不断变换定义两国关系时的交流和外交努力，不难发现，中美两国在如何定位两国关系的认知上存在明显差别。但可以肯定的是，无论具体用什么概念，两国的决策层还是希望保持合作的态势，以及在亚太地区继续开展合作，避免发生对抗。同时，中美两国也能找到合作的基本动力和基础，如从经贸合作到反恐再到地区安全、全球问题等。但如今这些似乎都在改变，反恐合作的动力减弱了，经贸合作这个“压舱石”动摇了，气候变暖等全球性议题美方越来越不感兴趣了。虽然两国决策层仍然在努力保持合作的态势，但显然在通过对话合作解决矛盾分歧方面，美方表态多于政策，言论大于行动，而选择与中方对抗、对中国持续施压的一面日益凸显。

回顾历史，中美关系从对抗到和解到正常化再到日益成熟，走过了一条曲折的发展道路。中美关系一直充满着矛盾，有时甚至是非常尖锐的矛盾，也存在着诸多合作的历史性机遇，但即使在合作的进程中，也伴随着矛盾。历史一再证明，两国不论是发展合作还是寻求对抗，都可以找到足够的理由，但最终都选择了合作。这是因为，只要是对两国人民负责、对地区和世界和平稳定负责的政治家和学者都明白，只有合作才是中美两国唯一的相处之道，否则不仅给两国也将给亚太地区和世界和平带来灾难性后果。

二、美国对华政策正在进行重大调整

美国《国家安全战略报告》明确讲，面对全球范围内日益增长的政治、经济和军事竞争，需要重新思考过去的政策，“这个政策基于这样的假设，即与竞争对手接触并将其纳入国际机构和全球贸易，将使他们成为良性的参与者和可信赖的合作伙伴。在很大程度上，这个假设被证明是错误的。”虽然这里没有点中国的名，但其所指是显而易见的。特朗普“以实力求和平”的基本理念，决定其对华政策重点是与中国开展力量竞争，并在多个领域全面施压，而不再是试图塑造中国。在这个意义上，美国对华政策正在进行根本性的调整，但目前并未调整到位。鉴于中国力量快速发展及其与美国差距不断缩小的大趋势，维持对华力量优势将是美国对华政策的长期重点。特朗普政府正是为了维持美对华力量优势而加大对华竞争力度。虽然其《国家安全战略报告》声称“竞争并不总是意味着敌对，也不一定会导致冲突”，但特朗普执政团队的保守偏激思维和强势的行事风格有可能导致中美恶性竞争。比如：经济上，特朗普政府一意孤行，出尔反尔，挑起贸易摩擦，使中美关系的“压舱石”地动山摇。在越来越多的人看来，特朗普政府对500亿美元主要是中国高科技产品的加征关税和限制中国对美投资的决定，并不完全是为了解决对华贸易逆差问题，更像是要迟滞中国在高技术领域的进步，放慢中国实力增长的步伐，以达到维持美国对华力量优势的目的。这种基于相对收益思维的政策行为，不仅会使中美经贸关系的发展严重受阻，更会加剧中美战略竞争，甚至恶性竞争。从长远看，损人不利己。在安全上，美国鹰派主导的外交与安全团队默许甚至纵容美国军方在南海加大对华施压力度，这势必升高中美两军在南海的对峙；而“印太战略”构架下实质性安全合作的增强，必然增大地区地缘政治分裂与对抗的风险。更危险的是，由美国国会通过并由特朗普签署的《台湾旅行法》，提升美台官员交流层级。这些动作表明，美方在积极地打“台湾牌”，这将不可避免地对两岸关系和中美关系造成冲击。

三、合作是中美关系的唯一选择

未来中美关系走势取决于很多因素，其中既有常规变量，也有非常规变量。常规变量包括两国实力对比、两国战略基础（经贸关系、安全合作等）、两国战略环境（内部利益集团掣肘外交政策；外部的伊朗、乌克兰、菲律宾、朝鲜等都对中美关系产生影响）。非常规变量最突出的就是特朗普政府的对华政策走向。但万变不离其宗，决定中美关系走势的决定性因素主要包括：

一是台湾问题。台湾问题仍然是中美关系中最敏感最核心最突出的问题。由于中美建交后的历届美国政府都承认“一中”原则，并基本遵守了两国政府达成的共识和底线，这个问题在过去多年得到一定程度的控制，没有出现大的危机，或者出现问题后通过两国战略交流与沟通最终得到缓解，至少没有完全失控。虽然时常出现干扰，但最终没有突破这一底线。而特朗普政府上台一年半来，这条底线有被随时突破的危险。特朗普和蔡英文通电话，并扬言拿台湾和贸易问题做交易；美国会通过了《2018 年度国防授权法》，特别是通过了《台湾旅行法》，并暗示出售 F—35 战机等等。所有这些动作都给台独势力发出了极为错误的信号，客观上起到了鼓励台独发展的作用。可见，现在美国政府对“一中”原则越来越虚化、淡化。

二是中美关系的框架和定位问题。中方希望继续推进中美新型大国关系建设，在与特朗普团队交往之始就强调“相互尊重、合作共赢”的重要性。时任美国国务卿蒂勒森在首次访华时也表示美方愿本着不冲突不对抗、相互尊重、合作共赢的精神发展对华关系。然而在国内利益集团的压力下，特朗普的立场开始后退，提出要发展“建设性的、以结果为导向的”中美关系。现在关键的问题仍然是美国如何看待中国崛起，以及如何看待中国的战略意图，如果把中国崛起看作是对美国最大的挑战，把中国的所有内外政策都看作是针对美国的，中美关系框架和定位就将会继续向消极的方向发展。

总之，中美关系目前处在一个新的十字路口，中美都进入了新时代，需要有新思维和新举措，既要有高层领导的共识和引领，也要有新的基础和动力，更要在管控好分歧和危机方面加大力度。在当前国际形势呈现变和乱基本特征、和平解决朝核问题出现重大机遇、亚太安全形势错综复杂的背景下，中美两国关系如何，对地区形势的影响将越来越大。历史和现实一再证明并将反复证明，合作是中美关系的唯一选择，合作不仅关系到两国利益，也事关亚太地区和世界和平。从这个意义上讲，我们对中美关系的未来仍应保持乐观。

亚太地区形势演变中的中美关系发展动态

越南外交学院战略研究所高级研究员

丁氏贤良

一、中国崛起背景下的外交成就与发展挑战

第一，实现"中国梦"宏伟战略是推动中国走向世界舞台中央的基石。中国"新时代"概念的提出，意味着邓小平时期"韬光养晦"外交方针告一段落。但是，中国外交政策从根本上延续了维护和平稳定、避免摩擦冲突、利用现有合作机制处理大国关系的邓小平外交思想。军事方面，习近平主席提出深化军队改革、走"富国强军"之路，从另一个侧面展示出了中国政府希望加速推动中国走向世界舞台中央的决心。

第二，中国正变得越来越自信，逐步展现出推动塑造亚太新秩序的意愿。事实上，作为地区支柱国家，中国积极的外交政策反映出其日益走近世界舞台中央。过去由美国主导的地区局势已经发生了不可逆转的改变，中美力量对比正朝着有利于中国的方向发展。2014 年亚信峰会上，习近平主席表示亚洲国家自身应加强安全努力（这也暗指"域外大国"在亚太安全问题上始终存在）。此外，中国正通过"一带一路"建设特别是"21 世纪海上丝绸之路"建设来提升国家海洋实力。

第三，中国在提供全球性公共产品方面仍面临一定局限。当今中国已掌握更多全球性资源，为解决全球性问题积极贡献方案，提出了构建人类命运共同体等主张。二战以来，国际秩序的重要特点是美国主导，加之资源和效率方面的局限，中国在应对全球性挑战上仍存在一些短板，如中国高度依赖中东

油气资源，这不仅给中国经济带来风险，也对地缘战略格局产生影响；此外，中国地方债务、金融风险、贫富差距、三股势力威胁等也给中国内部、外部安全造成巨大挑战。

二、中美关系发展新动态

第一，中美关系仍将保持“整体稳定”和均衡发展。中美关系的特点可以概括成“竞争、合作与妥协并存”，两国在发展过程中依存度高。从中国方面看，其经济的巨幅增长离不开美国大量投资。习近平主席提出要构建中美新型大国关系来避免落入“修昔底德陷阱”。中国在朝核问题等安全挑战中积极应对并成功转危为机，得以增加与美国谈判的筹码。从美国方面看，虽然其国内存在对华质疑声音，但也有一部分人将中国视为“有用的对手”，高度关注中国的发展成果与经验。总体来说，由于中国在综合国力特别是军事实力上尚不能与美国匹敌，且中国始终以建设性态度发展对美关系，传统的两极格局并没有出现。但博弈还在继续，中美两国均需调整本国政策以适应新的动态平衡。

第二，美国总统特朗普及其政府的不可预测性给中国带来新挑战。中国无法根据美国传统战略思维来判断其外交政策。特朗普在贸易问题上选择了更具对抗性的应对路径，对美中贸易失衡大加指责，但同时又将中国视为亚太地区不可缺少的重要大国。特朗普声称多边合作对美国不利，更重视通过双边途径处理问题。美国只是在经贸领域采取单边手段，在政治、安全合作中仍强调政府间合作。此外，2017 年，美国时任国务卿蒂勒森提出美国与印度共建“自由、开放的印太”，将印太概念视为加强与盟国合作的战略平台，印、日、澳随之“上车”，试图遏制中国。特朗普在亚洲之行中亦向中国释放这个信号，表现出对中国崛起的忧虑与关切。过去，人权与民主曾是美国对中国加以指责的传统话题，亦是中美关系中的绊脚石。如今，美国把更多注意力放在了经贸领域。但是，中国已发展得更为强大，可以适时制定出反制措施予以回击。

第三，中国采取迂回策略处理对美关系，展现出战略定力和耐心。中国寻求将力量对比朝着有利于自身的方向引导，对美国及其盟国关系加以分化。特朗普的系列政策导致美国同亚洲盟国的关系热度不断下降，这给中国提供了前所未有的机遇。习近平主席支持全球化和贸易自由化，而特朗普则呼吁加强贸易保护。特朗普坚持“美国优先”逻辑，在经贸谈判上偏好双边而非多边谈判，这引起美国盟国和传统伙伴的不安与担忧，给了中国充分空间来扩大自身影响。

第四，以美国为首的西方国家对中国高新技术产业进行打压，制约了中国产业发展。中国重视通过扩大中美贸易吸引资金技术、推动科技进步，这是推进“中国制造 2025”的重要途径之一。美国方面，特朗普出台系列政策吸引境外资本，巩固美国在全球制造业和海外私人投资领域的头把交椅。此外，纵使美国对华贸易逆差巨大，其在科技领域依然遥遥领先。美国对中兴公司的制裁不仅是经济事件，更具有政治含义和战略意图。中国方面，在处理中美贸易摩擦和经济纠纷过程中，首要考虑始终包括如何维护战略稳定。中国希望同美国保持和谐的双边关系，营造稳定的国际环境，顺利实现“两个一百年”奋斗目标。未来五年，中美关系的基本面将是两国领导人达成战略共识的反映和体现。

三、对中美关系及推动东南亚地区秩序重塑的展望

第一，两国皆重视东南亚地区的战略意义，重视同东盟合作。近年来，中美轮番行动，角力加剧，争相扩大在东南亚地区的影响力。两国集团（G2）模式或许正在萌芽，但尚不会扩大至全球范围。美国提出“印太战略”，但其外交政策信奉实用主义，漠视无法给自身带来切实利益的机制。例如，东亚峰会是美国了解亚洲、体现影响力的重要平台，但 2017 年 11 月特朗普的亚洲之行跳过了在菲律宾举行的东亚峰会绝大部分议程。美国国内或许并没有很看重东盟，只是认为目前尚没有可以替代的合作机制。美国需要东盟的影响力，最终或将以某种更为强硬的方式加大对东南亚事务的参与。随着中国日

益强大，中美竞争会愈加明显，若出现任何冲突，中小国家必将遭受冲击和损失。

第二，中美两国都有比对抗更好的政策选择。对中美及东南亚地区国家来说，“竞争、合作与妥协并存”是当前阶段的最优局面。中美两国经济相互依存度高，在推动全球金融、货币、贸易、投资体系改革中共同发挥重要作用。中国致力于在国际政治经济秩序中发挥稳定器作用，或将在美国势力收缩的节点上将国际秩序和规则向有利于自身的方向引领，重新建构中美在亚太地区的地位和作用。

第三，中美两国都有不愿逾越的红线。美国对中国的举动会予以制约。海洋问题上，美国反复开展“航行自由”行动来反对中国在南海地区的特定主张和要求，阻挠中国同东南亚国家通过“21 世纪海上丝绸之路”扩大战略合作。朝核问题上，特朗普意识到没有中俄两国参与，朝鲜半岛问题只会陷入死循环并耗费美国大量军力财力，因此向中国施压，希望推动朝核问题向前发展。在动荡不安的国际局势下，中国要想实现“保持战略定力”“营造有利的国际环境”等主张，还将面临一定困难和挑战。

中美战略认知与东亚地区安全

中国人民争取和平与裁军协会常务理事
中国社会科学院台湾研究所所长、研究员
杨明杰

伴随世界战略格局的深刻调整，东亚安全形势也在发生复杂深刻的变化。作为本地区至关重要的两个大国，中美两国对彼此的战略认知不仅影响双边关系的未来，而且将对地区形势与秩序产生深远影响。当前，中美之间相互的战略认知总体看仍是相对积极的，且有一定共性，但在一些关键问题和领域上仍有重大分歧，甚至是潜藏危机。新形势下，中美双方共同努力探索构建新型大国关系的实施路径任重道远。这一努力同样需要得到地区其他力量的支持与合作。

一、中美两国对国际战略格局的深刻变化有相当共识

中美之间对国际战略格局的深刻变化有相当共识，例如都认为当前战略格局的变化是巨大而影响深远的，都认识到维护国际安全环境稳定的迫切性和必要性，都认识到中美战略关系的重要性、避免全面战略对抗对双方的重要意义、在一些地区热点问题上必须加强彼此间的合作与对话、越来越多的非传统安全领域威胁必须采取合作措施、经济发展对国家安全的重大意义等。

二、在一些重大战略和地区问题上，中美双方仍存在相当大的认知差异，对双边关系和地区安全产生了现实或潜在的负面影响

首先，在全球化进程和现有国际秩序的认知上。中美都是全球化进程的主要受益者。当前，美国执政者将自己视为全球化的主要受害者，而将中国等新兴市场国家视为主要获益方，认为他们充分利用现有国际秩序或机制的漏洞不断获取利益，使得美国更加被动。中国则认为全球化是历史发展的必然，但其具有双刃剑效应，各国应加强在全球治理领域的合作，为新一轮全球化创造更坚实的基础和条件；应在尊重现有国际秩序的基础上不断对其进行调整，逐步建立新的国际政治经济秩序。在现实政策选择上，中国主张以更开放的胸襟进行更大规模更高层次的改革开放，倡议构建人类命运共同体。美国则更多采取单边主义措施，为新一轮区域化和全球化进程设置障碍，以“美国优先”消极应对地区和国际秩序的治理与调整，甚至将中国的国际贡献视为战略威胁。

其次，在彼此的战略定位和趋势判断上。美国明确将中国视为战略竞争对手，担心中国的进一步发展将直接挑战美国在东亚地区乃至世界的霸主地位。中国则认为美国仍是世界上唯一的超级大国，其影响力虽相对衰落，但对地区和世界的影响仍是重大的。在政策选择上，中国力图避免“修昔底德陷阱”，争取与美国建立新型大国关系，维护地区稳定和世界和平。美国则纠缠于战略两难，一方面在地缘战略上排棋布子，企图对中国形成更加有效的牵制和威慑，另一方面也担心与中国形成直接且全面的战略对抗，因此还在战略博弈中继续探索合作之路。

第三，在对地区热点问题认识上。中美共同致力于实现朝鲜半岛无核化，但双方对问题性质和实施路径仍存在不同看法。在南海问题上，中国和相关国家已经在和平解决的方向上取得重大进展，但美国却担心这种积极进展对其在南海地区的领导力和塑造力构成挑战，而继续以维护“航行自由”为借口抬升紧张局势。在台湾问题上，双方虽都认为台海的稳定极为重要，但美国国内政治局势变化造成台海问题再度升温，中国则从维护领土主权完整的角度

予以危机应对。

第四，在对盟国体系和冷战遗留问题看法上。中国虽认为美国在东亚地区的军事同盟是冷战时期的产物，但也充分认识到这一问题的复杂性，因而坚持反对美国针对第三方的同盟体系。而美国则有强化东亚地区军事同盟的优先战略考虑，并且提出“印太战略”，企图制造更大范围的价值观同盟体系，其中确有将中国作为主要因素的安全考量。

三、在新时代，面对繁纷复杂的安全形势，中美应从更高更广的层面加深战略共识

正如习近平主席所言，“我们正处在一个快速发展变化的世界里。世界多极化、经济全球化、社会信息化深入推进，各种挑战层出不穷，各国利益紧密相连。零和博弈、冲突对抗早已不合时宜，同舟共济、合作共赢成为时代要求”。作为世界上最大的发展中国家、最大的发达国家和前两大经济体，中美两国更应该从两国人民和各国人民根本利益出发，勇于担当，朝着构建中美新型大国关系的方向奋力前行。具体而言，中美两国可着重在以下四个方面增进战略沟通：一是加强对全球化和全球治理方面的共同研究和对话，切实找到在新一轮全球化中双方共同的战略定位和方向，为地区和国际新秩序的塑造发挥更大的合力。二是加强交流，在战略对话中沟通彼此的战略目标和意图，保持适度的透明化，加强与公众和媒体的沟通，防范彼此的战略误解在民间发酵。三是在地区热点问题的处理上加强战略沟通，特别是在涉及领土主权问题上要加倍小心，有效管控危机，防止危机升级。四是以更开放积极的姿态处理与其他相关国家的安全合作，避免新冷战思维泛起。

中美南海冲突的未来轮廓：地区冲突向全球冲突过渡

俄罗斯科学院东方学研究所东南亚研究中心主任
德米特里·莫夏科夫

今天南海的形势已不同于以往。过去一段时期该地区形势发生了重大变化，未来发展存在不确定性并且给全球安全带来危险。本文将谈及美国全面卷入南海冲突的演变情况。事实上，美国并非从一开始就全面卷入该地区事务。例如，2009 年美国—东盟峰会时，美方代表与东盟国家领导人交谈时用最严谨的措辞指出，东盟有关国家不应向华盛顿控诉北京，东盟国家的政治精英们应该自己寻求与中国妥协。但奥巴马上台后这一方针发生了变化，彼时新上任的美国国务卿希拉里阐明，美国必须重返东南亚。促使美国改变方针并将东盟国家视为潜在盟友的主要原因是中国在南海争议岛屿和水域采取了主动策略并寻求有别于美国的自主政策，其地区影响力明显上升。

美国介入南海事务是其“重返亚太”战略的一部分。美国军舰在争议岛屿附近中方限制的区域内航行，并威胁要与中国军队发生正面对抗。美中在南海的公开对抗使中国与周边相关邻国这一长期不为世界所关注的冲突被纳入到了大国对抗当中。

目前，由于美国的介入，南海冲突已经不再是地区性的而是全球性的，不但威胁着南海和亚洲的和平与稳定，而且影响全世界。事实上，美中之间的任何军事冲突都将引发世界一流大国间的大战。这种潜在的危险时常可见，因为美国军机频繁往返于中国防空力量的枪口之下，驱逐舰也经常在争议岛屿附近海域航行，而这些地区都是中方正式宣布的禁行区域。任何一次擅自或意外的袭击都将彻底改变地区局势。而且该地区的安全环境一直在恶化，特别是美国宣布卡尔·文森号航母舰队自 2017 年 2 月 18 日起在南海执行巡航任务后。这意味着东南亚地区发生冲突的可能性增加，时刻处于紧张和不稳定的状态。美中最近的一次对抗发生在 2018 年 5 月 27 日，美国“希金斯”号和“安提坦”号军舰擅自进入中国西沙群岛领海，激起中国舰机的强烈反应。

从软实力角度而言，具有侵略性和强大文化渗透力的美国文化的到来，改变了东南亚地区局势的现状，使这些国家多了一个可替代中国政治和文化主导性影响力的选项，地区文化变得多元，与美国的关系也更近。实际上，全球冲突不仅是指军事安全，也包括政治和文化对抗。域外大国往往通过政治文化影响力来获得东南亚地区各国的支持。提到文化影响力，有必要强调美国的文化软实力。虽然美国以其在世界上扮演的“救世主”角色为基础创造了美国式的文化“传奇”，但是也产生了新的内在矛盾，它过分夸大了中国在该地区的历史和文化影响力，导致美中互不信任。这一问题背后的原因是美国文化的定式与优势已在东南亚国家的某些政治精英中生根，破坏了东南亚地区的传统文化圈，使得域内各国间的互不信任和误解不断上升。

现在，中国已将南海政策摆在了国家安全的重要位置。循着中国军事发展的逻辑，我们可以看到，控制南沙群岛和南海的重要岛屿对于中国防止遭受美国导弹袭击，阻止美国及其盟友切断中国的海上经济动脉、封锁中国经济至关重要。而这些恰恰是美国媒体反复用于遏制和打压中国的例证。

最后，在中国与美国的对抗中，东盟国家发现自己并不在美国的阵营中，他们也不愿成为美国的傀儡。基于这一点，中国能够获得东盟国家相当一部分有影响力的政治精英的支持，这些人反复公开表明他们希望置身于美中全球冲突之外并保持选择外交伙伴的自由。东盟国家并不隐瞒希望与中国建立建设性伙伴关系的立场，且反对扮演帮助美国反华的前沿角色。这一立场对于中国未来在南海成功发展与美国关系具有决定意义。

印度视角下的中美关系

印度辨喜基金会副研究员
特舒·辛格

一、中美关系是当今世界最重要的双边关系

中美两国是世界上经济体量、军费开支最大的国家，双方经济依存度高、互补性强，在合作和竞争中共同影响着国际秩序与规范。正如美国前国务卿基辛格所说，中美关系是21世纪“起决定性作用”的大国关系，两国应携手共进，共促世界和平与人类发展。中美两国虽不是敌人，双边关系近来却面临贸易摩擦、朝核问题、台湾问题等挑战。中国驻美大使崔天凯表示，要警惕一些美国人试图在中美之间设置“玻璃幕墙”，对中美之间正常的经济、科技、人文交流合作设置障碍，甚至对中国在美国的留学生和学者疑神疑鬼。但可能出现的问题并不会改变中美关系的重要性及主流发展方向。

二、印度或成为中美贸易摩擦的最大受益者

一方面，如果中美贸易摩擦不断升级，印度可能会成为最大受益者。印度市场庞大，最可能成为中国大批制造商的下一个目标市场。2018年4月，印中举行第五次战略经济对话，两国一致认为印中作为两个最大的发展中国家应携手合作，成为推动地区和世界经济增长的“双引擎”。印度在资源禀赋特别是劳动力资源方面具有较强支撑，随着相关改革举措的推进落地，经济有望进入持续较快增长期。中国对大豆进口高度依赖，随着中国对美国征收

关税，印度大量大豆、白糖将首次低关税进入中国。另一方面，印太地区形势正朝着有利于印度的方向发展。印度话语体系倾向于使用“印太”概念来指代本地区，这是一个包容的地区性概念。印度洋连接太平洋和大西洋，贯通欧亚非及大洋洲，素有“海上生命线”之称，是世界上资源最丰富的地区之一。多年来，印度始终坚持不结盟，保持着清醒的“战略自主性”，这是印度的国家立场和影响力的一种体现。2017 年，美国特朗普政府发布的《国家安全战略报告》强调印太地区对美国的重要性，向世界传递出印度战略地位愈加重要的信息。2018 年，第 17 届香格里拉对话会突出强调“印太”安全概念；但莫迪总理认为没有其他双边关系能比印度和中国的关系层次更多，中方亦更加重视同印度的交流合作。

三、中美关系发展动向会对亚太地区产生重要影响

美国近期对华贸易政策是其对华安全战略心存担忧的体现。一方面，中国在南海的军事行动引发美方重大安全关切；另一方面，美国认为中国在美朝关系背后扮演一定角色，心存警惕。2018 年 5 月，美国突然取消邀请中国参加美方主导的环太平洋军事演习，以此方式向中国施压。中美关系恶化或将导致美元升值与实际利率上升，资金大量回流美国进而推动美元继续走高。在贸易和资本全球化的背景下，中美贸易摩擦必将给更大范围内的国家带来负面影响。可以说，本地区国家都在密切关注中美关系动态及两国的任何举动，担心由于任何一方造成的谈判破裂会给地区国家乃至全球各国造成冲击。印度希望中美两国通过和平谈判方式解决争议，因势利导，实现互利共赢。

中美关系恶化的结构性原因

中国人民争取和平与裁军协会常务理事
中国现代国际关系研究院院长、研究员
袁鹏

一、中美关系正处在比较严峻的时刻

过去十年来中美关系已经发生根本性转变，随着中国综合国力日益强大，中美难免形成战略竞争格局。由于美国当前的执政基调是“美国优先”，加之对中国和平发展政策的误读和误判，美国至今难以建立真正与时俱进的对华战略。

当前，一场冷战结束之后规模空前的对华战略大辩论、大反思、大调整正在美国上演。其参与者众多，政界、学界、商界、军界无不介入其中；议题广泛，从经贸、安全到人文、科技几乎无所不包；程度深入，辩论直逼一个主题，那就是美国对华战略是不是需要来个根本性的大调整。几个初步共识正在形成：其一，中国成为美国未来必须全力应对的主要战略竞争对手，而且这个对手已超越经贸领域和亚太区域，是全方位和全球性的；其二，美国既有对华战略虽难说完全失败，但可以说基本失效，亟须改弦更张进行调整重置；其三，未来五至十年是中美战略竞争的关键期，如不有效应对，中国将势不可挡，超越美国只是时间问题。

白宫《国家安全战略报告》公然将中国定性为“修正主义大国”“战略竞争对手”，宣告既往对华战略彻底失败；五角大楼《国防战略报告》声称美国安全的首要关切不再是恐怖主义，而是大国间的战略竞争，中俄首当其冲；

《核态势评估》报告则将中国同俄罗斯、朝鲜、伊朗并列，视为美国核安全的主要威胁。官方权威报告如此高密度、赤裸裸地将中国列为主要挑战甚至威胁，对塑造美国对华战略辩论的环境产生了非常恶劣的影响。

参与辩论的各方普遍认为，中美关系进入复杂敏感时期，有恶化的趋势。在经贸问题上，中美双方都想避免贸易战，但是特朗普政府一意孤行对华挑起贸易摩擦战，对 340 亿美元中国商品加征关税并发布新的征税清单，限制中国对美高科技投资，指责中国经济侵略、窃取知识产权等。在台湾问题上，美国通过了《台湾旅行法》，美访台的国务院官员、国会官员层级升高，次数增多，美国会还通过《2019 财年国防授权法案》，强化美台关系特别是军事关系，承诺将与台共同面对“挑战”。在军事领域，美军取消邀请中国参加环太平洋军演，作为对中国在南海持续军事化行为的回应。在人文领域，美国认为中国目前有意轻视美国实力，巧妙松动美国秩序，并开始逆向影响美国思想文化教育领域，施行所谓“锐实力”，所以美国必须施以颜色、晓以利害，让中国知所进退。

中美关系正常化以来，两国关系发展得比较好。既没有发生热战，也没有发生冷战，经贸总量从 25 亿美元发展到 5000 多亿美元。为什么会出现当前中美全面竞争的态势？

二、中美关系恶化的深层次原因是结构性矛盾

第一，中美两国力量对比的变化。2017 年中国的 GDP 是美国的 63%，苏联发展最高峰时期与美实力对比数值是 58%，日本是 69%。如果中国按照目前的节奏继续发展，其 GDP 很可能会达到美国 GDP 的 70% 到 80%。这一变化是最根本的，导致美国各界的心态不像原来那么自信、包容，而是显得敏感、焦虑。中美两国关系从以往的“（一）超（多）强”关系变为“老大老二”关系，形成战略竞争格局也就在所难免，这是不以人的意志为转移的客观现实，也是难以回避的历史基本规律。“修昔底德陷阱”命题之热炒概源于此。

第二，双方战略态势变化。美国的战略重心全面转向亚太或者印太，甚

至已经转到了中国的周边。美国认为中国对待世界的态度已经从原来的“韬光养晦”发展成“奋发有为”，将从陆地走向海洋，从自我发展走向“一带一路”。这一变化导致双方在亚太地区全方位的对峙，但双方既没有历史经验可以遵循，也没有现实路径可以走，只好以怀疑的心态揣测对方的战略意图，彼此的猜忌比较明显，恐怕将陷入恶性循环。

第三，双方战略基础变化。长期构成中美关系压舱石的经贸关系现在反而成为最突出的问题，而类似冷战时期共同应对苏联、“9·11”事件后联合反恐这样的安全基础目前也基本不存在。朝核危机本应成为凝聚中美两国战略合作的契机，但目前的情况是合作和嫌隙并存，还难说是深度的战略合作。特朗普执意退出气候变化《巴黎协定》，令支撑中美双边关系的应对气候变化的合作也受到侵蚀，在这种情况下，两国关系出现颠簸摇晃也就不令人意外。

第四，双方战略环境的变化。不同的、多元化的声音在影响两国高层的决策。中美关系对内受各利益群体的掣肘，对外受“第三方”因素的滋扰，双边关系的主轴或主航道往往由不得自己，可谓树欲静而风不止。

中美关系已经发展到了新的阶段，新的阶段要有新的应对之策，中国提出的办法是构建“新型大国关系”，但是没有得到美国热烈的呼应。在这一背景下，特别是特朗普上台后，中美关系既有的竞争趋势不断恶化，加之特朗普本人的不可预测性、“美国优先”的自私性、其外交与安全团队对华的敌视态度的不可改变性，使得中国与美国打交道比较困难。实际上，日本、韩国、欧洲与特朗普都不好打交道，但是中美关系与其他国家同美国的关系有本质区别，因为中美之间具有大国权力转移的特点，因此要承担的更多。

第二篇

东北亚安全形势及前景

特朗普对朝政策的变化与选择

中国人民争取和平与裁军协会常务理事
中国国际问题研究院美国研究所所长、研究员
滕建群

朝鲜半岛出现的缓和与美、朝、韩等国直接互动密切关联。其中，美国对朝政策的变化是重要原因之一。美国总统特朗普别出心裁、打破常规，试图在朝鲜问题上有所建树，但受地缘战略和国内政治束缚。当下，美国对朝政策不可能发生根本性调整，各国关系也不会出现剧烈变化，维系现有的稳定局势是有关方努力的重点之一。

一、特朗普对朝政策的基本演变

从 2016 年总统大选至今，特朗普总统的对朝政策可分为四个阶段：

第一阶段：试图另辟蹊径，通过“电话”或“汉堡”解决朝核问题。2016 年的美国总统大选被认为是突破底线的“超级真人秀”，是“最肮脏的战斗”。最后辩论成为特朗普和希拉里的相互攻击，两人涉朝的辩论内容不多。2016 年 6 月 15 日，特朗普在亚特兰大称：“如果朝鲜最高领导人金正恩来美国，我会和他一边吃着汉堡，一边就核问题进行更好的协商。”他说，虽然通过对话让金正恩弃核可能性只有 10% 到 20%，但不是完全没可能，他会与金正恩就核问题进行更好磋商。“希拉里批评我想和‘独裁者’进行沟通，但我认为，这是对话的开始，虽然这种对话的可能性不是很大。”特朗普还强调，和金正恩对话，不是他去朝鲜，而是金正恩来美国见面，但他不会为金正恩举行国宴，只是和他边吃汉堡边协商。上述表态是特朗普认识朝鲜问题的开始。

第二阶段：对朝决策权旁落国防部，美国对朝“极限施压”。2017 年 2 月初，时任美国国防部长马蒂斯出访韩国，这是特朗普内阁成员首次外访。马蒂斯强调，朝鲜半岛局势影响美国利益。他重申美国对韩国安全承诺，指出“萨德”导弹防御系统是为抵御朝鲜导弹威胁。马蒂斯指出，美国深知解决朝核问题的紧迫性和发展韩美军事同盟的重要性，因此他上任不久即访问韩国，表明特朗普政府重视与韩同盟关系，显示美国将继续参与亚太安保事务。马蒂斯警告朝鲜，任何针对美国及盟国的攻击必被挫败，美国将以压倒性优势反制一切核攻击。

军事威慑和向朝鲜施压成为马蒂斯此访首要任务。美韩决定继续在半岛举行大规模军事演习，同意提高美国对朝鲜延伸威慑的执行能力，通过定期出动和轮换，实现战略核武器在韩常驻，防范朝鲜核导挑衅。马蒂斯访韩当天，美国务院批准 1.4 亿美元的对韩军售案。

在特朗普当选和马蒂斯访韩前，朝鲜没有进行核导试验。但马蒂斯老调重弹使朝鲜失去耐心。2017 年 2 月 12 日，朝鲜在平安北道向半岛东部海域发射导弹。此后，半岛局势升温，美朝相互指责。特朗普政府提出向朝鲜“极限施压”，强化美韩同盟，进行大规模军事演习，频繁派战略兵器抵近朝鲜半岛。朝鲜除进行系列导弹试验外，还于 2017 年 9 月进行了第六次核试验。

第三阶段：美朝领导人实现会晤并达成四点共识。2018 年 2 月平昌冬季奥运会重新打开韩朝互动大门，但美国并不看好这种互动。开幕式和闭幕式上，美朝官员近在咫尺，但没有直接接触。美国副总统彭斯和国家安全事务助理博尔顿等认为，冬奥会圣火熄灭时就是朝韩交往结束之际。冬奥会结束后，韩国与朝鲜继续联系，派高官访问平壤，带回金正恩愿与特朗普见面信息。特朗普则迫不及待宣布将与金正恩会晤。2018 年 6 月 12 日，特朗普和金正恩在新加坡会晤，双方达成四点共识。可以看出，美朝领导人新加坡会晤各有所图。特朗普建功心切，希望能在朝核问题上有突破。

第四阶段：有关方陷入僵持，如何前行仍不确定。尽管美朝在新加坡达成共识，美韩同意停止 2018 年下半年在半岛举行联合军事演习，朝鲜继关闭丰溪里核试验场后也在拆除导弹试验场，但特朗普的阁员放风说朝鲜应该有弃核时间表和路线图，朝鲜则希望美国兑现安全承诺，尽快签署《终战宣言》。美国中期选举结束后，特朗普明显地放慢了与朝鲜互动的节奏，甚至发推特称，朝鲜核问题的解决可能需要 25 年，而不是之前所言的两年。

从发展趋势看，在结束中期选举之后，美国已经进入 2020 年的总统选举周期，特朗普的任何作为都将瞄准这个时间节点。在国内没有太多腾挪空间的背景下，特朗普将继续关注朝鲜半岛的局势演变，确保朝鲜不再进行核导试验。

二、特朗普对朝政策调整的主要原因

特朗普入主白宫后采取与以往任何一位总统不同的对朝鲜政策。从竞选期间声称一个电话或汉堡解决朝核问题，到提出对朝“极限施压”，再到在新加破与金正恩会晤，特朗普对朝政策的多变性体现了其外交政策的不确定性。

第一，美国对朝鲜核导威胁的判断发生重大变化。

美国认为，朝鲜目前已初步掌握核导技术，且部分导弹已可覆盖美国本土目标。美国情报机构对朝鲜核导能力表示担心。对美国来说，任何能对美国本土构成的直接和现实威胁，其领导人必会竭尽全力应对，如 1962 年苏联把导弹部署在古巴后，时任美国总统肯尼迪拉开不惜打第三次世界大战的姿态，逼苏联从古巴撤走导弹。特朗普在 2018 年《国情咨文》中指出，朝鲜导弹“很快就能威胁美国本土”。他强调，“朝鲜对核导弹的鲁莽追求很快就会威胁到我们的家园。为了防止这种状况发生，我们要发起一场运动，施加最大的压力。过去的经验告诉我们，自满和让步只会带来侵略和挑衅。我不会重犯过去那些让我们深陷危险的错误。”

第二，军事打击手段难以达到预期目标。1953 年以来，美国一直研究对朝作战计划。从 5027 到 5015 作战计划，作战样式由防守反击转为先发制人。由于对朝鲜核导威胁判断的变化，特朗普上台后就一直琢磨如何从根本上清除朝鲜的核导能力。

军事上看，特朗普政府已把对朝“先发制人”打击摆在桌面，但也面临很大风险。特朗普在其《交易的艺术》一书中写道：“我做生意的方式简单又直接。我给自己定很高的目标，然后为此不断付出，直到成功。”从 2017 年 2 月开始的半岛紧张局势似乎应验特朗普这种商人的行事风格：做高投入交易。

第三，韩朝积极互动给美对朝政策带来冲击。2018 年，特朗普对朝政策被韩朝冬奥会积极互动所打乱。2 月 9 日，朝鲜最高人民会议常任委员会委员长金永南率领的高级别代表团乘专机抵达韩国，出席平昌冬奥会开幕式。次日，韩国总统文在寅在青瓦台会见朝鲜高级别代表团并共进午餐。金正恩胞妹金与正作为金正恩特使向文在寅转交关于改善朝韩关系的亲笔信，转达金正恩对文在寅访问朝鲜的口头邀请。

2018 年 3 月 4 日，韩国宣布将派出高级代表团访问平壤。特使团团长为青瓦台国家安保室长郑义溶。访朝期间，韩国特使团与朝方高层官员就促进朝鲜半岛和平、改善南北关系展开对话，特别就创造条件促成以半岛无核化为目标的朝美对话、促进南北交流等问题进行全面讨论。4 月 27 日，朝鲜金正恩委员长和韩国文在寅总统在板门店举行会晤并发表《板门店宣言》，给南北互动注入了新的动力，也为半岛缓和创造了条件。

三、特朗普对朝鲜政策的未来走势

尽管美朝领导人在新加坡达成四点共识，但要落到实处还有很长的路要走。2018 年 8 月 24 日，美国国务卿蓬佩奥公布第四次访朝计划仅过一天，特朗普突然取消这一计划。他在推特上称：“我已要求国务卿蓬佩奥这次不要去朝鲜了，因为我觉得我们在朝鲜半岛去核化上没有取得足够的进步。蓬佩奥期待在未来再次前往朝鲜，可能会在我们与中国的贸易关系解决之后。”突然叫停蓬佩奥访问朝鲜，确实让人们看到美国和朝鲜互动前景堪忧。

美朝关系经历 65 年对峙，很难马上冰释前嫌，建立新型关系，若要建交还涉及美国国会立法程序。实现和平机制的前提是美国不再对朝使用武力或以武力相威胁。特朗普政府并没在解除对朝经济制裁和放弃武力威胁上做出承诺。实现朝鲜半岛无核化是一个复杂过程。

总之，特朗普政府对朝政策的变化是各种因素相互作用的结果。美国是对东北亚地区有深刻影响的国家，其一举一动会带来地区局势的变化。对东北亚地区国家来说，维护朝鲜半岛和平与稳定，实现半岛无核化应是共同目标。因此，各方应团结起来，防止特朗普对朝政策出现倒退。

朝鲜迈入后核武时代的战略影响

菲律宾外交关系委员会研究员
亚伦·雷宾纳

朝核问题和南北统一问题是影响朝鲜半岛局势的两大核心因素。半岛无核化进程体现着朝鲜内政外交走向。中、美、朝、韩围绕半岛无核化采取了系列动作，特别是美朝元首的历史性会晤，推动朝鲜开始迈入后核武时代，对地区安全形势产生了重大而深远的影响。

一些学者就朝鲜发展路径作出预判：首先，朝鲜集中力量发展经济后，其国家形象会向"遵守国际规则、秉持合作态度"的开放形象逐渐转变。其次，为掌握更多战略机遇、追求更多经济利益，朝鲜或将迈出国际化、市场化步伐，同国际社会加强互动，更大程度上融入国际市场，拥抱境外资本、先进技术和管理经验。再次，为给国家经济发展创造良好的外部环境，朝鲜或将积极加入国际多边机制，甚至重新加入《核不扩散条约》，逐步申请加入世界贸易组织、国际货币基金组织、亚洲开发银行等机构，以及东亚峰会、"一带一路"倡议等平台。从中长期看，朝鲜最终或能实现签订双边自贸协定，进而推动多边自贸谈判。东南亚国家欢迎一个无核、开放的朝鲜，欢迎朝鲜加入东盟主导的地区性倡议并探索开展合作。

冷战时期，美国将苏联视为在价值观、国家安全、全球主导权方面的最大威胁，利用中苏分歧加强同中国的联系以遏制苏联，推动中美关系正常化，助力中国推进改革开放和经济发展。当前，美国转而将中国视为最大威胁。在2018年美国《国防战略报告》中，美方多次提及中国，指称中国为战略竞争对手。同期，越南同美国开展更为紧密的战略和军事合作；朝鲜也迈出同美国和解的步伐，希望在外交上争取更多战略自主和回旋空间。但是，美韩联系紧密让朝鲜担忧。可以预见，美韩经济、军事等各维度联系不会减少，这在未来是否会再度引起美朝分歧，始终是横亘在朝鲜面前的一个问题。

朝鲜外交和安全政策的重大调整，对地区安全形势产生一定积极影响，但总体来看仍充满不确定、不稳定因素，包括“萨德”反导系统、日本安全政策、美韩同盟的结构性调整、中美关系演变等。具体来说，第一，如果“萨德”反导系统没有被撤走，其战略意图更多是指向中国。第二，日本谋求军事正常化一直动作频频，或将进一步引起中俄不适。第三，美朝关系是否会受到美韩关系的影响，我们还需拭目以待。第四，中美关系紧张升级，台湾问题、东海问题、南海问题等仍在发酵。推动朝鲜向无核化方向发展只是迈出了缓解地区紧张局势的第一步，我们需对地区安全形势谨慎地保持关注。

东北亚需要谋求可持续安全

——基于朝美领导人首次会晤后的思考

中国人民争取和平与裁军协会常务理事
清华大学国际关系研究院教授
刘江永

2018 年 6 月 12 日，美朝两国在新加坡成功实现了历史上首次领导人会晤。这是具有重要历史意义的一件大事、一件好事。朝鲜半岛有可能告别朝鲜进行核导试验与美韩不断加强联合军演的恶性循环。今后最为重要的是如何巩固朝韩、朝美峰会的成果，具体落实朝韩《板门店宣言》和朝美联合声明，实现朝鲜半岛完全无核化与建立永久和平的安全机制。

一、2018 年东北亚大变局的真正动因

迄今，朝鲜和美国、韩国尖锐对立是朝鲜战争历史因素和意识形态因素造成的，但三国决策者都坚信，只有拥有能够毁灭或威慑对方的军事手段，才能确保自身的安全。这种传统军事战略理论与权力政治现实主义的决策思维，必然导致朝核危机与美韩军演轮番升级，是一种高成本而不安全或安全状态不可持续的“死胡同”。

那么，在历史的十字路口，究竟怎么做才符合美国、朝鲜、韩国的国家安全利益？这是三国决策者必须重新认识和思考的重大问题。朝核问题要走出“死胡同”，首先需要相关各方摆脱囿于传统军事理论与现实主义政治思维的“死胡同”，共同树立可持续安全观，并在此基础上提出解决问题的新思路、新举措。舍此，朝鲜半岛完全无核化与东北亚持久和平与稳定，恐怕都将

难以实现。那种不惜一战也要优先解决朝核问题的鲁莽想法或所谓“利比亚模式”，既不现实也不会得到任何负责任政府的采纳。

旧的传统思维使一些人陷入了“制裁有效论”的误区，深信朝鲜最高领导人金正恩重返无核化轨道是“极限施压”的结果。然而，这种逻辑思维必然导致继续对朝制裁的政策选项而缺乏建设性，甚至适得其反。实际上，“制裁有效论”不过是美国及其追随者、盲信者对朝“舆论战”的一部分而非科学的研究。科学的研究是以大量事实为基础发现事物发展变化的内在规律，而不是为了证实自身偏见的主观想象。

回顾自20世纪90年代初以来朝核问题26年走过的历程，可以发现一个规律性现象：只要美韩同步对朝实施和解、包容的“阳光政策”，朝鲜半岛就可开启无核化进程；只要美韩任何一方对朝实施敌视、打压的“北风政策”，朝鲜就会搞核试验、导弹试射。冷战后初期，美国总统克林顿和韩国总统卢泰愚对朝鲜同时采取“阳光政策”，促使朝鲜半岛无核化迈出重要一步。然而，遗憾的是，2001年小布什政府执政后推翻了克林顿的政策，对朝实施“北风政策”，导致金大中、卢武铉政府推行的对朝“阳光政策”受挫。从那时起至2018年的近20年中，美韩两国对朝政策一直不同步，结果朝鲜加快了拥核步伐。2018年，美韩两国领导人终于统一步调，开始同时对朝采取“阳光政策”。这正是朝鲜领导人和半岛所有爱好和平的人民所期盼的。

尽管有些人还企图对朝实施“北风政策”，主张继续对朝制裁，继续针对朝鲜进行例行联合军演，但在新形势下，这些做法既有违于联合国安理会1718号对朝制裁决议第15条，也违反美朝领导人会晤联合声明所肯定的朝韩《板门店宣言》。2018年以来，金正恩在中朝、朝韩、朝美“三峰会”期间，均明确承诺实现朝鲜半岛完全无核化，并主动废弃核试验场，并将废弃导弹试验场，宣布朝鲜将集中精力发展经济。这种积极的变化应得到肯定。

有鉴于此，朝鲜半岛局势良性循环的逻辑起点，应该是美韩适时停止针对朝联合军演和联合国安理会讨论有关如何解除或减少对朝制裁问题。如果2019年朝鲜半岛能实现“双全停”，联合国开始取消制裁，朝核问题“六方会谈”就有希望恢复，并具体商讨朝鲜如何分阶段弃核，以及如何给予朝鲜经济援助等问题。中美朝韩四国签署朝鲜半岛永久和平协定，以取代朝鲜半岛停战协定也将会为期不远。

二、东北亚安全迫切需要树立可持续安全观

朝美峰会成功的重要因素之一是，金正恩和特朗普的安全观念同时发生了重要变化。2017 年 9 月 19 日，特朗普曾在联合国大会一般性辩论上发表演讲称，朝鲜的核武器与弹道导弹是对全世界的威胁，“如果美国被迫自卫或保护盟国，那么将别无选择去彻底摧毁朝鲜”。针对特朗普的这番“彻底摧毁朝鲜”的言论，金正恩怒怼称，“将坚决采取行动予以回击。”这种隔空叫板直到 2018 年 5 月仍未停止，并险些坏了“特金会”的大事。

然而，2018 年 6 月 12 日，金正恩在新加坡初次见到特朗普后发自内心地说了一句话：“来到这里不容易。历史扯了我们的后腿，过去的偏见和做法也阻挡了我们前进。但这些我们全都克服了，我们今天来到了这里。”对此，特朗普表示赞赏。

当然，并非所有人都会反思“过去的偏见和做法”，特别是在美国，传统的权力政治现实主义的惯性思维方式在“建制派”中仍占据主导地位。因此，特朗普与金正恩达成的联合声明在美国国内受到质疑和抨击是预料之中的，未来美国政局变化后会否翻脸仍有不确定性。

值得庆幸的是，2014 年 5 月中国国家主席习近平在上海举行的亚信峰会上首次提出“共同、综合、合作、可持续的亚洲安全观。”此后，习近平还在许多重要国际场合不断倡导和强调这一新安全观。

2015 年 9 月，习近平在联合国大会的重要讲话中指出：“我们要摒弃一切形式的冷战思维，树立共同、综合、合作、可持续安全的新观念……我们要推动经济和社会领域的国际合作齐头并进，统筹应对传统和非传统安全威胁，防战争祸患于未然。”这是中国领导人首次在联合国正式提出可持续安全观，从而使这一新的安全理念具有全球意义。

2017 年 9 月 3 日，习近平出席金砖国家工商论坛开幕式并发表主旨演讲

重申："要倡导共同、综合、合作、可持续的安全观，建设性参与地缘政治热点问题解决进程，发挥应有作用。" 2018 年 5 月 22 日，习近平在上合组织青岛峰会期间再次强调："要继续秉持共同、综合、合作、可持续安全观，推行综合施策、标本兼治的安全治理模式。"

笔者认为，中国提出的可持续安全观对朝美两国领导人的安全观也会产生重要影响，在处理国际热点问题方面可以形成标本兼治的安全治理模式。可持续安全观是一种新的国际安全和国家安全理论思维，可以在国际安全的实践中不断丰富和发展。其基本定义是，国家、地区乃至全球以较低成本长期确保和平与安全状态。可持续安全的范畴包括传统安全和非传统安全两大领域、国内和国际两大方面。在传统安全领域长期维护本国与世界的和平；在非传统安全领域长期加强双边及多边国际合作。可持续安全观就是要保持和平与安全状态的可持续性。可持续安全观追求的是通过国际社会的和平合作，争取各国以较低的安全成本保障较高水平的安全状态和本国安全与国际安全利益平衡的最大化，其特点是具有全球视野，既是某个国家的安全战略问题，也是关系到人类前途命运的国际社会共同的安全战略问题。可持续安全观的原则是：重视综合安全，提倡合作安全，谋求共同安全，争取持久安全。

可持续安全观注重以人为本，强调国家生存的安全环境与生态环境的统一性。可持续安全观要求不得用战争解决主权国家之间的纠纷，反对使用核武器或其他大规模杀伤性武器、核扩散、军备竞赛，尤其反对以破坏社会、文化、经济和生态环境为代价换取某一国家或国家集团片面的安全利益。可持续安全观采取的措施应具有预防性、综合性和协作性。

可持续安全的目标既包括持久和平也包括政权安全，其最低目标是维护朝鲜半岛和平，而朝鲜半岛更为需要的是在和平状态下政权的安全感、领导人之间的互信感与人民的稳定感。因而可持续安全观对于朝鲜半岛和东北亚的未来具有更为重要的现实意义和指导意义。

当今世界，国家面临的安全威胁日趋多元化。传统安全因素与非传统安全因素相互交织，任何一个国家都难以单独应付上述威胁的挑战，需要各国在社会、文化、宗教、经济、政治等多方面加强合作，综合治理，以消除安全威胁的根源。可持续安全观如果能得到美、朝、韩领导人的认同，势将在巩固朝韩、美朝峰会成果方面发挥重要作用。

可持续安全观涉及朝鲜半岛无核化与和平安全的顶层战略设计。为防止类似中东、欧洲的战乱在东亚上演，以可持续安全观为指导，重启“六方会谈”，共建东北亚安全合作机制显得越发重要。否则，即便未来在东北亚建立类似欧洲的多边安全机制，也难保东北亚安全的可持续性。

三、东北亚构建可持续安全的新因素和新方向

（一）当前东北亚安全新的有利因素在增加

——2018 年美朝、韩朝领导人双峰会开创了朝鲜半岛新的历史，中国、新加坡等国在其中发挥了重要作用，得到国际社会的普遍赞赏。

——该地区国家没有像美国为首的北约军事集团，没有在冷战后多次对外发动局部战争或军事介入。

——除少数宗教极端势力、民族分裂势力和国际恐怖势力以外，该地区广大穆斯林与其他宗教信众，长期和睦相处，没有大规模宗教冲突引发的新仇旧恨。

——该地区重视经济发展、就业与民生，各国政府有效维持着本国的社会管理与秩序而未失序、失控。

——尽管中国海峡两岸、朝鲜半岛尚未实现统一，本地区仍有一些领土领海争议问题，但有关各方大都认同以和平方式处理。

——该地区的安全与繁荣得益于中国的改革开放与和平发展，与邻为善，以邻为伴。中国经济发展、市场扩大，人民生活水平提高，带来的是中国企业与游客大量走出去，直接或间带动了世界各国特别是东北亚的经济。

——2020 年日本东京奥运会、2022 年北京—张家口冬奥会的相继举办，中日韩都要与有关各国合作确保赛事安全，也将促进本地区的安全、合作与发展，朝鲜半岛北南双方也可利用国际体育盛事改善彼此的关系。以此为契

机，东北亚可持续安全的航船就可驶出危险水域而扬帆远航。

——尽管日本在前一阶段鼓动特朗普对朝制裁，但只要安倍改变以往对朝政策，伸出橄榄枝，金正恩也不会拒绝，而且有可能当面听取日方关于“绑架”问题的想法。问题的关键在于，如果日本只是出于本国国内政治考虑而策略性地调整对朝姿态，将难有收效。在同朝鲜的交往中，只有从共同、综合、合作、可持续的安全观出发平等协商，才能达到预期目标。

（二）东北亚应谋求可持续安全的新方向

作为东北亚安全战略的顶层设计,有关各国要有长远战略的沟通与协调，而不能仅拘泥于眼前利益与得失。未来 30 年，东北亚应努力建立可持续发展的经济命运共同体、可持续安全的和平命运共同体、和谐与友爱的社会文化共同体。

为此，要提倡和坚持“和平的多边主义”，抵制“暴力的多边主义”，促进共同安全；提倡海洋国家与陆地国家和平合作的“海陆和合论”，抵制各种服务于战争和霸权的传统地缘政治思想。中国作为海陆兼备的大国，提出共建“一带一路”倡议，就是谋求海洋国家与陆地国家、陆地国家之间、海洋国家之间的和平合作。其中自然应包括朝鲜半岛，也欢迎海洋国家美国、日本的参与。

1、朝鲜半岛无核化与和平机制的建立，必须以共同安全为基础，尊重和保障东北亚每个国家的安全。2014 年 5 月 21 日，习近平主席在上海亚信峰会上指出：“安全应该是普遍的，不能一个国家安全而其他国家不安全，一部分国家安全而另一部分国家不安全，更不能牺牲别国安全谋求自身所谓‘绝对安全’。否则，就会像哈萨克斯坦谚语说的那样，‘吹灭别人的灯，会烧掉自己的胡子’。安全应该是平等的。各国都有平等参与地区安全事务的权利，也都有维护地区安全的责任。任何国家都不应该谋求垄断地区安全事务，侵害其他国家正当权益。安全应该是包容的。应该把亚洲多样性和各国的差异性转化为促进地区安全合作的活力和动力，恪守尊重主权独立、领土完整、互不干涉内政等国际关系基本准则，尊重各国自主选择的社会制度和发展道路，尊重并照顾各国合理安全关切。强化针对第三方的军事同盟，不利于维护地区共同安全。”这段讲话用在朝鲜半岛问题上也十分贴切。

2、朝鲜半岛无核化与和平机制的建立，必须重视综合安全，即用综合手段维护东北亚各国的传统安全和非传统安全。习近平指出：“我们应该通盘考虑亚洲安全问题的历史经纬和现实状况，多管齐下、综合施策，协调推进地区安全治理。既要着力解决当前突出的安全问题，又要统筹谋划应对潜在的安全威胁，避免头疼医头、脚疼医脚。”东北亚安全问题极为复杂，现实问题与历史问题相互交织，既有敏感热点问题，也有跨国犯罪、环境安全、网络安全、能源资源安全、重大自然灾害、跨国传染病等带来的挑战等。那种仅凭军事优势就可确保安全的思维方式已经落伍。因此，未来的“六方会谈”或东北亚多边安全机制，不应仅拘泥于讨论朝鲜半岛无核化问题，还可为东北亚的综合安全发挥积极的建设性作用，在互信与共赢中最终找到实现朝鲜半岛完全无核化的出路。

3、朝鲜半岛无核化与和平机制的建立，需要探索合作安全。习近平指出：“合作，就是要通过对话合作，促进各国和本地区安全。有句谚语说得好，‘力量不在胳膊上，而在团结上’。要通过坦诚深入的对话沟通，增进战略互信、减少相互猜疑，求同化异、和睦相处。要着眼各国共同安全利益，从低敏感领域入手，积极培育合作应对安全挑战的意识，不断扩大合作领域、创新合作方式，以合作谋和平、以合作促安全。要坚持以和平方式解决争端，反对动辄使用武力或以武力相威胁，反对以一己之私挑起事端、激化矛盾，反对以邻为壑、损人利己。”东北亚各国可在预防传染疾病、打击走私贩毒、防止重大自然灾害、改善生态环境等非传统安全领域展开安全合作。

4、东北亚的可持续安全，有赖于发展经济、改善民生。习近平提出：“可持续，就是要安全和发展并重，以实现持久安全。‘求木之长者，必固其根本；欲流之远者，必浚其源泉’。发展是安全的基础，安全是发展的条件。贫瘠的土地上，长不出和平的大树；连天的烽火中，结不出发展的硕果。对亚洲大多数国家来说，发展就是最大的安全，也是解决地区安全问题的总钥匙。”他主张：“要建造经得起风雨考验的亚洲安全大厦，就应该聚焦发展主题，积极改善民生、缩小贫富差距，不断夯实安全的根基。要推动共同发展和区域一体化进程，努力形成区域经济合作和安全合作良性互动、齐头并进的大好局面，以可持续发展促进可持续安全。”

我们衷心期待，朝鲜半岛无核化与和解进程不发生逆转；中国同朝鲜、韩国的关系进一步得到改善、巩固和加强；朝鲜半岛与东北亚迎来可持续安全与可持续发展的新时代。

建立朝鲜半岛和平机制面临的问题与挑战

韩国世宗研究所研究企划本部长、韩国核政策研究会会长
李相铉

一、对美朝领导人会晤成果的评估

2018 年 6 月 12 日，美国总统特朗普与朝鲜领导人金正恩在新加坡举行历史性会晤。美朝两个敌对国家的领导人第一次面对面会谈。

新加坡峰会达成了四点共识：第一，美国和朝鲜将遵照两国人民的愿望，致力于建立“新型朝美关系”，推动和平与繁荣；第二，两国将共同努力，建立持久稳定的朝鲜半岛和平机制；第三，朝方重申将遵守《板门店宣言》，承诺继续推动实现“半岛完全无核化”目标；第四，美朝致力于找回战俘和失踪人员遗体，包括立即遣还已确认身份者。

在这些内容中，没有涉及无核化的时间表、检查与核查机制。这意味着美朝谈判小组需要进行一系列长期而艰巨的后续谈判。此前，美国国务卿蓬佩奥第三次访朝，访问成果非常有限。访问结束后，外界得到了截然相反的信息：朝方指责美国采用“流氓般的策略”并提高了“战争风险”，蓬佩奥则表示双方进行了“善意、富有成效的对话，并将在未来几天和几周继续对话”。

从蓬佩奥第三次访朝后朝鲜方面的反应来看，无核化进程似乎面临不确定性，很难将“特金会”制定的朝鲜半岛无核化这一宽泛目标具体化。美朝两国对于蓬佩奥访朝这一事件的不同说法证明了这一点。

二、在朝鲜半岛建立和平机制的考虑

早在核危机出现之前,韩国就把建立半岛和平机制作为长期追求的目标。1953 年 7 月 27 日,朝鲜战争停战,联合国军总司令与朝鲜人民军司令员、中国人民志愿军司令员签署《朝鲜停战协定》。此后,朝鲜半岛的和平仅由一纸停战协定维系,而非和平条约,这意味着从技术层面来讲,各方仍处于战争状态。

朝鲜半岛和平机制包括“半岛完全无核化”、美对朝提供安全保障、各方正式结束朝鲜战争(终止《朝鲜停战协定》)、签署永久和平条约。朝鲜方面一直宣称,他们开发核武器的原因是美国对其采取敌对政策。因此,无核化的关键是美国必须结束对朝鲜的“敌对政策”,即停止在政治、安全和经济方面与朝鲜对抗,以换取朝鲜消除核武器,包括:政治方面,承认朝鲜是一个主权国家,允许朝鲜与韩国、美国等建立外交关系;安全和军事方面,正式结束朝鲜半岛的战争状态,用永久和平条约取代停战协定,停止使用(或威胁使用)反对朝鲜的战略武器;经济方面,解除自朝鲜战争结束以来的几十年里,美国和联合国安理会对朝鲜实施的贸易限制和制裁。

为了回应朝方关切,结束对朝敌对政策,美国可以考虑提供临时性安全保障,宣布结束朝鲜战争,做出美朝互不侵犯的承诺。这样的承诺是一个协议,而非一个条约,是朝着签署美朝永久和平条约迈出的具有象征性的一步。接下来,关于和平机制的谈判需要国际机构的支持和认可,例如多边安全磋商机制、国际金融组织等。当然,建立半岛和平机制应该与推进无核化进程保持同步。

三、朝鲜半岛建立和平机制面临的问题与挑战

目前,解决朝核问题还面临诸多挑战。如在推动建设和平机制的同时,韩美联盟的地位和作用,驻韩美军、联合国军司令部等未来都存在争议。美国总统特朗普已经宣布只要继续谈判,就会停止美韩联合军演。而在落实半岛

和平机制的过程中，谁将承担朝鲜无核化的代价；韩国、日本和中国是否会如特朗普所愿为此买单仍是未知数。

未来，实现半岛无核化与建设和平机制将会涉及三个层面，十分复杂：在朝鲜半岛层面，朝韩两国将讨论如何真正实现友好，改善双边关系；在美朝层面，两国领导人需要细化无核化的方案，且为稳固朝鲜政权提供保障；在朝鲜与国际社会层面，需讨论取消制裁和建立核查与监管机制。三个层面需有机整合，保持适当步调，这样才有利于永久解决朝核危机。

东北亚地区安全治理：重大机遇及其把握

国际关系学院校长、教授
陶坚

2018 年 6 月 12 日，朝美两国领导人在新加坡举行会晤并签署了《美朝联合声明》（下称《声明》），他们以巨大的勇气跳出常规，一举扭转了朝鲜半岛安全恶化的势头，重启半岛全面无核化进程。当前，各方应当把握住朝美关系改善所带来的难得机遇，切实加强东北亚地区的安全治理。

一、朝核问题解决的新进展及其未来前景展望

多年以来，朝核问题一直制约着东北亚地区安全环境的改善，而朝美关系是导致朝核问题难解的主要矛盾。此次美朝关系的大逆转，必将引起积极的连锁反应。在韩朝、中朝、美朝领导人会面之后，俄朝、日朝领导人的会面可以期待。以首脑外交为牵引，东北亚地区将出现新变局，地区安全治理迎来新机遇。

2018 年初，朝鲜最高领导人金正恩以元旦社论的方式抛出南北和解的“橄榄枝”。继承了韩国前总统金大中、卢武铉“进步派”政治路线的韩国现任总统文在寅，迅速接过了“橄榄枝”。4 月 27 日，韩朝两国就实现了第三次元首峰会，签署了《板门店宣言》，达成了一系列协议，为朝鲜半岛的未来设计了和平和新经济蓝图，超越“维持和平”，走向“创造和平”。朝韩领导人改善北南关系的决心之大、行动力之强，给人留下深刻印象。

朝鲜半岛局势取得上述进展，除了韩国的大力推动和朝鲜展示的外交灵活性之外，中国的坚定支持是极其关键的。2018 年 3 月以来，金正恩连续三

次访华，与习近平主席举行了历史性会晤，中国成为朝鲜半岛局势转变的巨大支持力量。美国总统特朗普也作出重大调整，从美朝元首会晤后签署的《声明》内容可见一斑。特朗普上台执政一年多来，在“破”的方面多有“建树”，比如退出《跨太平洋伙伴关系协定》（TPP）、伊朗核协议等，但在“立”的方面，即对国际和地区事务的建设性贡献方面乏善可陈。美朝关系的突破，可谓特朗普的一大政绩。同时，《声明》的内容也证明了中方先前提出的“双暂停”方案，即朝鲜停止核导试验，美韩停止大规模军演，以及无核化与和平机制“同时并举”的倡议，具有合理性和前瞻性，是经得起历史检验的。

展望未来，一是不能忘记处理朝核问题的历史波折。比如六方会谈“9·19共同声明”，以及朝美“2·29协议”之后，都曾出现过非常乐观的气氛，却没能持续多久。有鉴于此，各方也不能过于乐观，对美朝关系和朝核问题中的不确定性要保持高度警惕。二是必须注意细节。所谓“魔鬼存在于细节之中”。朝核问题的本质是安全问题。要实现半岛完全无核化，并从以朝鲜停战协定为基础确立并延续至今的安全框架，转向以和平协定为标志的、更具包容性和可持续的安全框架，需要进行大量艰苦细致的谈判工作，任务远比想象的要复杂严峻，耗时费力。美国是想从一开始就占据制高点，即制订一揽子计划，分阶段实施，实现目标明确、全程可控。朝鲜要的是分阶段进行，以行动对行动、同步对等，始终保持自己的主动权。可以预见，即使“框架性”协议确定之后，双方之间的交锋仍将是不间断的和激烈的。

二、东北亚安全治理机遇与挑战并存

推进地区安全治理，需要凝聚共识。东北亚地区安全治理能否进入正轨，取决于各方能不能抓住朝美关系改善的契机，恢复并建立起全面信任关系。东北亚地区是美、俄、中、日等大国利益的交汇点和竞争博弈的场所。尤其在朝鲜半岛，极度缺乏互信机制和有效的安全机制，“冷战思维”严重，“安全困境”突出。

从地区层面看，各国之间除了不信任，还互相恐惧。2017年12月19日，特朗普政府发布新的《国家安全战略报告》，将中国和俄罗斯并列为国际体系的“修正主义国家”，是美国国家安全面临的主要挑战和“竞争对手”。特别是 2018 年 7 月 6 日中美“贸易战”正式开打且加速升级，对两国多年来好不容易形成的战略互信损耗极其巨大。日本政府发表的 2017 年版《防卫白皮书》，涉华部分篇幅长达 34 页，强烈指责、肆意歪曲中国常规军事活动和正当国防建设。诸如此类，东北亚国家之间的互不信任如同“连环套”一样难解，成为影响东北亚地区安全治理的最大阻碍因素。

从安全治理实践看，美国依托美日韩同盟，试图复制北约模式，打造亚洲版的小北约，而中国和俄罗斯则主张在东北亚地区建立基于平等伙伴关系的多边安全体系。这两种不同的安全治理思路，使得东北亚地区安全体系的建设步履维艰。特别是美国作为世界上唯一的超级大国，试图通过扮演“离岸平衡者”的角色，掌控东北亚局势，利用中日历史认识和领土纠纷以相互制衡，利用台湾问题遏制中国崛起，利用朝核问题控制东北亚安全局势走向，谋求“美国统治下的和平”。正因为如此，使得东北亚地区安全问题上的大国协调难以取得成效。与此同时，随着地区各国实力消长，出现了新的利益矛盾，也给该地区固有矛盾的解决带来了新的变数和困难。

国际信任是形成国际秩序的重要因素之一，任何条约、协定都建立在国与国彼此信任的基础之上。二战后欧洲地区保持长期和平稳定，很重要的一点就是形成了彼此信任的关系，欧洲为此还特意建立起一系列信任措施。相形之下，东北亚地区的信任关系极为薄弱，必须作为当务之急予以建设，要从建立安全互信开始，逐步过渡到积极的区域安全合作和治理机制建设，最终实现该地区的“长治久安”。

中国倡导的以“共同、综合、合作、可持续安全”为主要特征的“亚洲安全观”，为建立东北亚地区信任关系提供了基本思路。建设命运共同体是实现东北亚安全稳定的终极目标。尽管东北亚地区安全治理困难重重，但只要有促进和平稳定的坚定决心和化解地区难题的坚强毅力，遵循“合作共赢”的原则，推动东北亚安全从“不信任”走向“信任”，由“不确定”走向“确定”，实现东北亚命运共同体的前景可期。基于命运共同体的东北亚地区信任关系，才是真正可持续的。

三、东北亚安全治理应坚持“多边加双边，安全加经济”的路径和方式

当前东北亚地区形势的发展，迫切要求有关各方积极、平等和建设性地参与到完善东北亚地区安全治理的现实任务中来。从路径和方式上讲，应坚持“多边加双边，安全加经济”。

多边合作是东北亚地区安全治理的主要模式。多边主义模式有助于提高透明度，缓解国家之间的利益纷争和相互猜疑，增进互信和对合作规则的集体认同。东北亚地区安全合作的实践证明，单靠某一大国主导和发声，无法维持东北亚安全秩序的持久性，这也是中国力推六方会谈的重要原因。东北亚地区各国在解决棘手问题的时候应共同商量、平等对待、互谅互让，不能把某个当事方排斥在外。

实现东北亚地区的和平稳定，必须处理好几对双边关系。其中，中美两国是实现东北亚和平稳定大格局的关键国家，如果两国关系不好，东北亚必然成为其较量的前沿阵地和主要地区。中美两国都要尊重对方在东北亚的重大战略关切和核心利益，构建“总体稳定、均衡发展”的中美关系框架，扩大“兼容共存”和合作共赢的空间。当下特别要防止中美关系因为“贸易摩擦战”而快速下滑，只有全力避免中美两国正面冲撞，才能防止“新冷战危险”重降东北亚地区。另外，2017 年以来中日双方都展现出改善关系的意愿且势头良好，互动有所增加。中日安全冲突下降的局面来之不易，应当悉心呵护。

建立地区安全治理机制，符合东北亚所有国家的共同利益，也只有通过机制化的制度建设，才能从根本上保证地区安全治理的稳定性和有效性。治理机制应该是多层次和多样的，既有法律化的，又有宽松灵活和弹性的，关键是让各参与方能够获得足够的安全感和舒适度。从任务上看，既要有以具体问题为导向的小型多边对话机制，又要有高层次的强大机构来讨论大国之间的安全关切、安全与和平协议方案等重大议题。更为重要的是，所有安全合作的参与者都应践行共同、综合、合作、可持续的安全观，摒弃冷战思维、

零和博弈的陈旧理念，以开放包容精神推进地区安全治理。只有这样，才能保证东北亚地区安全合作和政治信任的进程扎实向前推进，不会因各种原因停滞或倒退。

东北亚是世界重要经济区域，其主要特征是各国经济发展多样性和差异性所带来的地区经济互补性。东北亚地区是经济互补性最强的地区，其中，中日韩三国之间的经贸关系极为密切，互为主要的贸易与投资伙伴。朝鲜、蒙古的经济发展对中日韩的依赖较大，而俄罗斯远东地区是东北亚经济未来数十年内最可依赖的能源基地。这种特征使东北亚各国相互依赖程度不断加深，中期可望出现中日韩三国合作带动俄朝蒙三方的“3+3”合作机制。功能主义理论指出，行为体在合作过程中很容易出现“外溢”效应，即行为体在一个领域合作利益的增长会吸引参与者把合作推广到另外一些领域。在东北亚地区，以经济合作制度化为先导，产生示范效用并“外溢”到政治、安全领域，是可行和必然的。

综上所述，当前东北亚有关各方在朝鲜半岛局势好转的情况下，要以时不我待的态度，积极行动起来，激活已有的对话机制，创设新的合作平台，大力增进互信，多边和双边合作、安全和经济合作并举，推动东北亚地区安全治理进入正轨，维护好地区安全稳定的良好局面，确保地区和平和繁荣。

东北亚需建立地区安全机制

瑞典斯德哥尔摩国际和平研究所研究员
蒂蒂·埃拉斯托

与其他地区不同，东北亚缺乏政治安全对话和地区合作机制，而2018年朝韩、美朝之间领导人的积极互动或将为建立地区安全机制创造良好机会。在2018年6月12日的美朝两国领导人会晤中，双方确立了宏大目标，提出实现朝鲜半岛无核化、美国向朝鲜提供安全保障。过去，尽管付出了很多外交努力，这两个目标仍未达成；而今，美朝领导人会晤取得明显进展，朝韩签署《板门店宣言》，表明美、韩、朝三国处理和解决冲突的政治意愿极大增加。

尽管这些成果具有历史意义，但并非史无前例。此前，朝鲜半岛核问题也曾取得过一些进展，如美朝两国在1993年签署了联合声明，1994年签署了《美朝核框架协议》；朝韩两国在2000年6月、2007年10月发表了《南北共同宣言》和《南北关系发展与和平繁荣宣言》，内容与《板门店宣言》如出一辙；还有2005年达成的“9·19共同声明”等。

美朝领导人会晤为新一轮的外交努力创造了机会，但解决朝鲜半岛问题仍面临许多不确定性：一是双方政治意愿的持续性仍未可知，二是涉及实际操作层面势必会产生分歧，三是两国政策受领导人个人特点影响，合作关系仍显脆弱。因此，初期的双边或三边冲突解决进程需引入其他利益相关方，增加稳定性，防止风向突变。

从朝鲜方面来看，美国是其国家安全的头号威胁。因此，无核化的前提必须是美国承诺现在及将来都不会对朝鲜发动攻击、颠覆其政权。对此，双方似已达成共识，并将其作为进一步谈判的原则和基础。据报道，新加坡会晤期间，美国总统特朗普承诺将为朝鲜提供安全保障，朝鲜最高领导人金正恩则重申了自己将坚定不移地致力于实现朝鲜半岛无核化的立场。这是一个重大进步，但接下来就朝鲜半岛无核化的细节和时间框架的讨论将是一个漫长且复杂的过程，可能仍会面临很多障碍，其中最大的挑战还是双方如何建立互信，协商谈判的结果如何能够得到双方尊重。美朝两国长期敌对，有过多次外交上的失败经历，彼此之间互不信任。同时，特朗普多次“退群”（退出伊朗核协议等）的行为，给美朝建立互信增添了新难题。总之，美朝双方的重中之重是将积极的势头保持下去。

在朝鲜半岛无核化谈判过程中，域内外国家都应该为美朝建立互信提供支持，必要时积极介入，缓和美朝谈判可能出现的紧张态势。如果对话的政治意愿能够持续下去，其他国家在实际谈判中也将发挥重要作用。举例来讲，半岛无核化问题与朝鲜战争停战协定紧密相关。尽管处理这两个议题的顺序还存在争议，但从目前情况来看，和平条约谈判已经与半岛无核化问题绑定，这就需要韩国和中国也加入到谈判中来（中国是 1953 年朝鲜停战协定的签字方之一）。其他国家也应为半岛无核化与和平机制建设助力，比如日本需要与朝鲜建立外交关系。同时，可以寻求设立更为远大的长期目标，例如构建地区安全机制，让所有东北亚国家都能基于共同原则和行为准则来缓和紧张局势、妥善处理争端。构建地区安全机制可以与半岛无核化谈判并行推进，也可以借鉴六方会谈的机制。这或许能够让东北亚地区的其他国家也加入进来，增强他们的“主人翁”意识，充分考虑并回应他们的关切。

当然，最重要的还是要解决核武器问题，这是朝鲜与美国及其盟友冲突和对抗的产物，是导致东北亚局势紧张的主要原因。半个多世纪以来，东北亚地区没有任何的地区安全机制来管控这类冲突，而现有的双边或更广泛的军事同盟反而增加了这个问题的复杂性。

近期，美朝、朝韩之间的互动说明有必要建立地区安全机制，也为解决核武器问题提供了机会。在不远的将来，各方很有可能对解决核武器问题作出一些临时性的安排，但最终目标应该设定为建立一个基于合作安全、包容性强的地区安全机制。考虑到东北亚的现实，这个安全机制并非一定成为十分紧密的共同体，具备常设机构和共同战略价值观，而是意味着地区国家间能够达成共识，无论彼此间关系如何，都会遵守一定的行为规范，用特定的方式解决争端。最重要的是，这种方式不包括使用或威胁使用武力。

战后欧洲在推进赫尔辛基进程时的一些经验可以为建立东北亚地区安全机制提供参考，包括：第一，召开覆盖全地区的会议，签署不具有约束力的文件，初步形成一些共同原则；第二，将会议固定化，成立国际组织，形式灵活多样，甚至欢迎以非正式的方式进行沟通协商。

东北亚地区国家都认为当前状况十分危险，都有构建地区安全机制的政治意愿，这是第一步。事实上，东北亚地区安全机制建设不会完全从零开始，目前该地区已经存在一些组织和机制，例如东盟地区论坛、上海合作组织、东北亚和平合作倡议、乌兰巴托对话等，都有助于在该地区构建安全机制。

最后，域内国家也需开始考虑东北亚无核区概念，涉及到朝鲜半岛和日本。若能签署类似的条约，再加上中、俄、美三方共同提供安全保障，会增加美国对朝安全保障的可信度，有利于把朝鲜纳入到多边条约框架中。同时，建立东北亚无核区，将通过引入共同行为规范，达成互惠承诺来解决安全问题，这本身也会促进地区安全机制建设。

蒙古视角下的东北亚安全合作

蒙古地缘政治研究所教授
噶尔山加姆茨·瑟利特

一、蒙古安全与东北亚安全

当前，蒙古处于外部安全环境较为稳定的时期。一方面，蒙古和邻国没有领土主权争议，另一方面，中俄两大邻国成为良好安全屏障。回顾历史，蒙古在探索国家安全的道路上也曾遇到波折。蒙古的独立是在苏联支持下完成的，因此在建国之初，蒙古在对外安全战略上受苏联影响极深。彼时的蒙古与东北亚各国在各领域联系甚微。中苏关系紧张时，苏联多次向蒙古派驻军队。用现在的观点来看，苏联在蒙古部署大量兵力和武器装备（甚至是核武器），可能会使蒙古成为他国发动“预防性打击”的目标。冷战结束后，蒙古所处地缘政治环境发生根本性变化。由于无法仅仅依靠自身资源和能力来预防所有潜在威胁，蒙古适时调整对外政策，努力在亚太安全、特别是东北亚安全框架下应对安全问题。20 世纪 90 年代起，蒙古开始逐步发展同西方国家、亚太国家、发展中国家更广泛的安全合作。蒙古拒绝接受直接军事援助，承诺在和平时期绝不加入任何军事集团、军事同盟，绝不允许他国在蒙古部署军力或部队经蒙过境，宣布蒙古为无核武器国家。这些都是蒙古对全球和地区安全进程作出的积极贡献。

二、蒙古外交政策的演变

上世纪 90 年代初苏东剧变后，蒙古开始对社会主义体制进行改革，并在外交上重新审视安全战略，其中一个首要问题便是如何处理好同中俄两大邻国的关系，用蒙古自己的方式维护本国安全。为此，蒙古选择同中俄两国开展平衡、全面的合作，并将此作为外交政策主要方向，并先后同俄、中两国签订友好合作关系条约。此外，蒙古还界定了不同内涵的“第三邻国”，在“第三邻国”框架下同美、日、印、韩等重要国家开展积极、理性的合作。这一政策构想对维护蒙古未来安全具有重要意义。

三、蒙古加强同中俄在安全领域的全面合作

蒙古虽然积极与“第三邻国”发展双多边关系，但始终把发展同中俄两国的关系放在外交政策首位，中俄两国亦对蒙古予以理解和尊重。签订友好合作关系条约以来，蒙古同中俄两国关系不断深化并取得务实成效，这对促进蒙古的安全与发展至关重要。为推动友好合作关系进一步升级，蒙古提出愿意成为中俄两国间可以信赖的桥梁。2014 年 9 月，中蒙俄三国元首在塔吉克斯坦首都杜尚别首次举行三方会晤，为进一步扩大三方共同利益、对接三方发展战略奠定了重要基础，并推动三边合作不断深化，取得成效。我们希望中俄两国亦能积极参与蒙古的基础设施建设，实现共同发展。

四、蒙古参与国际维和、反恐行动

蒙古一直积极参与国际维和、反恐行动，致力于维护地区和世界的和平与稳定。这不仅为蒙古赢得国际声誉，有助于提升蒙古维和行动能力与军事武装力量，更是蒙古努力维护东北亚地区和平安全稳定的积极尝试。

五、蒙古在朝鲜半岛核问题上的立场

蒙古同朝鲜保持友好关系，致力于推动朝鲜半岛局势缓和。我们支持朝核问题六方会谈，提倡以适当形式将六方会谈发展成维护东北亚地区和平稳定的安全对话机制。国际社会不应孤立朝鲜，而应采取措施让朝鲜逐步融入，这种融入和接纳是推动解决朝鲜半岛核问题的重要步骤。蒙古政府和人民乐见美朝领导人峰会取得积极进展。1992 年，蒙古宣布其领土为无核武器区。20 年之后，联合国安理会常任理事国才签署共同声明，通过书面形式对蒙无核地位予以确认。蒙古经历的历史阶段和进程或许可为朝鲜走向无核化道路提供一些参考和经验。

第三篇

亚太安全机制建设

构建亚太地区全面合作安全伙伴关系

巴基斯坦伊斯兰堡战略研究所研究员
马利克·穆斯塔法

一、亚太安全问题日趋复杂，亟需构建安全合作新架构

当前，亚太地区传统安全热点不时爆发，非传统安全挑战复杂多样，核扩散风险、领土争端、恐怖主义、跨国犯罪、非理性军事竞争、人道主义危机等问题跨越国界、相互影响。冷战结束初期，亚太各国集中力量发展经济，未能充分应对发展中衍生的安全问题。近年来，亚太地区的安全挑战复杂性、严峻性、极端性突出，依靠单一机制、单个机构无法有效解决。在复杂多变的安全形势下，亚太国家需要对既有安全体系加以调整，构建新的全面合作安全伙伴关系。这种伙伴关系是长期性和多边性的，需要各国共同承担责任，共同期许愿景，在形式与内容上和中国提出的“命运共同体”观念较为接近，但更强调安全与发展问题的关系。

2014 年中国国家主席习近平在亚信峰会上提出加强亚洲安全合作的主张，呼吁各方创新安全理念，搭建亚洲地区安全合作的新架构，提出“共同、综合、合作、可持续”的亚洲安全观。在 2018 年香格里拉对话会上，中方代表强调亚太地区需要重新审视安全观念，重新评估安全架构，探索从根本上解决安全问题。以伙伴关系为基础的安全架构不同于军事同盟关系。互利共赢的安全合作是推动构建共建共享、共同发展、共同捍卫安全的新型国际关系的重要基础。

二、巴基斯坦愿为维护地区安全稳定做出积极努力

巴基斯坦赞同中国的立场。我们认为，为了实现持久和平和稳定发展，需要协同处理内部、外部安全挑战，通过扩大合作和构建安全伙伴关系来打造命运共同体。巴基斯坦遵守国际规则和国际机制，呼吁国际社会特别是广大发展中国家构建共同、合作、全面的伙伴关系，采取积极外交政策，形成有效对话机制，应对传统和非传统安全挑战。巴基斯坦愿同国际社会开展多种合作。例如，参与阿富汗和平进程；呼吁地区国家在中巴经济走廊框架下开展更多合作；向他国介绍包括“利剑行动（Zarb-e-Azb）”在内的打击恐怖、极端主义势力的有效做法和经验。巴基斯坦致力于在双边、地区、全球等层面推动和平安全事业向前发展。

三、推动构建长期有效的全面安全合作伙伴关系

单边路径、单一策略无法实现全面安全。各国应重视大局、开放包容，将本国安全同本地区乃至全人类的安全与发展结合起来，从更宏观的视角应对这些挑战。一是重视和平进程中的深层次问题，改善国家间的战略互信，从双边和多边渠道加强政治互信；开展层级多样、高度协作、积极主动的合作；投入必要资源以化解传统争端与分歧，减少政治经济联系的脆弱性。二是在拉紧友谊纽带、打造命运共同体的基础上，推动各国真正对安全挑战形成清晰认识，“有安全才有发展，有发展才有和平”。三是从国家、次区域、区域等层面对现有安全机制予以适当调整，推动各国加强安全战略对接。四是推动地区组织发挥积极作用，加强自上而下的能力建设，在发展目标、政策机制、法律规范等方面搭建交流合作的平台，加强同世界各国的联系。

巴基斯坦倡导公平、正义、非歧视、平等的人人安全，遵守国际准则，尊重国家主权，坚持不干涉他国内政，反对侵略，主张用对话方式和平解决分歧。巴基斯坦愿充分利用现有资源，推动亚太地区朝着和平稳定的方向不断发展。

亚太秩序重构中的日本与中国

日本庆应义塾大学教授
细谷雄一

一、中国的快速发展给日本带来机遇和挑战

中国国力快速提升，从根本上改变了亚太地区力量平衡。这给日本带来了机遇，也带来了挑战。中国自2009年起便是日本最大的贸易伙伴，在2010年超越日本成为世界第二大经济体。面对美国总统特朗普上台后强调的“美国优先”执政理念，亚太地区国家期待中国承担更多责任，加强合作，推动本地区的和平与发展。作为美国在亚太地区关系最紧密的盟友，日本自身也面临严峻挑战。日本首相安倍晋三是与特朗普见面次数最多的外国领导人，两人已举行六次会晤。日本希望美国作为唯一的超级大国，在国际事务中发挥负责任大国的作用，安倍晋三为此同特朗普多次沟通，但效果有限。特朗普在美国对日贸易逆差问题上变得更为严苛，甚至准备采取一系列有损双边互信与友好合作的单边主义政策。

当前，日本和中国越发意识到加强地区合作的重要性。目前，亚太秩序正在重构且存在领导力真空，日本和中国均认为有必要在各自提出的地区性倡议基础上塑造一个更加稳定繁荣的亚太。

二、日本近年来提出一系列新的外交理念

（一）两大洋的交汇

早在2007年，安倍晋三初任首相时便在印度国会发表了关于“两大洋交汇”的演讲，认为今天太平洋和印度洋已经成为自由繁荣的海洋，一个打破地理界线的“广义的亚洲”正在形成，他呼吁印度洋、太平洋沿岸的民主国家在各个层级增进人民友谊。演讲之后五天，安倍晋三由于身体原因被迫宣布辞职，彼时两洋交汇的概念未能得到进一步发展。一些人士认为，“印太”概念是日印两国意在牵制快速发展的中国。亚洲其他国家更倾向于同中国保持紧密友好的合作关系，因此并未对印太概念表现出强烈兴趣。

2016年，安倍晋三在肯尼亚参加第六届东京非洲发展国际会议时强调，印度洋、太平洋连接亚洲和非洲，日本有责任推动两大洋成为“尊重自由、法治、市场经济且繁荣发展”的地区。在亚洲，生活在民主政权下的民众数量超过了世界上其他地区。民主、法治、市场经济原则在此深深植根，亚洲经济因此实现快速增长。

（二）推动印太地区经济发展有机统一

目前的“印太”构想同安倍晋三先前提出的“印太地区民主国家联合起来”概念有较大不同。首先，“印太”构想对包括中国、俄罗斯在内的所有地区国家持开放态度。其次，该构想的出发点是推动印太地区快速发展的经济体互相联通，在广义上将非洲、中东、北美国家也包括在内。

日本外相河野太郎在美国演讲时表示，日本希望通过投资建设高质量的港口、铁路、公路等基础设施，加强互联互通，推动地区经济发展。“印太”构想本质上就是要加强互联互通，让各国都从中受益。当前，随着老龄化等人口问题加剧，东北亚国家都面临着严峻的社会问题。因此，东北亚国家应把握住时机，加强同东南亚国家开展互利共赢的合作。正如2018年河野太郎在日本国立国会图书馆发表演讲时指出的那样，亚太地区沿着印度洋向中东和非洲地区延伸，构成范围更广的印太地区，这里居住着世界上超过一半的人口，是全球发展的核心区域。

可以看到，“印太”构想和中国提出的“一带一路”倡议具有一定重合相通之处，研究这两项倡议之间的关系，推动其相互促进、实现共赢，具有重要意义。

三、"一带一路"倡议

（一）安倍晋三支持中国提出的"一带一路"倡议

自 2014 年安倍晋三同习近平主席会晤以来，日中作为世界第三、第二大经济体，紧张关系得到缓解，各领域合作不断扩大。对日本来说，只有同中国开展稳定的合作，才能实现本国经济的可持续发展。对中国来说，日本对华直接投资是推动中国经济增长的重要动力之一，保持对日友好合作亦能使中国从中受益。继 2015 年宣布考虑加入亚投行后，2017 年 7 月起安倍晋三开始对"一带一路"倡议表现出合作意愿。

（二）两国关系不断改善

2017 年 7 月，安倍晋三同习近平主席举行会晤，双方一致认为日中关系健康发展关系着两国人民福祉，愿意探讨在"一带一路"框架内开展合作，在国际和地区事务中发挥重要作用，推动地区和平与发展。2017 年 11 月，安倍晋三同李克强总理会晤时，双方进一步达成共识。很显然，日本对"一带一路"倡议采取了全新的态度。安倍晋三立场出现转变的一部分原因是，他认为在特朗普时代有必要促进日中关系进一步发展，他也愿意在"一带一路"框架下拓展同中国的合作。

四、日中两国应携手努力，推动地区繁荣稳定

日中两国关系近年来不断改善，2018 年 5 月中国国务院总理李克强对日访问是两国政府扩大合作的重要体现。安倍晋三在与李克强的会见中言辞友好，展现出希望以此为契机推动日中改善关系的良好意愿。安倍晋三对李克强再次当选中国国务院总理表示祝贺，感谢他将日本作为新任期的首访国家，希望 2018 年日中和平友好条约缔结 40 周年可以成为两国关系的新开端。安倍晋三说，日本和中国共同承担着推动国际和地区和平与发展的重任，两国关系改善符合地区国家期待。李克强总理表示，中日关系出现改善向好势头，此访目的是同日方共同推动中日关系重回正常轨道，希望双方相向而行，努力

保持中日关系长期健康稳定发展。

然而，目前两国主要是开展政府间谈判和政治对话，两国民众对对方国家的印象没有大的改善。日中两国应共同承担责任，架起增进相互理解的桥梁，推动亚洲朝着更加稳定繁荣的方向发展。

南亚和印度洋对亚太安全的影响：机遇与挑战

英国伦敦国际战略研究所南亚及核安全问题研究员
安托万·莱维斯克

一、南亚安全越来越多地由更大范围的亚太局势塑造

近期南亚安全呈现以下新特点：一是“印太”框架日渐形成，域内和跨地区的政策关联性不断增强，特别是美国总统特朗普上台后这一趋势更加明显；二是南亚安全问题突出，印巴冲突持续存在，阿富汗和平进程进展缓慢，恐怖主义与极端主义势力在该地区相互激荡；三是中国因素增多，且对地区各国的安全政策产生结构性影响。“一带一路”倡议在客观上加强了南亚地区的互联互通，使南亚各国内部连通性明显增强，南亚与外部接触增多。

二、南亚的安全挑战继续受到域内外因素影响

南亚各国面临的新旧安全挑战不断增多：第一，印巴两国间的核威慑及可能爆发的核危机将直接影响印度次大陆和印度洋地区稳定；第二，阿富汗和平进程缓慢，成为阻碍整个南亚实现地区稳定和区域合作的重要因素；第三，非传统安全形势复杂严峻，国际恐怖势力向南亚回流或扩散，印、巴、阿被列为恐怖袭击最为严重和频繁的国家；第四，印中边境管控和危机预防出现新的不确定因素。

在处理南亚安全问题方面，中国像其他许多国家一样并没有采用“一刀切”的政策模式，而是认真审视各自国家的安全认知及政策制定者的困境，这

说明了“审慎评估地缘政治”的重要性。中国提出的“一带一路”倡议应更好地结合南亚地区的现实需要和发展前景。作为联合国安理会常任理事国，中国有必要就南亚地区事务寻求与主要大国开展“南亚对话”。

三、南亚国家将保持战略内向，但不会错失任何正在形成的安全架构

从经济层面来看，由于地区整合度较低，南亚各国的繁荣始终依赖于亚洲更大范围的经济财富，所以必须“向外看”；但从安全层面来看，大国之间以及大国与地区邻国之间的边界迟迟没有划定，南亚国家有着强烈的安全关切，需要“向内看”，持续关注政府制定政策是否“清醒”、危机管控能力是否足够、治国理政成效是否显著。当然，印度是个例外。在印度总理莫迪及其继任者的领导下，印度应该能够成功地为自身开辟空间，同时兼顾地区近邻及更为广阔的亚洲地区的繁荣与安全。

目前，在“共担责任”、做出“负责任行为”及其他任何可能形成安全架构的尝试方面，南亚国家的意愿和能力相当有限，特别是对马六甲海峡以东、在其自身政治影响力以外的区域。印度有望承担更大的责任，保护印度洋地区的“自由、开放、包容”。但是，南亚国家可能会加入多个“俱乐部”或“集团”（包括上海合作组织），而不是聚合在某个组织中。

在塑造南亚未来安全格局的过程中，中国将发挥关键作用；而南亚国家帮助塑造或被纳入范围更广泛的亚太安全合作架构的意愿和能力也很重要。作为全球性大国、联合国安理会常任理事国、南亚地区近邻、南亚各国的主要债权国，中国在南亚地区的政策优先方向及其连续性，将会决定自身在该地区是面临机遇还是面对挑战。

“无冲突”应成为印太战略的底线

印度和平与冲突研究所所长、退役中将
阿尔文德·辛格·兰巴

印太地区已成为21世纪地缘政治的中心，域内外大国彼此积极竞争和协作，以应对他国影响、扩大自身影响。

一、亚太概念的演进

“亚洲—太平洋”这一概念可追溯到20世纪60年代，当时美国、日本、澳大利亚等国大力提倡，将其作为连接东亚与太平洋地区的一种手段。“亚太”这一概念在某种程度上强调了亚洲维度，而“太平洋地区”却没有。再者，从政治角度而言，美国无法扮演亚洲大国的角色，但通过广泛介入太平洋地区事务，其作为亚太地区一部分的身份具备了合理性。

亚太地区的政治制度多样化，包括自由民主主义、社会主义、威权制度等，这是导致该地区大国间竞争和对抗突出的原因之一。二战后，该地区经历了东南亚去殖民化、美中两国在朝鲜战争中直接冲突、中苏关系破裂、美中重新修复关系、东南亚地区主义兴起以及后殖民主义冲突等。冷战结束后，美国将中国视为其在亚太地区主要竞争对手。

二、现有机制的失效

澳大利亚前总理陆克文说，亚太地区的机制不像欧洲逐步形成的机制那样健全。我们隐约可见亚太地区正成为21世纪的战略要塞，所以我们需要比现有机制更为健康有效的机制。

我们需要建立适合彼此和可持续发展的大国安全机制，从而保证地区稳定，防止冲突。美国直截了当地表示印度是其维护地区稳定最可信赖的伙伴。在小布什总统时期，美国国务卿赖斯宣布要帮助印度成为21世纪的世界大国。蒂勒森担任美国国务卿期间，也在不同场合，以不同形式明确美国所期待的亚太地区未来发展方向和主要依靠力量。该地区的中心行为体——澳、中、印、日、美等国之间安全利益的竞争和重叠促使"印太"成为令人关注的地区概念。

三、地区实力的架构和机制

如今，连接印度洋和太平洋的"印太"概念使得该地区成为单一的地缘政治空间，绘出了亚洲的新地图，更使该地区的外交安全政策和战略伙伴关系发生了重大变化。

我们清晰地看到，印太地区在战略均势方面的重要性不断增加。最重要的是，中国的"海上丝绸之路"倡议、印度的"东向政策"、美国的"亚太再平衡"战略和日本的"两洋汇聚"概念等，目标都是要在印太地区发挥积极作用。虽然不可能存在某种完美的模式能够同时满足域内外大国的所有要求，但是我们迫切需要形成一种全面、共同、客观的机制，使得所有大国都能够互相尊重、预防冲突、维护海洋（航行）自由，从而确保这一关键地区的和平与稳定。

当前，"印太战略"热度不减。我们认为，这一战略应结合现有机制发挥作用，而非另起炉灶。作为新兴大国和正在崛起的国家，印度应独立地参与国际事务，以平等的姿态为全球治理贡献印度的智慧。中国正在崛起，但印度的发展也不容忽视，我们始终支持建立基于规则的全球和地区安全治理架构，愿为此发挥积极作用。

印太必须成为无冲突地区。为此，美、印、日、澳和中国应该共同努力，建立如文所述的控制机制和架构。美、中两国不能持续对抗下去，否则对地区和全世界有百害而无一利。

后 记

当今世界正处于大发展大变革大调整时期。世界多极化、经济全球化、社会信息化、文化多样化深入发展，各国相互联系和依存日益加深，国际力量对比更趋平衡，和平发展大势不可逆转。与此同时，世界面临的不稳定性不确定性突出，冷战思维、强权政治、单边主义、保护主义等阴霾不散，地区动荡、恐怖主义、网络安全、气候变化、难民潮等风险层出不穷，世界经济增长动能不足，贫富分化日益严重，人类面临诸多共同挑战。分析研判复杂变化中的国际安全形势，对促进全球安全治理，有效应对各种问题和挑战十分重要。

作为中国最大的民间和平组织，中国人民争取和平与裁军协会（简称“和裁会”）积极发挥特色优势，努力打造国际安全问题研究品牌，举办万寿国际安全研讨会，立足于高端、专业特色，邀请世界主流智库的知名安全问题专家，共同交流研讨国际和地区安全形势问题，把脉特点及深刻复杂变化的动因、发展演变趋势等，提出应对问题挑战的意见建议，为维护世界和平与安全，实现各国发展与繁荣凝聚共识、贡献智慧。万寿国际安全研讨会拟每年举办一届，主题根据国际和地区安全形势的变化和国际社会的关切设定。

首届万寿国际安全研讨会于 2018 年 6 月 20 日至 21 日在北京成功举行。来自美国、英国、法国、德国、俄罗斯、日本、韩国、加拿大、澳大利亚、瑞典、印度、巴基斯坦、越南、菲律宾、印度尼西亚、马来西亚、泰国、斯里兰卡、蒙古等 19 个国家及中国社会科学院、国防大学、中国现代国际关系研究院、中国国际问题研究院、清华大学、中国人民大学、国际关系学院等单位的 50 位知名安全问题专家参加。会议主题为“亚太安全”，议题包括“中美关系与亚太安全”“东北亚安全形势及前景”“亚太安全机制建设”。中共中央对外联络部部长宋涛出席研讨会并作主旨讲话，前国务委员戴秉国与部分外方参会代表进行深入交流，全国人大外事委员会副主任委员傅莹出席研讨会晚餐会、发表专题演讲并与外国专家现场交流互动。中外代表围绕主题和议题进行了深入研讨。

与会代表积极评价并充分肯定首届万寿国际安全研讨会，希望万寿国际安全研讨会这一平台越办越好，汇聚世界知名智库安全问题专家，就国际和地区安全治理问题展开深入交流互动，寻找应对安全问题的最大公约数，探求有利于各国长远利益的理性选择，让更多理性的声音影响甚至引领社会舆论和影响政府决策，为实现世界和地区的和平与安全贡献智慧和力量。

为进一步体现首届万寿国际安全研讨会成果，和裁会对部分专家的发言和提交的会议论文整理编辑后结集出版，供交流参考。

和裁会秘书长安月军、副秘书长陶涛对论文集进行了策划和统筹，陈湘源、侯红育牵头负责组稿和统稿，林欐、羊蕾、宋一鸣、沈芳、林永锋、孙博文、王清、牛娜、王珊、冯伟、王瑞娟、吴克生等同志做了一些编辑和翻译工作。

由于经验不足，水平有限，论文集难免会有不妥之处，诚恳希望有关专家和读者批评指正。

编者

2018 年 11 月

Make Concerted Efforts toward a Secure Homeland in Asia-Pacific

——Anthology of the First Wanshou Dialogue on Global Security

Wang Yajun: Chief Editor

An Yuejun, Tao Tao: Executive Editor

BUILD CONSENSUS AND MAKE CONCERTED EFFORTS TOWARDS A SECURE HOMELAND IN ASIA-PACIFIC

Keynote Address by Mr. Song Tao

Minister of the International Department of the Central Committee of the Communist Party of China

Distinguished guests,
Ladies and gentlemen,
Friends,

Good morning! I am delighted to join you at the first Wanshou Dialogue on Global Security and share with you our view on the security situation both internationally and in the Asia–Pacific region.

Our world is undergoing profound changes unseen in a century. The trends of global multi–polarity, economic globalization, IT application, and cultural diversity are surging forward; changes in the global governance system and the international order are speeding up; countries are becoming increasingly interconnected and interdependent; relative international forces are becoming more balanced; and peace and development remain irreversible trends. On the other hand, our world faces acute instabilities and uncertainties. The humanity is confronted with many common challenges. Against such a backdrop, Xi Jinping, General Secretary of the Central Committee of the Communist Party of China (CPC), pointed out clearly at the 19th CPC National Congress that China will stay on the path of peaceful development, work to forge a new form of international relations and build a community with a shared future for humanity. To forge a new form of international relations means creating new prospects for state–to–state relations based on mutual respect, fairness, justice and win–win cooperation. To build a community with a shared future for humanity involves each and every nation and country in sticking together through thick and thin and making concerted efforts to build an open, inclusive, clean, and beautiful world that enjoys lasting peace, universal security, and common prosperity, so that the people of all countries shall see the realization of their aspirations for a better life.

The vision to forge a new form of international relations and build a community with a shared future for humanity is both forward–looking and profound. It has not only become the aim and objective of China' s diplomatic agenda, but also offered Chinese wisdom and a Chinese approach to solving global problems. Today, this vision is being translated into concrete actions. In particular, the Belt and Road Initiative (BRI), under the banner of building a community with a shared future for humanity, has become the most popular international public good and the largest platform for cooperation among countries to realize common development.

As long as we follow the trend of the times, work together to address challenges, and seize opportunities amidst changes, we human–beings will be able to build synergy for the first time in history and enjoy unprecedented abilities and conditions to build a community with a shared future for humanity.

It is of great significance that the first Wanshou Dialogue on Global Security focuses on security in the Asia–Pacific region. As the largest block of the world economy, the Asia–Pacific cannot achieve growth and prosperity without regional peace and stability. Security in the region is not only critical to the wellbeing of people of all countries in the region, but also is something that matters to peace, stability and development of the whole world.

The overall situation of Asia–Pacific today remains stable. Settlement of differences and disputes through dialogue and consultation increasingly becomes an important policy option of countries in the region. An Asia–Pacific with steady growth still serves as the "locomotive" for global economic recovery. Nevertheless, it must be noted that new security challenges keep cropping up while old ones are yet to be addressed, which further complicate peace and development situation in the region.

Looking into the future, it is important for Asia–Pacific countries to keep pace with the times, reject outdated mentalities of zero–sum game and practices of the law of the jungle and beggar–thy–neighbor, work together to introduce new security concepts, expand security cooperation and build security mechanisms. There is an urgent need for countries in the region to work together, with a vision to forge a new form of international relations and build a community with a shared future for humanity, towards a path of Asia–Pacific security in the spirit of collaboration for shared benefits and win–win results. Here, I would like to share with you some of my understanding.

First, common development needs to be promoted through win-win

cooperation so as to consolidate the economic foundation for security in the Asia-Pacific. Security is the precondition for development, and development is the foundation for security. Many security issues in the Asia–Pacific originated from the lack of development and can only be addressed through development. Common development provides basic guarantee for peace and stability and holds the "master key" to regional security issues. Countries in the region need to focus on development, expand cooperation, increase connectivity and convergence of interests, so that development achievements are shared by all countries and peoples in the region and sustainable security is maintained through sustainable development.

China will continue to pursue a mutually beneficial strategy of opening up to share with the rest of the world opportunities brought about by our own development. Countries in the Asia–Pacific are welcome to get on board the "express train" of China's development so that we work together for broader cooperation to realize common prosperity and security. Countries in the region are also welcome to align their development strategies, devise development blueprints and share development benefits with us by participating in the BRI so that BRI is built into a new platform and growth pole for Asia–Pacific cooperation.

Second, mutual respect, equality and mutual trust need to be promoted to consolidate the political foundation for security in the Asia-Pacific. Political mutual trust is the bedrock of security mutual trust. Through years of practice, countries in the Asia–Pacific have developed some effective models and practices for cooperation, such as treating each other as equals, respecting each other's sovereignty, reaching consensus through consultation, proceeding in an orderly and gradual way, accommodating each other's comfort levels, all of which have served as important precondition for deepening political mutual trust and strengthening cooperation on security. Countries in the Asia–Pacific should carry forward these good practices in forging a new model of state–to–state relations which embraces "dialogue instead of confrontation, partnership instead of alliance" and break new ground in shaping regional security.

China actively develops friendly relations with its neighboring countries in accordance with the principle of amity, sincerity, mutual benefit and inclusiveness, and the policy of forging friendship and partnership with its neighbors. In recent years, China has expanded its "circle of friends" in the neighboring region, deepened its cooperation with neighboring countries on the basis of mutual trust and injected positivity to the security cooperation in the Asia–Pacific. We stand ready to continue political dialogue and strategic communication with countries in the region to enhance mutual understanding. We should always respect each other' s core interest and bottom line, understand in the right way each other' s development intentions so that political mutual trust can be built and further enhanced.

Third, mutual learning among civilizations and sincere heart-to-heart bonds need to be promoted to consolidate the opinion base for enhancing common security in the Asia-Pacific. The Asia–Pacific region boasts great diversity of ethnicity, religion, and culture. It is also home to countries of different social systems, development paths and economic development levels. Diversity should not be seen as the root cause of conflict but rather the driving force behind progress. Countries in the region need to take the lead in opposing confrontation or clashes of civilizations and advocate dialogue and interaction among civilizations. Efforts need to be made to enhance mutual understanding and trust among different peoples in the region transcending different ideologies and social systems and misperceptions thereof, so that diversity and differences are transformed into vitality and dynamism for regional cooperation on security.

We Chinese believe that in handling relations among civilizations, estrangement shall be replaced with exchanges, clashes with mutual learning, and superiority with coexistence. We are willing to work towards greater mutual understanding, mutual respect and mutual trust among different countries. We' ll actively engage in people–to–people dialogue, exchanges and cooperation with open mind and heart and ensure that the seeds of people–to–people friendship grow into big trees and bear fruits of shared security and growth. Over the next five years, the CPC will invite political parties from around the world to send to China exchange visitors totaling 15,000 for more interactions. We hope to see that a great number of visitors come from the Asia–Pacific region.

Fourth, dialogue and consultation need to be promoted for innovative ideas to forge greater consensus for security in the Asia-Pacific region. In the context of new realities of more complicated security challenges, remaining rigid or insensitive to changes won' t work. Neither does following old paths with new shoes. Countries in the region need to adopt a multi–pronged, holistic and coordinated approach in managing and controlling conflicts and disputes and administering security governance. Efforts are needed not only to address immediate security challenges, but also to make plans to guard against potential security threats with an aim to maintain the overall stability of the region.

China has always been an important force for regional peace and stability. Thanks to the concerted efforts of China and the ASEAN, the situation in the South

China Sea is cooling down and moving towards a stable and positive direction. China, by urging relevant parties of the nuclear issue on Korean Peninsula to solve problems through peaceful means, has played an important role in bringing the nuclear issue on the Peninsula back to the right track of settlement through dialogue and negotiation. Meanwhile, China has actively engaged in the settlement of Iran nuclear issue and issues involving Afghanistan and Syria. China has worked with other countries to handle challenges of terrorism and enhancing maritime security. We' ve also contributed our share to safeguarding security in the Asia–Pacific region. Looking into the future, China will continue to pursue the new thinking on common, comprehensive, cooperative and sustainable security, and play a constructive role in maintaining regional peace and stability.

Fifth, consultation and collaboration need to be promoted on security cooperation to put in place an effective security framework for the Asia-Pacific security. Countries in the Asia–Pacific, guided by the principle of equal participation, openness and inclusiveness, and a step–by–step approach, need to accumulate mutual trust, increase consensus, and expand cooperation towards the building of an integrated Asia–Pacific security framework.

China is an advocate and champion for regional multilateral security mechanisms. We firmly support the central role of ASEAN in East Asian cooperation and the development of relevant mechanisms including, among others, Shanghai Cooperation Organization and Conference on Interaction and Confidence–Building Measures in Asia. As a supporter and guardian of existing regional security frameworks, China will not build new mechanism to replace existing ones, but rather support and improve them according to the principle of achieving win–win progress through discussion and collaboration. We are ready to work with all relevant parties to further develop regional security mechanisms so as to promote common and universal security in the Asia–Pacific.

Ladies and gentlemen,

Friends,

Development and security of the Asia–Pacific region call for our concerted efforts. China will continue to promote peace in the region, contribute to the development of the region, and uphold security for the region. We stand ready to work with countries in the Asia–Pacific to build a secure homeland in the region through consultation and collaboration and create a prosperous and peaceful future for all in the Asia–Pacific region!

Thank you for your attention.

Session I:
China–U.S. Relations and Asia–Pacific Security Situation

China-US Security Strategic Game: Common Evolution or Doomed to War

Jin Canrong

Council Member, CPAPD
Professor and Vice Dean of the School of International Relations, Renmin University of China

In November 2016, Republican presidential candidate Donald Trump beat Democratic presidential candidate Hillary Clinton and won the election unexpectedly. Considering Trump's tough stance on his China policy during the election campaign, some people believe that the Sino–US relations will be full of variables in the next four years. But when looking at the Sino–US relations, we should not only see the influence of leaders' administrative concepts and styles on the relations between the two countries, but also see the general characteristics of the Sino–US relations since normalization of relations between the two countries, and more importantly also see the trend of international development. As the most important pair of bilateral relations in the world, China and the United States will maintain the coexistence of competition and cooperation in the future, which is not something that any single leader can change. The Sino–US relations can only follow the trend of the times and take the path of common evolution and win–win cooperation.

I. The overall characteristics of China-US relations

First, the special importance of the Sino–US relations in today's China's diplomacy

1. From the state perspective: the Sino–US relations are the highest agenda of China's diplomacy.

In overview of the history of the Sino–US relations, we will find that as far as bilateral relations are concerned, there is an asymmetric relationship between China and the United States. China's influence on American foreign policy is rather limited while the United States is the most influential country on China since modern times. To a certain extent, China's modern history is almost parallel to the history of Sino–US relations development trajectory, which makes the US factor play an important role in China's domestic and foreign policy–making. Domestically, safeguarding and expanding national interests is an important criterion for China's foreign policy and diplomatic work, and China pays particular attention to the influence of the US factor on maintaining the administrative legitimacy and the maintenance of domestic order by the Chinese Government. Therefore the influence of the US factor can be felt in almost every aspect of China' diplomacy. Under some circumstances, as the Sino–US relations are well handled, we fell secure, relaxed, and inclusive, so its policies will be more flexible based on inclusiveness. But on the contrary as the Sino–US relations are not well handled, we see tight domestic and international policies. Internationally, the American factor is an important consideration in China's diplomatic layout. The major country diplomacy, neighboring–country diplomacy, developing country diplomacy and multilateral diplomacy constitute the four pillars of China's diplomacy. In this regard, major countries are the key, neighboring–countries is the priority, developing countries is the foundation, and multilateralism is the important platform. There is one more sentence that the Sino–US relations are the gravity of the overall China's diplomacy. This is because the quality of Sino–US relations depends to a large extent on the United States and China's sincerity in developing the Sino–US relations is beyond doubt, while the United States has more initiative in the Sino–US relations. The United States can exert greater influence on China's diplomatic relations, which is manifested in the following aspects: the key for major country relations is the United States; in China's peripheral diplomacy, the United States often restricts China by playing a role of a guardian or balancer for small and weak countries; the US attitude and behavior influence the policies of China's neighboring countries; the Sino–US games in African and South American developing countries, etc. exert impacts on China' s economic interests and soft power in developing countries. In addition, the United States is also the leading country in the most important international organizations.

2. From the system perspective: the United States is the biggest external factor for China's diplomacy.

The international political architecture has profound influence on relations between major powers. After the end of the Cold War, the pattern of "one superpower" emerged. Since the beginning of the new century, a multi–polar world has accelerated its development. From the perspective of comprehensive strength structure, the world is moving toward two super–major powers with several strong powers, forming a power structure characterized by economic strength including China, the United States, Europe, Japan, Russia, India and other countries and regions. In terms of total economic volume, China and the United States are leading the world economy, and the economic gap between Europe, Japan, Russia, India and other countries and regions with China and the United States is growing. From the perspective of development, despite the challenges of overcapacity, insufficient effective supply, unbalanced regional development and downward pressure on the economy, China's economy has maintained healthy and stable development on the whole.

In comparison, although Japan is still one of the strong powers in terms of economic strength, China with larger size can easily surpass Japan by taking advantage of its late development. Fundamentally speaking, Japan, Britain, Germany and a few other countries belong to what Paul Kennedy called "middle powers", which cannot be matched with China, the United States and others. Japan's best seller in 2009 – Be a 1/10 Country – warns Japanese people of the fact that China was the center of East Asia for most of the past 5,000 years, which is normal; but it is abnormal for Japan to be the center of East Asia for the past 100 years. Because Japan has fully studied and learned very well from the Western industrial civilization, so it became No.1 not only in Asia, but also in the non–western world countries, hence possessed advantages of an industrial country over agricultural countries, and become the geo–political center in East Asia. China was rather foolish for refusing to study industrialization for a period of time, especially in the 70 years of the late Qing Dynasty. Therefore, the author reminds Japanese that the advantages Japan has acquired are essentially the advantages of knowledge, because Japan has a good attitude towards learning, so it has a good grasp of knowledge. But this knowledge advantage is very fragile since knowledge can be compensated by learning. The premise that Japan can maintain its knowledge advantage is that the Chinese people foolishly refuse to learn. The conclusion in the book: since Deng Xiaoping's reform and opening–up policies, the Chinese begin to catch up with Japan technologically. It is only a matter of time before China levels Japan in technology and catches up with Japan. Once technology of the two countries is on the par, the strength between China and Japan will be determined by scale. Eventually Japan will return to normal, i.e., Japan's GDP is China's 1/10. So he warns Japan that day will come, Japan will be China's 1/10.

European countries are also facing multiple challenges in recent years: first, the negative effects of European integration, workers lacking competitive advantages under the pressure of intensified external competition are in the plight situation; second, the financial crisis and debt crisis have worsened the economic situation; and the third is the "refugee tide" from North Africa and Southeast Europe has intensified social contradictions. In the future, the primary task of European development is to focus on social governance. China–EU relations will meet opportunities to deepen cooperation and build a brand new bilateral relationship. China can "lock in" the strategic relationship between China and Europe through investment and financial cooperation, enhance the breadth and depth of factors flow between China and Europe, and lay a solid foundation for establishment of a large Asia–Europe market.

Russia's problem lies in its under–development of market economy, unreasonable economic structure and over–reliance on energy for economic growth, and is a "one–crop economy". From the perspective of social structure, the biggest problem facing Russia is the low birth rate, and the population growth rate was –0.06% in 2016. At present, China and Russia have established a comprehensive and coordinate strategic partnership. The complementarity of their economies is conducive to enhancing pragmatic cooperation and developing the stable bilateral relations.

From the above–mentioned, we can see that the major powers in the current international political architecture are either facing domestic crises and busy with domestic affairs or their development prospects and potential cannot be matched with that of China. In the long run, China will maintain a greater advantage in the future security strategic games but the Sino–US relations are different. As the two largest economies in the world, the gap of comprehensive strength between China and the United States is shrinking year on year. According to World Bank estimates, in 2015, the gross domestic product (GDP) of the United States was US$17.9 trillion, while that of China was US$10.8 trillion. China's economic growth grew rapidly not only in quantity, but also improved in quality. The World Intellectual Property Organization (WIPO) reported that in 2015, for the first time, the total number of patent by China exceeded 1 million applications in a single year, almost having totaled that of the United States, Japan and South Korea, which ranked second, third and fourth respectively in the world. As the strength level of China and the United States approaches and the conflicts of their interests increase, and the competition between the two countries will also further intensify. In the view of offensive realists, the major countries' growing strength will inevitably lead to the reconfiguration of international power, as a newly–emerging power in order to compete for a favorable space for development in the international system will try to challenge the existing international system, thus triggering conflicts and wars between the emerging powers and the hegemonic powers. Therefore, how to achieve peaceful coexistence with the hegemonic country has become the biggest factor for consideration in China's diplomacy.

In a word, how to define the Sino–US relations is the hardest problem at present. China and the United States will lead the international system in the coming decades, and the Sino–US relations are the decisive factor in international relations in the 21st century. China and the United States yield welfare with harmony, and generate losses with fight for both sides. If China and the United States fall into a geopolitical struggle, arms race or zero–sum confrontation, then peace and stability of the global system will be at stake. If they can seek common ground while reserving differences and find a broader common language in the fields of economic, political and security cooperation, the prospects for peace and stability in Asia and even in the world will be strengthened.

Second, Sino–US relations: competition and cooperation, important and complex, diversified risks and challenges, and multiple influencing factors

1. The Sino–US relations are both competitive and cooperative

Today's Sino–US relations are different from those between the United States and other major powers in the past. During the Cold War, the US–Soviet relationship was dominated by competition, and there was little cooperation between the two countries except for maintaining a fragile balance in arms control. Although there are differences and contradictions in trade and defense, etc., the current Japan–US relationship is a strong alliance, with cooperation as the mainstream for the two sides. The Sino–US relationship is somewhere between them, with both competition and cooperation between the two countries, which David Shambaugh calls "competition", but the balance between cooperation and competition is tilting to the latter recently.

In view of great repeatability and resilience of the Sino–US relations, we use to say that the Sino–US relations will neither get too good nor become too bad. But now scholars have proposed that there will be a period of mutual adaptation between China and the United States in the years from now to the time when China surpasses the United States as the world's No.1 economy, so the Sino–US relations will be either getting better or worse, either deepening cooperation or moving towards strategic competition, with conflicting factors between the two countries. Some scholars even call this Sino–US relationship neither a cold war nor a hot war, but a "cool war".

2. The Sino–US relationship is both an important and complex bilateral

relationship.

As far as importance is concerned, to a certain extent, the Sino–US relations determine the destiny of mankind in the 21st century, and is the gravity of China' s diplomacy, something like a slight move in one part may affect the whole situation, so which calls for great caution. As far as its complexity is concerned, on the one hand, China and the United States are highly interdependent economically. In 2015, China surpassed Canada in total imports and exports with the United States and became the US largest trading partner. On the other hand, China and the United States regard each other as competitors militarily and strategically, very rare in modern human history.

From the perspective of structural characteristics, the strategic interests of the two countries are confrontational and conflicting, seeming to have fallen into the "Thucydides trap". This so–called trap means that a new power will inevitably challenge the existing major powers and the existing major powers will respond to it, thus making war inevitable. After the end of the Cold War, the United States becomes the only superpower in the world, with an unchallenged hegemony and belonging to a defending power. Under the impetus of reform and opening–up and China's accession to WTO, China's domestic economy has developed rapidly, and its international influence continuously upgraded, its nominal GDP in 2010 surpassed that of Japan and became the second largest economy in the world, belonging to a newly emerging economy. The Sino–US relationship between a newly emerging economy and a defending power determines that their strategic interests are to a large extent conflicting. Moreover, besides geopolitical and economic conflicts, China and the United States still have political and ideological differences. China is the largest socialist country in the world, while the United States is the largest capitalist country in the world. In terms of civilization form, the United States is a Christian civilization in the West, while China is a Confucian civilization. The two countries have conflicting factors from the perspective of civilizations. Therefore, compared with the Thucydides trap in history, the "Thucydides trap" between China and the United States is more complex.

Third, the Sino–US Relations: both structural confrontation and interests binding

The structural confrontation between China and the United States is generated from the objective results brought about by their changing strength. The structural contradictions are embodied in following four aspects: the contradiction between a rising power and a defending power, the geopolitical contradiction, the political system and ideology contradiction, and the Taiwan issue. But meantime, there are common interests and global interests between China and the United States, with economic interdependence, social interconnection and international common threats to security. The two countries have achieved remarkable results in their multi–field cooperation, such as jointly combating terrorism, preventing problems in the world economy, maintaining stability in the global financial order, preventing the spread of Ebola virus, and jointly responding to global climate change, etc.. The Huffington Post once compared this Sino–US complex relationship to a marriage of convenience in the 19th century: the two sides must get together on the basis of common interests, and they have to maintain the relationship even if they don't love each other.

Fourth, the Sino–US relations are affected by many third party factors.

Looking back at the development process of the Sino–US relations, it is not difficult to see that the Sino–US relations are structurally an "external force–driven" relationship. The ups and downs of bilateral relations often depend on what kind of a "third party" involvement and the bilateral relations is adjusted to each other in this course of change. From the Anti–Japanese Invasion War to the Cold War, still to the end of the Cold War, the two countries had different cooperation due to the third–party factors. The third–party factor can become adhesives for the bilateral relations, but can also have negative impact on the bilateral relations. The outbreak of the Korean War had plunged China and the United States into nearly two decades of hostility, while in recent years, the strategic games between China and the United States are largely influenced by Japan, the Philippines, Vietnam, North Korea, Iran and Myanmar, etc. The relationship of China and the United States with these countries has often aroused mutual suspicion, even frictions sometimes. Therefore, how the Sino–US relations develop sometimes do not completely depend on the two countries themselves.

A new variable affecting the Sino–US relations is that in recent years, with China's peaceful rise, the United States increasingly shows its worries about China's future development intentions. Currently in the United States, a largest and most intense debate on China policy since 1989 is going on. Some American scholars and government officials believe that in the past, the United States wishfully believed that China's economic development would lead to urbanization, that urbanization would lead to the growth of the middle class, that the growing middle class would demand corresponding political rights, and that then China would change from one–party rule to an American style democratic society. In other words, economic and social development will lead to China's political liberalization; China will become a Western–style democratic and peaceful country without regional or global hegemonic ambitions, which is also a prerequisite for the United States to welcome China to become a "prosperous, peaceful and stable" country. But now more and more American elites believe that China's rising has brought a strong competitor to the United States and a destroyer of the US –led international system. China is becoming a "major country that will eventually drive the United States out of Asia and build itself a leader in Asia by weakening the credibility of US security assurance and undermining the US alliance." The policy of dialogue and engagement pursued by the United States in the past decades have basically failed, and in the future need changes or adjustments of the policy towards China substantially. There are even some extreme views that the United States should clearly abandon its engagement with China and counterbalance China in various fields. Therefore, in the debate on China policy, the American containment and hostility mentality towards China is on the increase.

II. Significant opportunities for developing China-US relations

In the second decade of the 21st century, the rapid rise of China has brought challenges to both China and the United States, and the United States is not ready to deal with the growing influence of China's strength, while China is also faced with how to explain to the world that China will not threaten the United States, but the strategic trust between the two countries has declined, and bilateral relations are facing multiple challenges, in addition to the "old" issue of trade, Tibet, Taiwan and human rights, etc., new frictions have also emerged between the two sides on such issues as leadership in the Asia–Pacific region, China's military modernization, new frontier space, ocean issues and China's development model, etc. Although there are still many problems between the two countries, the inherent feature of the two countries and the historical experience accumulated in bilateral exchanges help lay an indispensable foundation and conditions for the two sides to control differences and avoid conflicts. This makes it possible for China and the United States to establish a new form of major powers relations, which is different from "confrontation and conflict" characterized by the traditional model of relations between major powers in the past.

First, the first category of opportunities: old games, new players

Firstly, both China and the United States are super–large countries of continental scale, which means that neither side can overwhelmingly conquer the other side. John J. Mearsheimer pointed out in his book The Tragedy of Great Power Politics that international politics is major power politics, and the distribution of power decides the political pattern of major powers, i.e., if a country tries to acquire a major power identity so it must have the military strength to fight a large–scale conventional war with the strongest powers in the world. As far as scale is concerned, the two countries rank first in the international community in terms of hard power factors such as population, territorial area, natural resources, production capacity, economic scale and military strength, as well as soft power factors such as cultural, artistic and social attractiveness. Compared with the major competitors of the United States in history including Britain, Germany and Japan, China and the United States are all "all–round champions", and neither of them can ensure complete destruction of the other side, which constitutes the foundation for competition and cooperation. Especially since modern times, with the evolution of international politics, declined number of states and expanded average state territory, conquest has become more and more difficult, "coexistence" has become the main feature of the major powers politics in today's world, particularly for major countries. Both Chinese and American governments and elites recognize that an outbreak of a large–scale conflict or war between the two super–large countries is a disaster for the world. Therefore, even if there are frictions or contradictions emerging between the two sides, both sides will try to exercise restraints and avoid escalation of conflicts.

Second, unlike nation–states in history, China and the United States are both civilized states, which are more inclusive. Compared with Germany, Japan, which are composed of a single ethnic group historically, China is a multi–ethnic country based on Confucian civilization, and has a long history and rich experience of peaceful coexistence of multi–ethnic groups for thousands of years, and with attention to civilization inclusiveness like a sea taking water from all rivers. The United States is a multi–ethnic multi–cultural country based on Christian Protestant civilization. Both China and the United States have developed and grown in the process of cultural exchange and integration, full of confidence in their own cultures, neither has narrow nationalist egoism or great power chauvinism, and lack objective conditions and subjective conditions of the clash of civilizations. Even though, we do not exclude a certain nationalist emotions in a given period, yet, it is entirely different with extreme nationalism.

Thirdly, both China and the United States are secular countries, although their political systems and ideologies are quite different, they all emphasize pragmatism, materialism and individualism. Both China and the United States are multi–ethnic countries. Alexis de Tocqueville, in his book On American Democracy, points out that Americans are concerned with pragmatism to the neglect of theory in practice, are generally interested in material welfare, and in the firm defense of individual freedom and democratic rights. It is these characteristics that make the United States strong and prosperous, and has achieved the national pride and advantages Americans are proud of. Similarly, China's philosophy of accommodation and flexibility in handling things is pragmatism. The Chinese people attach more importance to the present life rather than to the future life, and this materialism makes people more active in the secular life. China' s tradition stresses that Chinese people advocate collectivism, but since the late Ming Dynasty, the idea of encouraging individualism is gradually nurtured and propagated. For example, it is Li Qi' s idea that a man must be selfish pioneered the enlightenment movement of Chinese individualism thinking. It is true that China and the United States have different religious theories, but shared similar internal "capitalist" features such as stress on hard work, making vigorous efforts, continuously pursuing welfare, which derive time and credit concept, efficiency and economical concept, equality and competition concept, sincere and cautious concept, planned disposal incomes, etc.

Fourthly, both China and the United States emphasize soft power, cultural identity and self–improvement to enhance attractiveness and influence. The United States regards itself as "a city on the top", emphasizing its own moral commanding height. While China advocates Confucianism's "subduing people by virtue", and influences the world by leading examples and following good inducements. When confronted with provocations, China can exercise restraint and always put national development and economic construction in the first place, which is entirely different with the hegemonic countries likely to show their muscles everywhere, treat small and weak countries with coercion and intimidation, and often over–react in the face of conflicts. In addition, it is worth mentioning that while China tries to get some achievements tactically, it also insists on keeping restrained strategically. Responding to the US provocations, except for issues like Taiwan, maritime territory, and those affect the legitimacy of China's political system which China regards as its core interests, China has generally adopted a stimulus–response to respond to the challenges of international security, global governance and others to avoid stimulating the United States.

In a word, this is the first kind of opportunity since the United States regards China as a power competitor in the real global society, but does not get into conflict or war as Britain, Japan and Germany did in the past. The game tactics of the two countries are different, and the competitions between the two countries are quite different from that of the former great powers' rivalry for hegemony.

Second, the second category of opportunities: new background for old games

The first new background is the balance of nuclear terror in the nuclear age.

Since mankind enters the era of nuclear weapons, the great lethality and destructive power of nuclear weapons have pushed the cruelty and destruction of human war to the extreme. Human fear of nuclear states' ability to "mutual assured destruction" plays an important role in restricting the outbreak of war between nuclear states. During the Cold War, the United States and the Soviet Union were very cautious in dealing with their contradictions and conflicts because of their fear of each other's nuclear capabilities. Similarly, China and the United States are both nuclear powers. Although they are asymmetric in terms of nuclear deterrence, both sides have nuclear arsenals sufficient to completely destroy the other side. Meantime, both countries are rational and responsible actors, and neither side will use nuclear weapons to break the balance or the "strategic stability" between the sides.

The second background is that since the end of the Cold War, globalization has reached an unprecedented level in breadth and depth, and has had a far–reaching impact on the international system. Firstly, in the era of globalization, economic activities of various countries transcend national boundaries and form intricate network relations world–wide. Globalization enhances the degree of interdependence between China and the United States, various interests are intertwined, and form a natural restraint relationship, and any targeted policy of containment or isolation will jeopardize one's own interests. Secondly, along with economic globalization comes the globalization of governance issues, any single country alone is unable to respond to the global challenges of climate, resources, terrorism and disease control, etc., and they must work together.

The third background is the growing influence of civil society in the two countries. Both China and the United States have strong civil society. With the advancement of informationization and globalization, the consciousness of political participation and voice of ordinary people are gradually strengthened, whose influence on the decision–making process of the government is growing. Both peoples are concerned about the government's distribution of rights, obligations and interests, and advocate business heroes such as Buffett and Bill Gates. The disgust of war and the concern for personal interests are the general characteristics of civil society. In the United States, a large number of social groups and active community activities have an important impact on American political practice. American people's dissatisfaction about the Iraq war and Afghanistan war launched during George W. Bush Administration and their anti–war sentiment made the Obama Administration change the past aggressive policy and reduce overseas direct military interventions. In recent decades, China's urbanization has developed rapidly, civil society has grown very fast, and the influence of media, opinion leaders and even ordinary people on policy has been increasing. Naturally, the public demands personal freedom, happy life and a peaceful and stable development environment. Particularly, China's long–standing one–child policy has made people more opposed to casualties and war.

The fourth background is the rigidity of the United Nations and international law plays an important role in restraining major powers' conflict. Firstly, since the end of World War II, the process of institutionalizing the international community has accelerated. State behavior has been increasingly constrained by international organizations such as the United Nations and international law. More and more international organizations and international laws and regulations have mandatory restraints on state behaviors. States often have voluntary accession to certain mandatory or binding international organizations because of worries about the violation costs and international credibility. Secondly, in the era of peace and development as the theme, all countries in the world tend to solve international disputes in an open, fair, just and more authoritative way, and the existence of international organizations and international laws provides a useful platform. For contradictions and frictions between China and the United States, various international laws and international arbitration institutions provide a solution mechanism and means for arbitration or negotiation between the two countries. So, states do not need to resort to force to resolve conflicts. For example, the dispute settlement mechanism of the World Trade Organization provides an important platform for trade anti–dumping lawsuits and intellectual property disputes between the two countries.

The fifth background is the evolution of "anarchy culture" in international politics is conducive to the peaceful development between the two countries. In the views of Alexander Wendt, there are Hobbesian, Lockean and Kantian three different anarchic cultures under anarchism. Correspondingly, the relations among major powers in the international system identify "enemy", "competitor" and "friend". From the perspective of historical development of international relations, the United States, since World War I, intervenes in international affairs, advocates decolonization, promotes the rule of law, persuades various countries to seize the world market share through peaceful means, expands the market through technological innovations, and achieves prosperity, which undoubtedly has played an important role in gradually transforming international politics from Hobbesian anarchic culture to Lockean anarchic culture. At the end of World War II, the US gross domestic product (GDP) accounted for half of the world's GDP, but it still established an open economic order that allowed other countries to flourish and compete. After World War II, the United States led and promoted the revival and prosperity of Europe, and meanwhile promoted establishment of a series of international organizations and systems conducive to peacekeeping and development worldwide. It is under the Lockean anarchy culture that various countries in the world have increasingly shifted their focus to economic development and social progress rather than on territorial rivalry, so the overall peaceful international environment has created the preconditions for global economic prosperity. A typical case in this process is Japan's rise twice after the Meiji Restoration. Its first rise is before World War II, Japan learned from the Western powers to occupy its surrounding territory, invade China, Korea and other countries, plunder the Taiwan of China, and seize the opportunity to conquer the Asian continent to establish a "Greater East Asian Co–prosperity Circle", but ultimately defeated by the United States. Japan's second rise took place in the Lockean anarchy culture, through the market economy and the rule of law, Japan has continuously expanded its market share in Asia and the world, and realized the transformation from a soldier to an excellent engineer. Therefore, the international community advocated by the United States after World War II is generally peaceful, open and fair. Similarly, China's reform and opening–up has benefited substantially from this peaceful international environment under the Lockean anarchy culture. Undoubtedly, China's future development is bound to support and maintain this environment as the objective, and China has no reason to destroy or change this environment.

Third, the third category of opportunity: historical legacies in the Sino–US relations

Since Nixon's visit to China in 1972, China and the United States have gone through the end of the Cold War and the breakthrough of bilateral relations, and gradually developed into the most important and complex bilateral relations in the world. For more than 40 years, the Sino–US relations have provided five historical legacies for further cooperation between the two sides.

Firstly, China and the United States are economically interdependent. According to the statistics of the US Department of Commerce, China is the largest importer and the third largest exporter of goods with the United States. In 2015, the bilateral imports and exports of goods between the United States and China are worth US$598.07 billion. The Chinese goods accounted for 21.5% of the total imports of the United States. From 2007 to 2015, the annual average growth of American direct investment in China (FDI) was 12.2%, and the total FDI reached US$111.7 billion in 2015. Although China's FDI to the United States is lower than that of the United States in China, which has grown rapidly in recent years. FDI to the United States increased from US$11.9 billion in 2014 to US$15 billion in 2015, an increase of 25.8%. Similarly, the United States is China's largest trading partner. As of September 2016, China holds US$1.15 trillion in US bonds and is the largest holder of US Treasury bonds. Some even call this financial interdependence between China and the United States a balance of financial terror. To some extent, economic interdependence has made China and the United States develop into a pair of "community of destiny". Therefore, Trump had China listed as a "trade manipulator" and tariffs raised substantially to punish China, which will not only raise the production and living costs of American entrepreneurs and ordinary people, and multinationals in China will also be difficult to find alternative production bases, and the US economy will also confront more uncertainties. Therefore, the bilateral close economic exchanges have become the "ballast stone" for the Sino–US relations. Although some academics question whether trade may not necessarily lead to peace, and may even be the root cause of conflict, yet interdependence at least makes both sides pay a big price, thus alleviating the impulse for conflict, and becoming the main force for peace.

Secondly, China and the United States have extensive social and interpersonal contacts. Cultural and personnel exchanges can ease tensions between countries and promote mutual trust. Currently, there are about 6 million Chinese Americans, including overseas Chinese, who, equal to the number of Jews in the United States, have become a special bond between China and the United States. There are more than 200 pairs of sister provinces (states) and sister cities between China and the United States, which are rarely found with other countries, and have very deep direct contacts. The two countries have close personnel exchanges, with the number of personnel exchanges between the two countries reached 4.75 million in 2015, and more than 5 million in 2016, and the number of students studying in either country reaches 0.5 million. China and the United States also hold activities such as the Year of the United States (China), the Year of Tourism and so on. To a certain extent, personnel exchanges have become independent of the political and economic relations, and become a "regulator" restricting political and economic frictions between the two countries. The personnel and cultural exchanges, political mutual trust, and economic and trade cooperation have jointly constituted the three pillars of Sino–US new–type major country relations, which provides an important guarantee by common aspirations for the long–term sustainability of bilateral relations.

Thirdly, on the issue of global governance, China and the United States have jointly responded to many challenges and formed a good cooperation mechanism. In recent years, China and the United States have expanded their scope and areas of cooperation worldwide. In addition to cooperation on counter–terrorism, China and the United States have achieved results in international cooperation on Iran's nuclear deal "5+1" negotiations and the denuclearization of Korea Peninsula. In 2014, the two countries signed the Sino–US Joint Statement on Climate Change, which broke the deadlock faced by various countries in their efforts to reach an effective global agreement to respond to climate change for decades, and China' s cooperation also made an important contribution to the Paris Agreement on Climate Change led by the two countries at the Paris Climate Change Conference. Generally speaking, in the process of participating in global governance, China and the United States have "reached a certain consensus, built a solid foundation for cooperation and accumulated rich experience in working with each other", which means that it is possible and feasible for China and the United States to "establish a more stable and reliable sound interactive framework and create a new form of major countries relations."

Fourthly, Deng Xiaoping made a correct strategic choice. Looking back at the beginning of the reconciliation between China and the United States, it is not difficult to find that normalization of the Sino–US relations was linked to China's adoption of reform and opening–up. Deng Xiaoping combines the handling of Sino–US relations with China's modernization process and regards the building of stable and peaceful Sino–US relations as the primary external condition for China to achieve prosperity and strength. Based on this judgment, since Deng Xiaoping's era, the successive leaders' strategic choices for China's development have remained unchanged, i.e., having chosen to develop within the existing international system instead of trying to make a new start and to challenge the authority of the current international order. This decision has created a prerequisite for the Sino–US win–win cooperation.

China's rise is realized in the current existing international system, thus, China is its participant, builder and contributor. The rise of China is a new variable for the international order in Asia, but this does not mean that China is a revolutionary and to lead the establishment of a China–centered Asian order. In fact, China upholds the authority of the UN Security Council, the international law, and the free and open international trade system. As Jeffrey Bader, the former Director for Asian Affairs, National Security Council, said, Xi's foreign policy is quite different from that of previous leaders, the main reason is that China's capacity and strength are totally different from those of the past, but he still continues the past China's development path, especially that since the year 1978.

Fifthly, China and the United States have established fruitful dialogue mechanisms. Over the past 10 years, the two countries have established very mature and effective mechanisms. According to the statistics of the Ministry of Foreign Affairs, China and the United States have nearly 100 dialogues and exchanges at or above the deputy ministerial level. Senior officials of the two countries have maintained close communication with each other, even exceeding the ties between the United States and its allies. Since Trump assumed the office, China and the US have maintained frequent communication and interaction, the two sides have established the diplomatic and security dialogue, the comprehensive economic dialogue, the law enforcement and cyber security dialogue, and the social and people–to–people dialogue. These dialogues provide platforms for communication between the two sides, and conducive to deepening mutual understanding, reducing information asymmetry, controlling differences and managing conflicts.

In short, the bilateral relations of the two countries in recent years is characterized by complexity, i.e.,intensified competitions, and even spiraling of contradictions and differences between the two sides in some aspects. With inauguration of a new US president, especially Trump's unconventional game–playing may increase variables for the Sino–US relations, but given the abovementioned existing opportunities, the overall framework of Sino–US relations will not change significantly, and cooperation remains the mainstream of the bilateral relations. If we can make full use of opportunities and deepen cooperation, the Sino–US relations can go beyond differences and can ensure that bilateral relations maintain the correct direction of development.

III. China's long-term security strategy maintains consistency, continuity and sustainability

As mentioned above, Trump, the new president of the United States, has neither experience in politics nor policy statement on international governance, so the future US long–term strategy is uncertain. But it should also be noted that the political system of the United States contains a strong inherent resilience derived from the reform tradition, and Trump is bound to adjust the US policies. On the other hand, the long–term security strategy of China's diplomacy will keep consistent, continuous and sustainable, as it is being constantly innovated. This strategy is embodied in the following aspects:

First, actively responding to internal challenges

Diplomacy is the continuation of internal affairs, China's foreign policy is always characterized by "introversion". It is embodied in promoting economic development, realizing modernization, safeguarding the unity of multi–ethnic country, and maintaining the legitimacy of decision–making. For China, despite the rapid economic growth since the reform and opening –up, there are many challenges, such as unbalanced economic development growth, structural contradictions and cyclical problems intertwined, sluggish demand and excess capacity in coexistence, and the foundation of sustainable economic development is not yet solid. If domestic problems are not solved properly, it will affect the development of China's soft and hard power and drag down its external impact, and China will become a so–called "fragile superpower". By then, just as Joseph S. Nye said, the only country that can contain China is China itself. In the future, whether China can grasp the initiative of the Sino–US relations will ultimately depend on China's domestic development. Only by alleviating domestic social contradictions, improving the quality of people's life, achieving honest and efficient governance and realizing the great rejuvenation of the Chinese nation, can China play a greater role in the Asia–Pacific and global landscape, shoulder more responsibilities and gain more far–reaching impact.

Second, actively expanding diplomatic layout without direct conflict with the United States.

The core issue of China's diplomacy is to strive for a peaceful international environment to achieve its own development while promoting world peace through its own development. Fundamentally speaking, China's diplomatic strategy embodies and coincides with the theme of peace and development. Faced with the new environment and challenges, China is no longer just a participant in the international order, but strives to become a constructor of the international order and the international governance system. On the one hand, the foreign policy layout pays more attention to autonomy and independence. At the 2014 Central Foreign Affairs Work Conference, Xi Jinping stressed that diplomatic work should adhere to an independent and peaceful foreign policy, adhere to putting state and national development on the basis of our own strength, unswervingly follow our own path and the path of peaceful development, while, we must never give up our legitimate rights and interests, and never sacrifice the national core interests." Under the guidance of this idea, China firmly safeguards its legitimate right and interests while launching a series of concepts and measures such as the Belt and Road Initiative, BRICS Development Bank, Asian Infrastructure Investment Bank and the East China Sea Air Defense Identification Zone, etc. On the other hand, the foreign policy layout reflects respect for the US interests. The proposition of "new form of major country relations" defines "mutual respect" -- respecting the social system and development path of the respective choices, respecting each other's core interests and major concerns, seeking common ground while reserving differences, pursuing inclusiveness and mutual learning, and common progress -- as the important connotation of this new form of relations. Not only that, China has repeatedly stressed its respect for the existing international system led by the United States, also emphasizes that the two countries have a wide range of common interests and cooperation space and stresses that peace and prosperity in the world, especially in the Asia–Pacific region, cannot be separated from in-depth communication and frank cooperation between the two countries, and also welcomes the United States to play a constructive role in the Asia Pacific region.

Third, expanding the cooperation areas and reducing the stock of competition with the increment of cooperation.

Deng Xiaoping said that reform is China's second revolution. Over the past 4 decades of reform and opening–up, the most important reason why China has achieved profound social change but not experienced major social and economic turbulence in a short period of time is that China's reform is an incremental reform, while reform in the USSR is a stock reform. Taking the reform of state–owned enterprises in the 20th century as an example, Deng Xiaoping proposed to encourage development of private economy and diversified business, whose pilot effect and competitive pressure promote the reform of state–owned enterprises. Meantime, the gradual increase of the proportion of private enterprises in GDP assures that the social instable factors emerging in the process of state–owned enterprises reform could be controlled and major social upheaval be avoided.

Incremental reform provides a useful reference for handling Sino–US relations. Currently, the competitive factors in Sino–US relations are extensive, and some problems cannot be solved in the short term. China is trying to establish a partnership based on common interests to minimize the competitive factors affecting bilateral relations whenever possible. If we build the Sino–US cooperation bigger and stronger, stabilize the Sino–US relations and then settle the competitive differences, the foundation of bilateral cooperation will not be shaken, and the relationship will not become deteriorate or turbulent.

Fourth, actively assuming international responsibilities

China and the United States share the same views on whether China should actively assume international responsibility, but there are great differences on what kind of international responsibility or how much international responsibility it should assume. In the United States in recent years, more and more voices demand

China to fulfill more obligations and take on more responsibility. In 2005, Robert B. Zoellick, US Deputy Secretary of State, delivered a speech entitled "Whither China: From Formal Membership to Responsibility" to the National Committee on US–China Relations, formally urging China to become a responsible stakeholder in the international system. Especially as C. Fred Bergsten, director of the Peterson Institute for International Economics, in 2008 proposed the concept of "Chimerica" (G2), which was rejected by the Chinese Government, a considerable number of people in the United States criticized China for assuming inadequate international responsibility and for its "options", i.e., only fulfilling those responsibilities beneficial to China. On the Chinese side, one general view holds that China is still a developing country with limited capacity, so it is unable to shoulder responsibi lities beyond its ability.

In recent years, having actively participated in global governance, China has strengthened cooperation with the United States in the areas of environment, climate, nuclear security, major diseases, counter–terrorism and cyber security. Among them, China has cooperation with the United States in nuclear security, undertakes the responsibility in the work of assuring regional nuclear security. Therefore, the Sino–US nuclear security cooperation is regarded as the most successful area in bilateral, regional and global cooperation between the two countries. Similarly, at the Marrakech Climate Change Conference in 2016, China and the United States and other countries reached agreement on implementing the Paris Agreement. These cooperation helps to "share responsibilities" with the United States, thereby alleviating the US dissatisfaction on "sharing power" with China. Meanwhile, China also adheres to transparency and fairness in the process of assuming responsibility, which is conducive to enhancing mutual understanding and reducing misunderstanding of each other's intentions with the United States that adheres to the rule of law and transparent procedures.

Fifth, adhering to mutual benefit and win–win cooperation and actively promoting the Sino–US relations

In order to develop the Sino–US relations, it is important to reject zero–sum thinking and adhere to mutual benefit and win–win outcomes. In recent years, in spite of China's strength growth, industrial upgrading and the return of manufacturing industry back to the United States, but in overall view, there emerge some new changes in the Sino–US economic cooperation, China and the United States share more complementarity than competition economically. Particularly, the US economic growth requires a large investment, while China has the largest foreign exchange reserves. The Bilateral Investment Treaty (BIT) will help Chinese enterprises enter the US market, thus promoting US employment and economic growth.

With the steady increase of China's investment in the United States, the American public, enterprises and interests groups will gradually change their views on China. If China invests in every congressional district in the United States, and these investments can produce good economic benefits, bring employment and economic growth to American society, improve the lives of residents and share the dividends of China's economic development with ordinary Americans, then the American people will also welcome Chinese investment instead of seeing it as a "monster and flood", thus creating a situation of "Chimerica" concept -- Sino–US economic and cultural integration. Just as Japan invested heavily in the automobile industry in Ohio and Kentucky in the 1980s, abundant employment opportunities can cool bilateral tensions and help improve and promote healthy and positive development of bilateral relationship.

In short, China's long–term security strategy toward the United States is like "walking on two legs", with the positive side to advocate the development of the Sino–US new–type major country relations, strive to expand cooperation between the two countries and promote the realization of common interests and with the negative side to control the crisis, reduce and eliminate strategic mutual suspicions and avoid conflicts and confrontations.

IV. A new prospect of Sino-US relations is to establish functional partnerships or to achieve bilateral coordination

The complexity of Sino–US relations determine that there is no definite answer to the prospect of the Sino–US relations, i.e. we are unable to make a definite forecast that either there will be doomed to war between the two countries, or the two countries will definitely jump over the Thucydides trap and can live in peace. The Sino–US relations ultimately depend on the joint efforts of both sides, but also on whether the top leaders of both sides can seize the current opportunities. Now there is some consensus at the elite level of both sides, so we should work together in a number of directions for win–win cooperation.

In the United States, some scholars, represented by Henry Kissinger, propose that the United States with China should engage in co–evolution. Kissinger believes that China's development potential is unlimited, and the United States must make changes to adapt to China's rise, while China should also make some changes. Specifically, China and the United States need to continuously develop the tradition of consultation and bilateral trust, and jointly handle well the relations in three perspectives: They through consultations safeguard the common interests of the two countries, eliminate tensions, comprehensively enhance the cooperation framework between the two sides, and jointly build the Pacific Community. This idea finds a large market in some elite of the United States. It is worth mentioning that although the idea of "co–evolution" has not yet been implemented at the strategic level, it has been reflected more and more among the people between the two countries. In 2013, the discussion of "tiger mother phenomenon" between the two countries was a case in point. In education, China and the United States learn from each other and make up for each other's weakness, which is the co–evolution. In culture, diet and pop music, etc. China and the United States share co–evolution.

This paper holds that the most likely future prospect for the Sino–US relations is to establish functional partnership or to achieve coordination. The so–called coordination between the two countries stems from the European coordination in early 19th Century. Back then, rising France swept across Europe under Napoleon's leadership and established a huge empire, but was defeated by the European countries under British leadership. After the war, the major powers held a conference in Vienna and decided to deal with major European issues through consultation. Europeans believe that there is a need to establish a bottom line between major powers, i.e., controlling contradictions, avoiding military confrontation, and choosing cooperation on important issues and achieving win–win results. The European coordination system enabled Europe to maintain nearly a century of peace before the First World War from 1815 to 1914.

The functional partnership between China and the United States is similar. i.e., China and the United States do not aim at establishing an alliance, but will strengthen cooperation in all areas of common interests, concretely including: the two sides jointly maintain the regional balance of strength, jointly respond to transnational and global issues threatening human survival, assume common responsibility for the sustainable development of human kind through consultation, while control differences in the areas of competition, be cooperation or competition, maintain institutional communication to avoid misjudgment, and strengthen strategic cooperation. On this basis, the two sides will gradually expand the scope of cooperation by establishing the mutual trust through cooperation, and ultimately resolve the deep–seated contradictions and disputes between the two countries. In this regard, the "functional partnership" and Kevin Rudd's proposal on "constructive realism with the same dream and mission" between China and the United States are similar. To achieve this historic mission, which concerns the future of the two peoples, requires top leaders of the two countries to have a broad vision and extraordinary wisdom, to recognize the need for friendship between the two countries, and to show their great resolve as in the early 1970s to make collaborate efforts to overcome the mutually spiraling suspicions and lead the two countries and the two peoples to common prosperity and peace.

U.S.-China Great Power Rivalry: Turning Back to the Future a Cold War Situation?

Jun Osawa

Senior Research Fellow
Nakasone Yasuhiro Peace Institute (NPI), Japan

Will U.S.-China Great Power Rivalry fall into a trap?

Taking a long–range view of history, the rise of a challenging power and fall of a hegemonic power leads to an upset in the balance of power in the region, sometimes resulting in a struggle.

◎ Rivalry between emerging and established powers that upset the previously stable balance of power in the region results in a struggle for regional supremacy.

◎ So the big question is that will this great rivalry between a rising power and a ruling power in world history be applicable to the U.S. and China?

◎ Graham Allison describes that in 12 of 16 cases of a rise of emerging powers, confrontation and war broke out between the emerging and the established powers. He also poses a question in his new book: "Can America and China Escape Thucydides' Trap?"

◎ In his famous original book, Thucydides finds that the cause of Peloponnesian War was "the growth of the Athenian (sea) power, which putting the Lacedaemonians (Sparta) into fear necessitated the war."

◎ From the era of Thucydides to this 21st century, sea power provides the basis for a state' s prosperity and security, and therefore a rapid rise of a state as a maritime power evokes a sense of caution among its neighbors and the ruling power.

Will Chinese "defensive" actions in the sky and the sea become the cause of conflict with U.S.?

◎ As its economic and military power increases, China has begun to expand its periphery outward into the ocean to protect the prosperous industrial areas along the east coast of China.

◎ With the emerging "maritime power strategy," which intends purely to ensure its national security, China is in the process of setting up buffer zones on its coastlines both in East and South China Sea.

◎ The Air Defense Identification Zone that China introduced November 2013 is one of the efforts at creating these buffer zones. I have put a name to the new China' s Adiz: "Great Wall in the Sky."

◎ To protect Taiwan, and the East China Sea, the South China Sea, from incursion by the U.S. military in times of emergency, if China were to take a buffer zones strategy or "counter–intervention operation" strategy, widely known among western experts as "anti–access/area denial" strategy (A2/AD), vis–à–vis America' s "freedom of navigation" or "freedom of the sky," struggle over coastal and littoral areas where land power China meets sea power United States will be inevitable.

U.S.-China struggle in the cyber domain

◎ In these recent five years, the U.S. and China have waged a long battle to protect their respective cyber domains, not only in the digital field but also in the diplomatic, judicial, and international arenas.

◎ The U.S. suspects that the Chinese government and military support Chinese cyber espionage groups in spying into intellectual properties and business secrets of American companies.

◎ China also suspects that NSA, the U.S. military intelligence authority, has been hacking into China, after the leaks by Edward Snowden.

◎ Allowing that President Xi and Obama once agreed that the U.S. or Chinese government wouldn' t conduct or knowingly support cyber–enabled theft of intellectual property, including trade secrets or other confidential business information, there has been a tug–of–war between the U.S. and China for gaining technological advantage in the coming Internet of Things (IOT) era.

BRI from the viewpoint of geopolitics

◎ The Chinese government intends to improve connectivity and cooperation between Eurasian countries under the Belt and Road Initiative (BRI).

◎ Even though Chinese President Xi Jinping defends BRI as "China has no geopolitical game calculations" in his keynote speech at the Boao Forum in April 2018, BRI carries a risk of being regarded as geopolitical strategy, because the Road and Belt of BRI straddle completely what Spykmans called "Rimland."

◎ The most influential scholar in geopolitics, Nicholas J. Spykman, describes his "Rimland Theory" as: 1) "Who controls the rimland rules Eurasia; who rules Eurasia controls the destinies of the world." 2) "The great threat to U.S. security has been the possibility that the rimland regions of the Eurasian land mass would be dominated by a single power." 3)Therefore, the United States was "obliged to safeguard her position by making certain that no overwhelming power is allowed to build itself up in these areas."

◎ Sometimes in history, one side' s misperceptions about the intentions of another makes things seriously worse, consequently leading to war as in the case of the Munich agreement in 1938.

◎ Rivalry emerges not only from a realistic view of IR theory or structural realist thought; there is also a risk that it could develop due to misperceptions about the intentions of the other, caused by some incident—action and reaction—between China and the U.S., and its allies, in a wide variety of fields from the maritime arena to cyber domain in which both great powers interact.

◎ What kinds of incident or factors influence these misperceptions and reactive policies and strategies? And how can we avoid a negative spiral of misperceptions and wrong assessments of the intentions of the other side? These are our serious questions.

Conclusion

◎ Rivalry between great powers emerges to a great extent from misperceptions about the intentions of the other, easily caused by even a small incident—action and reaction—in a wide variety of fields from maritime arena to cyber domain.

◎ Unfounded fears from distrust of each other easily cause countries to miscalculate the intentions of the other. That would drive China and the US in a dangerous direction—confrontation or even war.

◎ To avoid a descent into a negative spiral of misperceptions and wrong assessments of the intention of other side, China, the U.S., and its allies have to take measures as follows:

1) Handle every incident—even a small case—carefully;

2) Refrain from assertive activities—such as military drills near other countries;

3) Conduct a net assessment about the capability and intentions of the other without any prejudgment;

4) Enhance communication between any and all levels—from top leaders, navy–to–navy and people–to people.

Major Changes of China-US Relations and their Impacts on the Asia-Pacific Security

Meng Xiangqing

Council Member, CPAPD
Professor, Institute of Strategic Studies, PLA National Defense University

Since Trump in power for about one year and half, the United States has released several documents including the National Security Strategy report, the National Defense Strategy report, Nuclear Posture Review, etc. which have made new judgments on the US security threats, and new adjustments on its diplomatic strategy. Regarding relations with China, the Trump Administration has frequently adopted tactics, imposed sustained pressure in many areas and aspects, launched disputes one after another, even challenged the bottom line for the "one China" principle, and made it more and more difficult for China and the United States to control differences, and to resolve crisis. Currently, scholars in China and the United States as well as the international media take pessimistic attitude to China–US relations.

I. The Asia-Pacific Security to a great extent determined by China-US relations

In overview of the Asia–Pacific security situation in the past 70 years, its developments and changes are determined by many factors, but China–US relationship factor carries fairly heavy weight, which can be divided into two phases. The first phase is from the founding of New China in 1949 to 1979 as China and the United States established diplomatic relations. During this phase, the basic feature of the Asia–Pacific security was confrontational, which is earmarked by China–USSR alliance signed in February 1950, and the US–Japan military alliance signed in April 1951. Then, the two confrontational blocs in different forms and at the different levels were expanding in the Asia–Pacific region. Down to the 1960s, the United States established a military alliance system, while the China–

USSR alliance existed in name only, not long afterward China and the United States took onto a reconciliatory path. The second phase is about 40 years from establishment of diplomatic relations between the two countries in 1979 up to now. During this phase, the Asia–Pacific security situation is showing cooperation from confrontation, and the cooperation is the mainstream, which has brought about 40–year basic stability and peace, and also the backdrop for the region to maintain development and prosperity. The Asia–Pacific regional sustained development and prosperity are historic and leave an impact on the world. Whether the future Asia–Pacific regional stability and peace can be maintained is a matter of concern to the entire world, and is also one of the important reasons for China–US relations to attract more and more attention.

Undoubtedly, over the past 40 years, China and the United States are not allies, but have established very close strategic cooperation. This close strategic cooperation shaped during the medium– and later period of the Cold War are analyzed by many systematic academic studies in both China and the United States, and are being proved by more and more decoded files. The quality of Sino–US strategic cooperation in some areas even surpassed that between the United States and its European allies, so which is also defined as "quasi–alliance" . The profound changes of the international situation and geopolitics produced by the end of the Cold War once triggered a negative inclination for the Sino–US strategic relations, which have made their relations an element of uncertainty in the Asia–Pacific region. In the Asia–Pacific region, there is no possibility for a sharp contradiction to emerge between the United States and Japan, but there is a possibility between China and the United States. The contradictions and even conflicts China has with Japan, Vietnam, the Philippines, etc. on territorial disputes will not change the basic feature and security order of the Asia–Pacific security situation, but if China–US relations see a fundamental change even a reversal of the bilateral relations, the Asia–Pacific security may be overturned, a confrontational security pattern may come into being.

With the end of the Cold War, the special Sino–US strategic cooperation shaped during the Cold War late period also disappeared. But the two sides soon began to search for a path and means to maintain cooperation in strategic security areas, both sides try to learn its counterpart intentions. Both countries have made proposals for defining the Sino–US relations, for example, building constructive and cooperative partnership, being stakeholders, establishing constructive cooperation, and then a new type of major countries relationship, etc. Comparing these concepts, and looking at the exchanges and diplomatic efforts as both sides continuously change their definitions for the bilateral relations, it is not difficult to find that there are obvious different identities of the two counties on defining the bilateral relations. However, it can be certain that the decision–makers of the two countries also wish to maintain the cooperation momentum and continuously carry out cooperation in the Asia–Pacific region to avoid confrontation no matter what concrete concept to use. Meanwhile, the two countries can find basic impetus and foundation for cooperation, for example, from economics and trade cooperation to anti–terrorism still to regional security, global issues, etc. But, it seems that all these are changing these days, the anti–terrorism driver is weakening, the economics and trade as the ballast stone is shaking, the US side is becoming less and less interested in global issues such as climate change, etc. The Korean Peninsula nuclear issue is having an opportunity of settlement. Although decision–makers of the two countries still vigorously maintain cooperation momentum, yet, regarding settlement of contradictions and differences through dialogue and cooperation, the US side expresses attitude more than adopting policies, speaks louder than acting, but choosing to counter China and putting pressure on China become more prominent.

In overview of history, China–US relations, from confrontation to reconciliation to normalization still to increasing maturity, have experienced a path of twists and turns. China–US relations are full of contradictions and sometimes very sharp contradictions, but also many historic opportunities for cooperation, and cooperation is accompanied with contradictions in the process. The history proves again and again whether the two countries develop cooperation or pursue confrontation can find enough reasons, but ultimately choose cooperation. That is because those statesmen and scholars working responsibly for peoples of the two countries, and for regional and global peace and security clearly know that only cooperation is the only way for the two countries to get on well with each other, otherwise a disaster will be generated not only for the two countries, but for the Asia–Pacific peace and global peace at large.

II. The US China policy is under a major readjustment

The US National Security Strategy report clearly states that in the face of worldwide growing political, economic, and military competition, the United States needs to reconsider its past policy. This policy is based on such assumption i.e., the engagement with the counterpart and integrating it into the international organizations and global trade, and enabling it to become a good participant and trusty cooperative partner, this prerequisite is proved wrong to a great extent.

Though no China is named there, yet, its reference is quite clear. The Trump' s basic concept of pursuing peace with strength determines its China policy focus is to carry out competition in strength with China, and impose comprehensive pressures in many areas and no longer attempt to shape China. In terms of these, the US China policy is under a fundamental readjustment, which is not completed yet. Because of the megatrend featured by rapid growth of China' s strength and the gap with the United States continuously narrowing, to maintain strength superiority over China is the long–term focus of the US policy to China. It is to maintain strength superiority over China that the Trump Administration strengthens its competition with China. It is true that the US National Security Strategy report states that competition does not always mean hostility, and nor necessarily leads to conflicts, but the conservative radical thinking and forceful style of work of the Trump Administrative team may trigger Sino–US vicious competition. For example, economically, the Trump Administration acts willfully, and launches the trade conflicts, which shakes the ballast stone for China–US relations, but more and more people believe that the US Administration' s US$50 billion tariff focuses on China' s high–tech products, restraining China' s investment, and not on settling the US trade deficits with China, but more likely to slow down China' s high–tech progress and growing strength steps, so as to reach the goal of maintaining US strength superiority over China. This policy based on the relative returns thinking does not only severely obstruct the development of China–US economic and trade relations, but will intensify the Sino–US strategic competition, even vicious competition. From a long–term perspective, harming others is not in the interests of oneself. The US Hawk–led diplomacy and security team will acquiesce in or even wink at the US military to increase pressure on China in the South China Sea, which is bound to increase spiral confrontation between the military of the two countries; while the growing substantial security cooperation under the Indo–Pacific strategy framework is bound to enhance the risks of the regional geo–political split and confrontation. What is more dangerous is the Taiwan Travel Act, adopted by the US Congress and signed by President Trump, will upgrade the ranking of official exchanges between the United States and Taiwan. All these acts prove that the US side actively plays the Taiwan card, which will inevitably produce severe impacts on the relations between the two sides of the Taiwan Straits, and China–US relations.

III. Cooperation is the only option for China-US relations

The future China–US relations are determined by many factors, among which there are conventional variables and non–conventional variables. The conventional variables include the balance of strength, the strategic foundation (economics and trade relations, security cooperation, etc.) and strategic environment (constraints of domestic interests groups on foreign policy; impacts of external factors such as Iran, Ukraine, the Philippines, the DPRK, etc. on China–US relations) between the two countries. The most noticeable non–conventional variable is the Trump Administration' s China policy direction. No matter how things are changing, the decisive factors determining the direction of the China–US relations are as follows:

First is the Taiwan issue. The Taiwan issue is the most sensitive, most central and most prominent issue in China–U.S relations. Since the US Administrations recognize the "one China" principle after the establishment of diplomatic relations between the two countries, and basically abide by the consensus and the bottom line reached by the two countries, the Taiwan issue is brought under control to a certain extent over the past decades, so no major crisis has emerged, or any emerged problem is finally mitigated through bilateral strategic exchanges and communications, and at least does not get out of control. It is true that disruptions often occur, but the bottom line is never broken. However, since Trump came to power, this bottom line may be broken up at any time. Trump had a phone call with Tsai Ing–wen, clamoring to make a deal with the Taiwan issue and trade issues; the US Congress adopted the Defense Authorization Act 2018, and especially passed the Taiwan Travel Act, and hitting for a sale of F–35 fighters, etc. All these acts have sent out wrong signals to the Taiwan separatists, subjectively playing a role in encouraging the Taiwan separatists. It is noticeable that the "one China" principle is getting weaker within the current US Administration.

Second is the framework and positioning of the Sino–US relations. China hopes to continuously promote the construction of Sino–US new–type major–country relations, and emphasizes the importance of mutual respect, and win–win cooperation from the very beginning of its contacts with Trump's team. During his first visit to China, former Secretary of State Tillerson also expressed the willingness of the United States to develop relations with China in a spirit of non–conflict, non–confrontation, mutual respect and win–win cooperation. However, under domestic pressure, Trump's position began to back out, proposing to develop "constructive, result–oriented" Sino–US relations. Now the key issue remains how the United States views China's rise and its strategic intentions. If China's rise is regarded as the greatest challenge to the United States and all China's domestic and foreign policies aimed at the United States, the framework and orientation of the Sino–US relations will continue to develop in a negative direction.

In a word, the Sino–US relations are at a new crossroads. Both China and the United States have entered a new era, need new thinking and new measures. They need not only high–level leadership consensus and guidance, but also new foundations and momentum, and also call for greater efforts in controlling differences and crises. Under the background of the current international situation showing the basic characteristics of change and chaos, a great opportunity for peaceful settlement of the DPRK nuclear issue and the complex security situation in the Asia–Pacific region, the impact of Sino–US relations on the regional situation will become greater. History and reality have proved and will prove repeatedly that cooperation is the only option for the Sino–US relations. Cooperation is not only related to the interests of the two countries, but also to peace of the Asia–Pacific region and the world at large. In this sense, we should remain optimistic about the future Sino–US relations.

Sino-US Developments amidst the Evolving Strategic Dynamics of an Extended Asia-Pacific (Indo-Pacific)

Julia Luong Dinh

*Senior Research Fellow,
Institute for Foreign Policy and Strategic Studies, Diplomatic Academy of Vietnam.*

I. Chinese foreign policy in the context of China's rise

Firstly, "China Dream" grand strategy will help China "approach closer to power centre". The 19th Congress of the Communist Party of China (CPC) proposed a development path to achieve the 'two–hundred–year goals' by 2050 under President Xi's core leadership, marking Xi Jinping's long–term thinking for China's strategic development. President Xi has labeled the future as the "new era", with fulfillment of the "two hundred years" (2021 and 2049) a prerequisite for the "China Dream". The 19th Congress set about the goal and task of the CPC to lead China to realize the "China Dream", or "the Great Rejuvenation of the Chinese people" in order to establish a new role for China. While the new era may signal China's official termination of Deng Xiaoping's "keeping low profile and biding time" guideline, Chinese foreign policy has fundamentally embodied the continuities of Deng's policy in maintaining stability and avoiding conflict in great power relations through existing cooperation mechanisms. Militarily, President Xi has conducted restructuring of the People's Liberation Army (PLA) and set its goal to turn the PLA into a world class army based on the mantra of "Fu Guo Qiang Bing" or" prosperous nation, strong military".

Secondly, China is growing more confident, demonstrating its willingness to contribute to the shaping of regional order constitute as a main pillar of power. In other word, the proactive diplomacy testifies to the fact that China has long aspired to be located right in the world's center of power. The situation dominated by the US in the past has seemingly changed in an irreversible course, and balance of power has increasingly tilted in favor of China, at least in the Asia–Pacific.[1] At the Conference on Interaction and Confidence–Building Measures in Asia (CICA) in May 2014, President Xi suggested that Asian countries need to look after their own security, implicitly expressing reservations about the presence of any "outside powers" in the region.

Thirdly, China have yet to become a global power which may possess the power and resources to provide global public goods such as the US has long committed to maintain a US–led world order since the end of World War Two. China's dependence on oil supplies from Middle East transported through the Malacca Strait and the South China Sea (Chinese trade relies on 21/29 regional maritime routes) is associated with not only economic risks but also geopolitical and strategic ones. In terms of security, China must address increasingly complex domestic and external security challenges, notably the local debts, financial risks, the poor–rich gap and the threats of the three evil forces.

II. Sino-US Relations and China's vision in the Asia-Pacific

Firstly, while both countries have not yet found the new equilibrium, Chinese and the US leaders have so far still managed to ensure "overall stability and balanced development". Current Sino–US relations are highly interdependent and mutually beneficial, and China's rise has, to a large extent, been blessed by American investors over the past few decades.[2] President Xi puts an emphasis on "smooth" and "major country" relations with the US, avoiding the "Thucydides Trap" in which diplomacy plays an important role in promoting "[a] new type of international relations" ("major country relations version 2.0"). China has also adroitly made use of latest developments such as 9–11 terrorist attacks, North Korean nuclear tests etc. turning challenges into opportunities, improving Chinese

[1] Recently, China has been proactive in demonstrating its role as a responsible major power, in hosting Bo'ao in Hainan on April 8–10, SCO Summit in Qingdao on 9–10 June, President Xi held informal Summit with Indian Prime Minister Modi in Wuhan on April 27–28, Premier Li Keqiang joined China–Japan–South Korea Trilateral Summit in Tokyo on May 9, and shuttle diplomacy between Beijing and other stakeholders in Korean Peninsula in which President Xi received Chairman Kim Yong–un twice in late March and early May respectively.

[2] China's trade surplus accounting for two thirds of bilateral trade volume of 500 billion USD; 6000 visitors per day between the two countries; Chinese investors' wielding influence in Wall Street etc.

leverage in negotiating with the Americans. While this situation generates much domestic concern, the US has also recognized China as a "useful adversary". [1] While the US has been on a relative decline, the traditional bi–polar order has not emerged as China has yet to stand on the same par with the US, particularly in military capability. While the game has not changed, both players must adapt themselves to the new dynamics. Sino–US relations can be summed up as "a mixture of competition, cooperation, and concession". Today, both China and the US aspire to promote cooperation and certain concessions or compromise may be made. During 2 recent summits, and through exchanges on the sideline of multilateral meetings, Trump and Xi have established personal relationship and struggled to advance their country's interests respectively.

Secondly, China is confronted with new challenges from the US foreign policy under an unpredictable President Trump and the Trump administration's departure from the traditional approach which relied on past American grand strategy thinking. On the one hand, Trump has opted for a confrontational approach, denouncing China as a competitor and an irresponsible partner and criticizing unfair Chinese trade practices at the expense of global trade. On the other hand, the Trump administration also recognizes China as an indispensable player in the Asia–Pacific. While Trump's rhetoric has given more weight to bilateral dealings, and disparaged multilateral cooperation allegedly not in America's favor, the US has indeed prioritized unilateral approach only in the commercial sphere and still placed emphasis on the need for governmental cooperation in multilateral political and security cooperation mechanisms. At the recent APEC 2017 summit in Danang, Trump announced the "Free and Open Indo–Pacific" concept, envisioning it as a strategic platform where Japan, India and Australia could be counted on to bandwagon with the US and turn the balance of power to restrain China. This is an important message that Trump has sent to China and the region during his visit to Asia, undoubtedly revealing American concerns about the rise of China. While currently President Trump administration may not be so attentive to Chinese records on human rights and democracy, which have traditionally served as stumbling blocks in Sino–US relations in the past, Trump may resort to other alternatives to contain China's rise. China is now strong enough to threaten and use retaliatory measures to respond to Trump's decision to levy tax on Chinese

[1] China has received President Trump with the highest honors ever – a State visit Plus; announced big agreements (253 billion USD worth of contract, acquisition of 5,000 Boeing aircrafts...), all aimed at symbolically reassuring the US.

products.

Thirdly, President Xi has applied "patience" taking steps backward and forward in handling the relationship with the US to take advantage of Trump. Xi Jinxing took the initiative in approaching Trump, meeting with him at Mar–a–Lago (Florida) in early April 2017. Whereas Trump is weakening American ties with allies in Asia and handing China unprecedented opportunities, China is seeking to shift the balance of power in its favor, and to divide American allies. Xi supports globalization, free trade while Trump calls for protection for American interests when faced with unfair trade practices. Trump is in favor of "America First" and prefers bilateral to multilateral economic negotiations (as evidenced by American withdrawal from the TPP, protectionist measures in aluminum and steel) and is causing much concern for allies and partners. American regional allies and partners have not been reassured by Trump's commitments made during his recent Asia trip. This has given China free rein to rally forces and expand its influence. [1]

Fourthly, China's efforts to open markets for investors in return for hi–tech transfer have largely been crippled by the West's policy, especially the US, in circumventing China's possession of hi–tech industries. China pays due attention to trade with the US, the center of the global economy, to make use of the economic, scientific and technological potentials to realize key development strategies for "Made in China" space technology, industrial strategies etc. by 2025. During his visit to Beijing in November 2017, Trump did not completely criticize China, and only stopped at lambasting previous administrations' fault for creating loopholes for countries such as China to take advantage of. Since his appointment, Trump has put forth a host of policies to attract capital, reinforced the American position in manufacturing and limited private overseas investment. While the US may run trade deficits with China of over 500 billion USD, American companies still own the advanced technologies and value–added processes. The case of ZTE is important to China not only in economic but also in political and strategic sense. If China does not invest in more modern technology, it will forever remain "a follower lagged behind". Xi has a good approach with President Trump, taking advantage of every opportunity to stabilize relations with the US, focusing on goals and circumventing American efforts to hinder the rise of China. Beijing

[1] In terms of security, China has had a strategic "good harvest" with regards to regional security hotspots. With the South China Sea, the US and China have varying degrees of interest. While China is ready to enforce an air defense identification zone (ADIZ) which would apply to all vessels in the sky, on the ocean surface and sub–surface, the US is only calling for maritime and aviation safety in the South China Sea..

criticized the US in resorting to the article 301 in the documents dated back in 2001 to conduct investigation of China' s violations, if any, with regard to Intellectual Property (IP) and technological transfers. In other words, China's preoccupation is coupled with maintaining political stability and the status quo. Sino–US relations in the next 5 years could be expected to reflect the common understanding between the two countries' leaders regarding strategic reassurance. President Xi would want to have harmonious relations with the US to ensure a stable international environment to grasp achievement of the first Centennial goal by2021, while President Trump have also expressed goodwill, reciprocating the "olive branch" offered by Beijing's leadership.

III. Strategic Implications on the Shaping of a future regional and global order

Both the US and China are stepping up efforts to tip the balance of power and to compete for influence. A G2 model may be in its nascent stages but cannot yet reach the globe in scope. Both China and the US are cognizant of the strategic importance of Southeast Asia and would want to court ASEAN and its members. While Trump may highlight the "Indo–Pacific" as the new American strategy for the region, his inclination for pragmatism will result in ignoring those forums that do not bring about realistic benefits for the US. This is particularly evident during Trump' s recent trip Asia, skipping the East Asia Summit in the Philippines; highlighting normative values of democracy and human rights, and hinting the possibility of setting up an axis of democracies in the Asia–Pacific. Domestically, the US may not view ASEAN in a bright light, but in the absence of an alternative, it has no other option than ASEAN. Trump needs ASEAN's centrality and the US will eventually come round with ASEAN. However, the way it takes part in the mechanism may differ. The US would not want ASEAN following its past, and will "get tougher" on ASEAN. This competition for influence will become even fiercer as China grows, and smaller powers will suffer the most collateral damage in case of major power conflict.

Both China and the US have policy options that are better than a confrontational scenario. A cooperation, competition, and concession scenario is the optimum scenario for all purposes of the parties involved, and the region. Due to the highly interdependent nature of the world's two largest economies, the new balance of power and the roles that both China and the US play in promoting reform of the international financial, monetary, trade and investment system China is ready to play an important, stabilizing role in the global political – economic order. China's recent foreign policy successes is an affirmation of its confidence in China's rising economic, political and military heft. China will take advantage of this strategic contraction of US power to renegotiate, reshuffle the world order and the rules more to its favor, proactively reviewing the role of the US in the Asia – Pacific.

However, there are redlines that both sides are not willing to cross. This means that China is not completely free to do as it pleases in the South China Sea. The US has conducted 4 FONOPs in the area over the past 10 months by the end of 2017. The Trump administration has also sought to restrain China' s realization of the BRI Maritime Silk Road. With regard to the Korean peninsula, Trump understands that no matter what the US, Japan, and Korea do to facilitate cooperation, without China and Russia, the issue of North Korean nuclear weapons will not be resolved. However, Trump also realizes that if the US does not quickly resolve this issue, it will be bogged down here and pay the costly price of strategic division of forces. Thus, Trump has taken a tough attitude, continually put pressure on Xi with regards to North Korea, demanding that China take action and put in place strong punitive sanctions with a clear message that "any company that does business with North Korea will not do business with the US" . For its part, the US positioned and put on patrol 3 aircraft carrier groups in the Korean peninsula at the same time for the first time in history. Chinese and American experts believe the chances of a "collision" between the two powers are high when China is no longer reluctant to stand up, wields knowledge of its own and its opponents strengths and weaknesses (including military deterrence, large domestic market and an economy transitioning to catering to domestic demands), and will renegotiate in its favor(22). This Sino–US foreign policy milestone is proof of "China' s overconfidence in the international context of chaos and turbulence" , while ensuring a "favorable international environment" and "strategic stability" to realize the "China Dream" and a "Risen China" in the era of Xi Jinping.

Sino-US Strategic Cognition and East Asia Regional Security

Yang Mingjie

Council Member, CPAPD
Director of Institute of Taiwan Studies, Research Fellow, CASS

Along with deepening adjustments and changes in the world strategic architecture, the security situation in East Asia is undergoing complex and in-depth changes. As two major countries of vital importance in the region, strategic cognition of China and the United States not only affects the future of bilateral relations, but also will have a far–reaching impact on the regional situation and order. At present, the mutual strategic cognition between China and the United States is still relatively positive and has some commonalities on the whole, but there are still major differences and even potential crises regarding some key issues and areas. Under the new circumstances, the two sides still have a long way to go for continuously exploring a road map for building a new form of major country relations. This effort also requires the support and cooperation of other regional force.

I. China and the United States share considerable consensus on profound changes in the international strategic architecture

There is considerable consensus between China and the United States on the profound changes in the international strategic architecture, i.e. both recognize the profound and far–reaching impact of the changes in the international strategic architecture, both recognize the urgency and necessity of maintaining stability of the international security environment, both recognize the importance of the strategic relationship between China and the United States, both recognize the importance of avoiding comprehensive strategic confrontation to either side, both recognize the need to strengthen cooperation and dialogue on some regional hotspot issues, both recognize the need for cooperative measures to address the growing non–traditional security threats, both recognize the importance of economic development to national security, etc.

II. On some major strategic and regional issues, there are still considerable cognitive differences between the two sides, which will exert practical or potential negative impacts on bilateral relations and regional security

First, on understanding the process of globalization and the existing international order

Both China and the United States have been benefited from globalization, however the U.S. administrators regard the United States itself as the major victim of globalization, and emerging economies such as China as major beneficiaries, which even make full use of the loopholes in the existing international order or mechanisms to continuously obtain benefits, thus placing the United States in a more passive position. While China, on the other hand, believes that globalization is an inevitable trend of historical development and has a double–edged sword effect, and the world should strengthen international cooperation in the field of global governance to create a more solid foundation and conditions for a new round of globalization. The international order should constantly adjust itself on the basis of respecting reality and gradually see establishment of a new international political and economic order. In terms of the option of practical policies, China stands for carrying out reform and opening–up at a larger scale and at a higher level with a more open mind and proposes to build a community with a shared future for mankind. The United States, on the other hand, has taken more unilateral measures to set obstacles in the way of a new round of regionalization and globalization. The United States uses the America First to passively respond to the governance and adjustment of the regional and international order, and even regards China's international contributions as a strategic threat.

Second, on judging each other's strategic positioning and projection

The United States has identified China as a strategic rival and is worried that its further development will directly challenge the U.S. hegemony in East Asia and even across the world. China sees the United States as the world's sole superpower, and its influence, though relatively declined, still remains significant in its impact on the regions and the world at large. In terms of policy option, China is striving to avoid Thucydides' trap, establish a new form of major–country relations with the United States, and safeguard regional stability and world peace. While the United States is entangled in strategic dilemma, on the other hand, it makes geo–strategic plans to intend to form more effective check and deterrence against China, and also worries about forming direct and comprehensive strategic confrontation with China on the other hand. Therefore, it continues to explore a way of cooperation in a strategic game.

Third, on understanding those regional hotspot issues

China and the United States have conducted in–depth cooperation on issues such as the Korean Peninsula nuclear issue and achieved remarkable results. However, they still have different views on the nature and road map of the issue. On the South China Sea disputes, China and relevant countries have made significant progress towards a peaceful settlement. However, the United States is worried that such positive progress will challenge its leadership and shaping power in the region and continues to raise tensions under the pretext of maintaining the so–called "freedom of navigation" . On the Taiwan issue, although both sides believe that stability across the Taiwan Straits is extremely important, yet the Taiwan issue is being heated up again by the main factors of the U.S. domestic political situation, so China has to respond to it as a crisis from the perspective of safeguarding territorial sovereignty and integrity.

Fourth, on viewing the alliance system and issues left over from the Cold War

Although China believes that the U.S. military alliance in this region is the product of the Cold War, it is fully aware of the complexity of this issue, so it firmly opposes the U.S. alliance system targeting the third party. The United States, on the other hand, has given strategic priority to strengthening military alliances in East Asia, and proposed the "Indo–Pacific strategy" in an attempt to create a broader value alliance system, which indeed takes China as a major factor in the security considerations.

III. In the new era facing complex security situation, China and the United States should deepen strategic consensus at a higher level more broadly

As President Xi Jinping says, we are living in a world of rapid development and change. The trend toward a multi–polar world, economic globalization and social normalization is gaining momentum. Various challenges are emerging one after another and the interests of all countries are closely linked. Zero–sum games, conflicts and confrontation have long gone out of fashion, and sharing thick and thin and win–win cooperation are called by the times. As the largest developing country, the largest developed country and the two largest economies in the world, China and the United States should act in the fundamental interests of the two peoples and peoples of various countries, take on responsibilities and work hard to build a new form of major–country relationship between China and the United States.

To be specific, China and the United States can enhance strategic communication in the following four areas. First, we should strengthen joint study and dialogue on globalization and global governance so as to find common ground of strategic position and direction in the new round of globalization, and to offer greater synergy in shaping the new regional and international order. Second, in the strategic dialogues, the two sides should enhance mutual exchanges of strategic goals and intentions with appropriate transparency, strengthen communication with the public and media, and prevent misunderstanding from being cooked up among the people. Third, we need to strengthen strategic communication on handling regional hotspot issues. Particularly, we need to be very cautious on territorial sovereignty issues, effectively manage and control crises and prevent escalation. Fourth, we should take a more open and active stance in handling security cooperation with other relevant countries and prevent a new cold war mentality.

Contours of the Future in the Conflict between the US and China in the South China Sea: the Transition of the Regional Conflict to the Global Conflict

Dmitrii Mosyakov

Head of the Centre for Southeast Asia, Australia and Oceania Institute of Oriental Studies at RAS, Russia

Today, the situation in the South China Sea is different from that it was in relatively recent times. In the last period in this region, conflicts have been proceeded quite radical changes, which indicates how uncertain the outlines of the future are and how dangerous they can be for global security. I speak about actual transformation of the US into a full participant in the conflict. This did not happen right away, there was a time, for example, at the first US–ASEAN summit in 2009, when American representatives spoke in strictest terms with the leaders of the member countries of ASEAN, and pointed out to them that they should not complain about Beijing to Washington, and that the political elites of the ASEAN countries should themselves seek a compromise with China.

However, this tough approach of the US administration to ASEAN changed when President Obama came to power. New US Secretary of State Hillary Clinton stated that the US must return to Southeast Asia. The main reason that forced the Americans to change their approach to ASEAN, and to move the country members of this organization into their potential allies, was China's apparent elevation when Beijing began to pursue an increasingly independent from the US and realized active policy in the region of the islands and in the waters of the South China Sea.

Today, as part of the policy of returning to Asia, US are intervened in the conflict. Their military ships are placing, in the restricted by Chinese authorities zones near the disputed islands, threatening the direct confrontations with Chinese troops. The unfolded US–China confrontation in the South China Sea has turned the sluggish conflict of the neighboring states, which for a long time was of little interest to the world, to the confrontation of modern superpowers. Moreover, interestingly, the growth of this conflict occurred as if the events were written off from the textbook on political science, when the conflict is born on the basis of very few understandable small contradictions, and then, if not quashed, begins to develop, gets its own logic, and, at the end ends, draws in itself all the new countries and peoples.

The arrival of Americans with their aggression, powerful cultural mythology literally crumpled the status–quo. As an alternative to the Chinese political and cultural domination US has activated the diverse modernist forces in the Southeast Asian countries, which have actively promoted the American cultural stereotype and, thereby, prepare the national communities for closer relations with the United States. Today, with the involvement of the Americans in the regional conflicts, the conflict in the South China Sea has ceased to be regional. It has become a global one, threatening stability and security in both the South China Sea, and in Asia, and throughout the world. The fact is that any military clash between Chinese and American forces can cause a big war between the world's leading powers. The threat of such a development occurs regularly, because over and over again either an American airplane will fly under the guns of Chinese air defense in the forbidden area declared by the PRC, or the US destroyer will pass under the barrels of Chinese cannons in the zone of bulk islands, which is also forbidden by China. Any unauthorized and accidental shot can drastically change the situation. Moreover, the situation in the sphere of security only worsens, especially after it was announced that from February 18, 2017, a patrol of a group of US warships began its mission at the South China Sea, led by the aircraft carrier Karl Vinson. This means that the entire region of Southeast Asia is literally doomed to constant nervousness and instability, the expectation of a conflict, as it has happened on more than one occasion and for the last time on May 27, 2018, when the American warships 'Higgins" and "Entitem" deliberately and demonstratively entered the waters of the disputed territories of the South China Sea, provoking Chinese coastal artillery to a devastating response.

Moreover, today we can talk not only about a new global quality of the conflict, but also a new round of cultural and political rivalry, when the great powers appeal to the countries of the region in search of support. And here it is necessary to say that the "soft power" of Americans, based on a well–developed cultural mythology about America's messianic role in the world, clearly overstates the mythology of the Chinese about the historical and cultural community, which has led to mutual distrust between China and the US. But the problem is that the success of American myth–making is seen as full of new conflicts, an atmosphere of mutual misunderstanding and tension. The reason for this is that American cultural stereotypes and dominants, taking root in the political elites of Southeast Asian countries, destroy the traditional cultural field of Greater East Asia, giving rise to mutual distrust and misunderstanding.

Today the issues of national security come to the forefront in China's policy in the South China Sea. If we follow the logic of the Chinese military, we will see that the control of the Spratly and a significant part of the South China Sea is necessary for the PRC to protect itself from US missiles, and prevent the United States and its allies from blocking the vital sea economic arteries and suffocate the country with an economic blockade, which is constantly being mentioned in the American press.

After all, in the context of confrontation with the US, China is extremely important that the ASEAN countries do not find themselves in the American camp or become Washington puppets. By the way, in this, China can find support among an influential part of the ASEAN political elite, whose prominent representatives have repeatedly publicly voiced their desire to be outside the global confrontation between Beijing and Washington and to remain free to choose foreign policy partners. The ASEAN members do not hide that they would like to have constructive relations with the PRC, they are against taking on the role of the advanced American front against China. This position can be decisive for Chinese success in future relations with US in the South China Sea.

Locked in a Spiral? Sino-US Relations in the Asia Pacific Region: An Indian Perspective

Dr. Teshu Singh

Associate Fellow, Vivekananda International Foundation, India

Overview of the Development

The Sino–US relations are the most significant bilateral relationship in the world today. They are the two largest economies in the world, as well as the two biggest military spenders. They are embroiled in certain issues, i.e. bilateral trade, the North Korean Crisis and Taiwan Strait issue. So far the US and China are not rivals, either. And the fact that their economies are interdependent dismisses the chance of any conflict. Both countries cooperate and compete in shaping international norms in a larger way. Consequently, the relationship is critical to the world order. Former US Secretary of State Henry Kissinger has said that the US–China relationship will be the defining relationship for the world of the 21st century, and both the countries should work jointly to promote peace and prosperity. [1]

The three flashpoints of the world: the Taiwan Strait, the Korean Peninsula and the South China Sea dispute, are located in this region. Recently, the rising US trade deficit and frictions over the technology issue with China have become a serious issue in the contemporary stage of Sino–US relations. These developments have bearing over the security of the region. The Chinese ambassador to the US Cui Tiankai has said, "There are some people in the United States who are trying to place a "glass curtain" between the two nations, so as to impede bilateral exchanges in economy, science and technology, and people–to–people engagements, and even stoke suspicion against exchange students and research

[1] Kissinger calls for cooperative U.S.–China relationship accessed at http://news.xinhuanet.com/english/2017–09/27/c_136643378.htm

fellows from China." [1]

An India Perspective

In the on–going trade friction between China and the US, India may be the biggest beneficiary. India being a huge market will only be the next destination for Chinese manufacturers. In the fifth India–China Strategic Economic Dialogue (SED), amid growing US–China trade frictions, India has offered to sell soybean and sugar to China in response to tariffs imposed by the Chinese on US imports. [2]It is the first time India has offered to China to sell a product in case the ongoing US–China trade friction turns serious. In the interdependent world order, a full–blown war between the US and China is not in any nations interest. Besides this, the concept of Asia Pacific is under discourse in India. The more widely used term is Indo–Pacific. Notably, India maintains its 'strategic autonomy' in such kind of grouping. Further, the National Security Strategy report in 2017 has stated the importance of the Indo–Pacific region for the US and eventually has also conveyed the strategic importance of India. At the 2018 Shangri La Dialogue in Singapore, Indian Prime Minister Narendra Modi outlined India' s vision of the "Indo–Pacific" Region. He expounded on the six component of the concept; all–inclusive region, the centrality of the Southeast Asian Region, rule–based order for the region, freedom of navigation, condemn protectionism and vitality of connectivity in the region. [3]During the discussion, Col Zhou Bo of China' s People' s Liberations Army, highlighted that if the "Pacific Ocean can accommodate China and the US, the Indian Ocean can accommodate both China and India, steering away from the debate of possible friction points."

Implications for the Region

Overall, the US trade policies toward China has been to an extent determined by its growing concerns about China' s military activities in the South China Sea and its perceived role in US relations with North Korea. The US has already revoked its invitation to China to join the Rim of the Pacific (RIMPAC) exercise

---

[1] Ambassador cautions against "glass curtain" between China, U.S. accessed at http://en.people.cn/n3/2018/0514/c90000–9459500.html

[2] SutirthoPatranobis, India offers to supply soybean to China at high–level economic dialogue accessed at https://www.hindustantimes.com/world–news/india–offers–to–supply–soybean–to–china–at–high–level–economic–dialogue/story–RKnbHYPVhvcDUE2YGuVu5I.html

[3] Prime Minister' s Keynote Address at Shangri La Dialogue (June 01, 2018) accessed at https://www.mea.gov.in/Speeches–Statements.htm?dtl/29943/Prime+Ministers+Keynote+Address+at+Shangri+La+Dialogue+June+01+2018

2018, and continues to build pressure on China.

Deteriorating US–China relations may lead to rising dollar and rising international interest rates and the flow back if capital flows. [1]Consequently, the outcome of the trade consultations will have ramifications for other countries as well. Any failure in the negotiations between the two sides is bad for the region and has larger ramification. India supports the peaceful resolution of the issues and believes in reciprocity based on the merit of the situations.

[1] Dollar, yen rise as US–China trade war worries perk up, accessed at https://www.cnbc.com/2018/08/02/forex-market-dollar-moves-and-trade-tensions-in-focus.html

The Structural Factors for the Deteriorating of China-US Relations

Yuan Peng

Council Member, CPAPD
Research Fellow and President of China Institute of Contemporary International Relations

I. China-U.S. Relations are in a rather grave period

China–U.S. Relations in the past decade have witnessed fundamental changes. With the growing China' s comprehensive national strength, it is inevitable for China and the United States to shape a strategic competitive pattern. Because of "America First" – the basic administrative tone of the current U.S. Administration, plus the misunderstanding and misjudgment on China' s peaceful development policy, it is difficult for the United States to genuinely adopt a China strategy in conformity with the times.

Nowadays, an unprecedented large–scale debate, reflection and readjustment on China strategy are going on in the United States after the Cold War. The participants are from so many walks of life that include politics, academics, business, military, etc., the topics are so many that covers economics and trade, security, humanity, science and technology, etc. the discussions are so deep that they straightforward go to one topic, i.e. whether or not the U.S. China strategy needs a fundamental readjustment. Few preliminary consensuses are being shaped. One, China has become a major strategic competitor for the United States to spare no effort to respond to in the future, and this competition has gone beyond the economics and trade, and the Asia–Pacific region, and is all–dimensional and world–wide. Two, the existing U.S. China strategy can hardly be defined as a total failure, but can be viewed as a basic failure, and urgently needs a fresh start and readjustment. Three, the forthcoming 5–10years is the key period for the China–U. S. strategic competition, if responding ineffectively, China will be invincible, and it is only a mater of time for China to surpass the United States.

The National Security Strategy report by the White House wantonly defines China as a "revisionist country", a "strategic competitor", and brazenly claims the complete failure of the past U.S. China strategy; the National Defense Strategy report by the Pentagon claims that a priority concern of the U.S. security is no longer the terrorism, but strategic competition among major countries with China and Russia bearing the brunt; the Nuclear Posture Review puts China on a par with Russia, the DPRK, and Iran, and views them as major threats to the U.S. nuclear security. The U.S. authoritative reports so frequently and openly list China as a major challenge or even a threat, which generate a very bad impact on the environment for shaping the U.S. China strategy debate.

Various sides commonly believe that China–U.S. relations have entered a complex and sensitive period, showing a deterioration sign. Regarding the economics and trade, both China and the United States hope to avoid a trade war, but the Trump Administration has wantonly launched the trade conflicts against China, increased tariff on the Chinese goods worth US$34 billion and will release a new list for tariff increase, restrained China's investment in the U.S. high–tech industry, criticized China engaged in economic invasion, and stealing intellectual property rights. Regarding the Taiwan issue, the U.S. Congress passed the Taiwan Travel Act, so the raking for officials of the U.S. State Department and the Congressional members to visit Taiwan is upgraded with higher frequencies. The National Defense Authorization Act for the Fiscal Year 2019 passed by the Congress strengthens the U.S.–Taiwan relations particularly the military relations, and shows commitment to jointly respond to "challenges" with Taiwan. In the military area, the U.S. military canceled its invitation to China to participate in the Pacific–rim military exercises, as a response to China's continuous military actions in the South China Sea. In the humanities, the United States thinks that China purposely overlooks the U.S. strength, ingeniously disintegrates the U.S. order, and begins reversing the U.S. ideological, cultural and educational impacts, and carrying out the so–called "sharp power", so the United States must show its expressions, warn it of the possible consequences so China knows how to move forward.

Over the past 40 years since the normalization of relation between China and the United States, the bilateral relations develops relatively smoothly, there is neither a hot war nor a cold war, the total volume of trade between the two countries grows to US$500 billion from US$2.5 billion. Why has there emerged an across the board competition posture between China and the United States? There are different interpretations between the two sides.

II. The in-depth reasons for the deteriorating China-U.S. Relations are the structural factors

First, the changing balance of strength between China and the United States.

China' s GDP of last year amounted to 63% of that of the United States, the balance of strength between the USSR at its peak and the United States was figured by 58%, while 69% for Japan. If China continues its growth at current rhythm, the figure may approach 70–80%. This change is the most fundamental, which leads to less confident and less inclusive but more sensitive and worrisome mentality of people in various walks of life in the United States. The two countries' relationship has become No.1 and No.2 from the past of one superpower with many strong powers relationship. So it is inevitable for them to form a strategic competitive pattern, which is the objective reality independent of man' s will, and is also the historical basic law that can hardly be avoided, which is the source for cooking up the Thucydides trap.

Second, the changing strategic posture of both sides

The U.S. strategic focus is comprehensively shifting to the Asia–Pacific or Indo–Pacific, or to the peripheral areas of China. The United States believes that China' s attitude to the world has developed to work hard to make progress from the past abiding time, moving to the ocean from land and to the Belt and Road from self–development. These changes are leading to all–dimensional confrontation between the two countries in the Asia–Pacific region, but the two sides have neither historical experience to follow nor a practical path to take, thus only figuring out the counterpart strategic intentions with suspicions. China regards the U.S. sending out warships as the U.S. strategic encirclement, while the United States views every action by China on the Belt and Road construction as an attempt to squeeze it out of the Western Pacific, so mutual suspicions are very obvious, falling into a vicious cycle is much likely.

Third, the changing strategic foundations of the two sides

The economics and trade relations as the ballast stone for China–U.S. relations for a long time has seen very prominent problems instead, the security foundation for cooperation such as joint response to Soviet chauvinism and to terrorism after the 9.11 terrorist attacks is basically nonexistent. The Korean Peninsula nuclear crisis should be an opportunity for the two countries to build strategic cooperation, but the current situation is the coexistence of cooperation and grudge, which can be hardly taken as in–depth strategic cooperation. Trump is determined to withdraw from the Paris Agreement on Climate Change, which has eroded the bilateral relations supported by the climate cooperation. Under such circumstances, the twists and turns of the bilateral relations are not surprising.

Fourth, the changing strategic environment of the two sides

Different and diversified voices influence the top–level decision–making. From the external perspective, the third party factors influence the U.S. policy–making. The Sino–U.S. relations is subjected to the establishment groups within the United States while troubled by the third party factors externally, so China–U.S. relations are often forced to divert from the main channel, -- things taking their course regardless of one' s will.

China–U.S. Relations have developed to a new stage, so there should be new tactics at the new stage and a China–proposed way is to build new type of major country relations, which however is not warmly responded by the United States. With this big backdrop, Trump comes to power, the existing competition within China–U.S. relations is intensifying, plus the unpredictability of Trump himself, the selfishness of the America First, and the rigidity of a hostile attitude to China shown by Trumps diplomatic and security teams, hence, it is rather difficult for China to work with the United States. Actually, neither Japan nor the ROK , nor Europe finds it easy to get on well with Trump, while China–U.S. relations is different with the relations between other countries and the United States, so should China shoulder more since major countries' power transition gets involved in China–U.S. Relations.

Session II:

Security Situation in Northeast Asia and Its Prospect

The Changes and Options of Trump's Policy Toward the DPRK

Teng Jianqun

Council Member, CPAPD
Research Fellow and Director of Institute of American Studies, China Institute of International Studies

The relaxation of the Korean Peninsula is closely related to the direct interactions between the United States, the DPRK and the ROK, among which the changes of the U.S. policy toward the DPRK is one of the important reasons. Trump tries to be distinctive and unconventional in his attempt to make some contributions to the DPRK issue. However, due to the constraints of geo–strategy and domestic politics, it is impossible for the United States to fundamentally adjust its policy toward the DPRK nowadays, and there will be no dramatic changes in relations among relevant countries either. So, maintaining the existing stable situation is the focus of the parties concerned.

I. The basic changes of Trump's policy toward the DPRK

Since the presidential election in 2016 up to now, President Trump' s policy toward the DPRK can be divided into four phases.

The first phase: trying to find a different way to solve the DPRK nuclear issue such as through "telephone" or "Hamburger" . The 2016 U.S. presidential election is regarded as "a super reality show" and as "the dirtiest fight" breaking through the bottom line. The final debate became slashing attacks between Trump and Hilary, but there was not much time given to the DPRK issue. On June 15, Trump said in Atlanta that if Kim Jong–un comes to the United States, he' ll have a hamburger with him and have better deals with him on the nuclear issue. He said that although the possibility for Kim Jong–un to abandon nuclear program through dialogue is only 10% to 20%, but it doesn' t matter. Kim Jong–un' s nuclear abandonment is not entirely impossible and he will have better deals with him on the nuclear issue. Hillary criticized him for intending to communicate with the dictator, but he thought it' s the beginning of a dialogue, although it' s not very likely. Trump stressed that he will not go to North Korea for a dialogue with Kim Jong–un, but Kim Jong–un should come to the United States for a meeting. Trump will not invite Kim Jong–un for a state dinner, but would simply talk to him over hamburgers–eating. The above statements are the beginning of Trump' s understanding of the DPRK issue.

The second phase: the decision-making on the DPRK policy is lost to the Department of Defense and the United States imposes "maximum pressure on the DPRK". In early February 2017, U.S. Defense Secretary Matisse visited South Korea, which is the first visit by Trump' s cabinet members. Matisse stressed that the situation on the Peninsula affects the U.S. interests, reiterated the U.S. security commitment to South Korea, and the THAAD system is to resist the North Korean missile threats. He pointed out that the United States is well aware of the urgency of resolving the North Korean nuclear issue and the importance of developing the ROK–U.S. military alliance. Therefore, he paid a visit to South Korea shortly after taking office, showing the importance Trump Administration attaches to the alliance with South Korea and demonstrating that the United States will continue to participate in the Asia–Pacific security affairs. Matisse warned North Korea that any attack on the United States and its allies would be foiled and that the United States would overwhelmingly counter all nuclear attacks.

Military deterrence and putting pressure on the DPRK are top priority task of Matisse' s visit. The United States and South Korea have decided to continue large–scale military exercises on the Peninsula. The two sides agreed to enhance the U.S. performance capability to extend deterrence against the DPRK, and to realize the permanent presence of strategic nuclear weapons in the ROK through regular dispatch and rotation, so as to prevent nuclear missiles provocations of North Korea. On the day of Matisse' s visit to South Korea, the U.S. State Department approved arms sales worth US$140 million to South Korea.

Before Trump was elected president and Matisse' s visit to South Korea, the DPRK had not conducted nuclear tests. Defense Minister Matisse played the same old tune, and the DPRK lost patience. On February 12, the DPRK launched missiles at P' yŏnganbuk–do to the sea east of the Peninsula. Since then, the situation on the Peninsula became heated up, and the United States and the DPRK accused each other. The Trump Administration put forward the "maximum pressure" on the DPRK. Militarily, the United States strengthened the U.S.–ROK alliance, conducted large–scale military exercises, and frequently designated strategic weapons to get close to the Peninsula. In addition to conducting a series of missile tests, the DPRK conducted the sixth nuclear test in September 2017.

The third phase: the U.S. and DPRK leaders meet and reach a four-point consensus. In February 2018, the Winter Olympics in Pyeongchang reopened the door of interactions between the two sides on the Peninsula, but the United States is not optimistic about such interactions. At the opening and closing ceremonies, the U.S. and DPRK officials were close to each other without any direct contact. U.S. Vice President Burns and National Security Adviser Bolton believe that it is when the Winter Olympics flame is put out that the contacts between the two sides will come to an end. After the Winter Olympics, South Korea continued contacts with the DPRK, sending senior officials to visit Pyongyang, bringing back information about Kim Jong–un' s wish to meet Trump. Trump can' t help announcing that he will meet with Kim Jong–un. At that time, former Secretary of State Tillerson was visiting Africa and said that there was no possibility for the U.S. President to meet with Kim Jong–un.

On June 12, President Trump and Chairman Kim Jong–un met in Singapore and reached a four–point consensus. It can be seen that Singapore meeting of the U.S. and DPRK leaders signals different intentions. After many rounds of sanctions, the DPRK is in difficulties. Domestically, the interests of the elite are damaged, and Kim Jong–un has to change his policies, while Trump is eager to show his capability for success and hopes to make a breakthrough in the DPRK nuclear issue.

The fourth phase: how to move forward is still uncertain since the relevant parties are in stalemate. Although the United States and the DPRK reached a four–point consensus in Singapore, the United States and South Korea agreed to stop holding joint military exercises on the Peninsula in the second half of the year, the DPRK was also demolishing the missile test site after closure of the Punggye–ri nuclear test site, yet Trump' s cabinet members signal to the DPRK for a timetable and a road map of its nuclear abandonment, while the DPRK hopes the United States to fulfill its security commitments and sign a declaration on ending the war as soon as possible.

For the United States, it is hard to accept the signing of the declaration on ending the war currently: the Trump Administration is unable to immediately lift the sanctions against the DPRK; nor is it to stop military pressure on the DPRK. Before resolving the DPRK nuclear issue, Trump' s policy of the "maximum pressure" on the DPRK will not change. The U.S. Government is anxious to see the DPRK' s nuclear disarmament results.

Under the agreement, the two countries have not reversed the situation on the Peninsula. There are two reasons: firstly, after having the nuclear power, Kim Jong–un needs to improve the domestic social and economic life, to improve its external environment, and is unwilling to immediately engage in a stalemate with the United States. Secondly, Trump knows that meeting Kim Jong–un violates the U.S. diplomatic principles, i.e., the incumbent president does not meet with North Korean leaders. The key is what the United States will get from the meeting. The direct result is the DPRK will return some of the remains of U.S. POW/MIA during the war.

In view of the growing situation, after the mid–term congressional elections, the United States again enters the 2020 presidential election cycle, any Trump' s move will target this occasion. President Trump will continuously show concern to the changing Korean Peninsula situation under the circumstances that there is not much room to move around domestically and guarantee that North Korea will not have nuclear test as the set goal for the two years to come.

II. Main reasons for Trump's adjustment of his DPRK policy

After taking over the White House, Trump made a policy toward the DPRK different from any previous president. From claiming a settlement of the DPRK nuclear issue over a phone call or hamburger–eating during the election campaign, to proposing "maximum pressure" on the DPRK, still to meeting with Kim Jong–un in Singapore, Trump' s changing policy towards the DPRK shows uncertainty of his foreign policy.

First, the United States has made significant changes in its judgment on the DPRK's nuclear missile threat.

The United States believes that the DPRK has acquired a preliminary mastery of nuclear missile technology, and some missiles are able to cover their U.S. domestic targets. The U.S. intelligence agencies are worried about the DPRK' s nuclear capability. For the United States, any direct and pragmatic threat to its homeland would be dealt with by its leaders with utmost efforts. For example, after the Soviet Union deployed its missiles in Cuba in 1962, Kennedy took the posture of not hesitating to launch World War III in order to force the USSR withdraw its missiles from Cuba. In his State of the Union Address 2018, President Trump pointed out that North Korean missiles will soon threaten the U.S. homeland. He stressed by saying that North Korean rash pursuit of nuclear missiles will soon threaten U.S. homeland, that to prevent this from happening, the United States needs to launch a campaign to exert the maximum pressure, that the past experience tells that complacency and compromise can only bring aggression and provocation, that he will not repeat those mistakes having left the United States deep in danger.

Second, it is difficult to achieve the expected goal by military operations. Since the year 1953, the United States has been studying a war plan against the DPRK. From the 5027 Operational Plan to the 5015 Operational Plan, the operational style was shifted from defensive counterattack to pre–emptive strike. As a result of changes in the judgment on DPRK' s nuclear missiles threat, Trump begins to figure out how to eliminate the DPRK' s nuclear missiles capability fundamentally as soon as he comes to power.

Militarily speaking, the Trump Administration has tabled the "pre–emptive" strike against the DPRK, which is still confronted with great danger. President Trump in his The Art of the Deal says that the way he does business is simple and straightforward, that he sets high goals for himself, and then continues to work for them until success. Tensions on the Peninsula since February 2017 seem to confirm Trump' s style of doing business: make a high–input deal.

Third, the positive interactions between the two sides on the Korea Peninsula have brought impacts to the U.S. policy toward the DPRK. In 2018, Trump' s policy toward the DPRK was disrupted by the positive interactions between the two sides during the Winter Olympics. On February 9, a high–level delegation led by Kim Yong–nan, chairman of the Presidium of Supreme People' s Assembly of the DPRK, arrived in South Korea on a special plane to attend the opening ceremony of the Pyongchang Winter Olympics. The next day, Moon Jae–in met with the delegation of the DPRK at Chong Wa Dae and had lunch together. Kim Yo–jong, as Kim Jong–un' s special envoy, handed in the Kim Jong–un–signed letter to Moon Jae–in for improving the two side' s relations and conveyed Kim Jong–un' s oral invitation to Moon Jae–in for a visit to the DPRK.

On March 4th, South Korea announced that a high–level delegation would be sent to Pyongyang. The chief of the envoy mission is Chung Eui–yong, Director of the National Security Office in Chong Wa Dae. During the visit, the special mission will hold a dialogue with senior officials of the DPRK on promoting peace on the Korean Peninsula and improving North–South relations, particularly, will have comprehensive discussions on creating conditions for the DPRK–U. S. dialogue aimed at denuclearizing the Peninsula and promoting North–South exchanges. On April 27, Chairman Kim Jong–un of the DPRK and President Moon Jae–in of the ROK held a summit in Panmunjom and reached the Panmunjom Declaration, which injected new driver into North–South interactions and also created conditions for relaxation of the Peninsula.

III. The future trend of Trump's policy toward the DPRK

It is true the leaders of the United States and the DPRK have reached four-point consensus in Singapore, but they still have a long way to go to implement it concretely. On August 24, 2018, Secretary of State Pompeo announced a plan for his fourth visit to the DPRK, but President Trump cancelled his travel plan just one day later. Trump said on his Twitter that he had asked Secretary of State Pompeo not to go to North Korea this time because he did not think enough progress in denuclearizing the Korean Peninsula had been made. Pompeo' s plan to go to North Korea again in the future is possibly after the settlement of U.S. trade relations with China. Abruptly calling off Pompeo' s visit to the DPRK did make people see that the prospect for interactions between the United States and the DPRK is worrying.

After 65 years of confrontation in the U.S.–DPRK relations, it is difficult for them to thaw the ice immediately and establish a new relationship. The establishment of diplomatic relations also involves the legislative process of the U.S. Congress. The premise for realizing a peace mechanism is that the United States no longer uses force and the threat of force against the DPRK. The Trump Administration does not commit itself to lifting economic sanctions and renouncing the threat of force against the DPRK. Achieving denuclearization of the Korean Peninsula is a long and complex process.

In short, the change of Trump' s policy toward the DPRK is resulted from interactions of various factors. After all, the United States is a country that has a profound impact on Northeast Asia, and its every move will bring about changes in the regional situation. For countries in Northeast Asia, maintaining stability and peace on the Korean Peninsula and realizing denuclearization of the Peninsula should be the common goal. Therefore, we should unite to prevent Trump from reversing his policy toward the DPRK.

Strategic Implications of a Post-Nuclear North Korea

Aaron Jed Rabena

Senior Consultant, Warwick & Roger
Program Convenor, Asia-Pacific Pathways to Progress
Associate Fellow, Philippine Council for Foreign Relations

Ever since, the Korean Peninsula has had two prevailing major issues: denuclearization and reunification. The two issues undoubtedly have correlation but the former is what has dragged North Korea' s economic progress and diplomatic relations. Recent groundbreaking measures taken by North Korea, under the auspices of its leader Kim Jong–un, is ushering in the country to the path of a normal state. Two landmark announcements he made in a speech last April, that caused tensions to die down, were the suspension of nuclear and missile tests, claiming that they have already allegedly mastered the technology for so doing, and the prioritization of the national economy. In support of these, North Korea has embarked on a series of diplomatic summits with his counterparts in South Korea and China, and has gone as far as Singapore for his historic meet with US President Donald Trump. A meeting with Japanese Prime Minister Shinzo Abe is also reported to be in the works. In other words, North Korea' s new policy would have wide implications for Asian regional development and security. The major implication would be the increase in North Korea' s foreign policy autonomy owing to accession to regional organizations and reception of economic partners.

Some experts predict that North Korea may finally overcome the challenges of political and economic isolationism. As North Korea puts premium on its economy, its national image will be seen as a normal, conformist, and cooperative state willing to work through the existing international system and be integrated with forces of globalization. And these would mark a sharp improvement in North Korea' s interaction and socialization with the international community in terms of strategic opportunities and economic gains. For instance, North Korea would be able to maximize its behavior in the market as it would have greater international market access and there will be an influx of capital, knowledge, and technology. But as North Korea does this, it will no doubt be absorbed domestically. And as North Korea normalizes its foreign relations and prioritizes image and economic–building, the country will join and be more active in international organizations, and be a signatory to multilateral treaties. North Korea may eventually rejoin the NPT and accede to international organizations and institutions such as the WTO, IMF, East Asia Summit, Nuclear Security Summit, Asian Development Bank, APEC, AIIB, and the BRI (which includes interconnectivity projects with Russia and South Korea). Over to medium to long–term, North Korea may eventually negotiate bilateral FTAs or agree to multilateral FTA processes. Regionally, North Korea' s denuclearization is a step forward in the creation of a Northeast Asian Community (and eventually an East Asian Community). For example, the Trilateral Summit may become a Quadrilateral Summit and the Six–Party Talks may become a formal peace regime. Similarly, the DPRK will be further integrated into ASEAN–led initiatives, as the Southeast Asian body welcomes as a denuclearized, inclusive, and prosperous region.

During the Cold War, the immediate threat to the US was the Soviet Union. The United States deemed the Soviet Union' s global communist agenda and formidable military force as a major threat to US values, allies, security, and global dominance. To safeguard these interests, United States needed balancers against the Soviet Union. This was easier done when the balancers had lingering political differences with the Soviet Union. One could note the famous Sino–Soviet split where Beijing and Moscow even went to the point of exchanging nuclear threats and accused each other as revisionists. This eventually resulted in China' s decision to align with the US through the Sino–US rapprochement and normalization of diplomatic ties, which basically goes to show that socialist countries should not be seen to be, by default, in the same bloc as they are also motivated by common national interests. Also, China had its reform and opening up, the US and Japan were instrumental in helping and engaging China.

The US, according to the latest National Defense and Security Strategies, considers China a strategic competitor, which threatens American values, alliances, security, and global dominance. It should thus not be surprising why Vietnam, a socialist country, is establishing closer strategic and military cooperation with the US. Not only this, Vietnam had also joined US–led regional initiatives such as the Trans–Pacific Partnership (TPP). As North Korea engages in rapprochement and détente with regional major powers, and decision end state of Cold War conflicts by replacing the 1953 Armistice Agreement, Pyongyang will gain more diplomatic and strategic autonomy and gain more choices and room for maneuver. Drawing from historical analogies, the United States will likely not leave South Korea just as they did not leave Asia when World War II ended with the defeat of Imperial Japan, and were eventually confronted with the emerging challenge of Communism during the Cold War. That is, American presence in South Korea will still be valuable vis–à–vis strategic rivals such as China and Russia.

As North Korea commits to major adjustments in its security and foreign policy, with far–ranging regional implications, it is important to take note of other issues that will continue to shape the interactions of the relevant stakeholders, namely: the THAAD missile defense system in South Korea, Japan's security policy, structural changes on US–South Korea alliance, and Sino–US relations. First, if the THAAD missile defense system is not dismantled, it would be seen to be more directed at China. Second, if Japan pursues its military normalization, it would also be perceived to be targeted at China (and even Russia). Third, it would be interesting to see how the nature of US–South Korea exercises and strategic priorities would be affected. Lastly, a win–win settlement of a nuclear–free North Korea for the US and China would simply cancel out one flashpoint in Sino–US tensions. Consequently, since the Korean peninsula would stabilize, other regional flashpoints may gain more attention (e.g., Taiwan, East China Sea, and South China Sea).

Northeast Asia Needs Pursuit of Sustainable Security: Thinking Based on the First DPRK-U.S. Summit

Liu Jiangyong

Council Member, CPAPD
Professor, Department of International Relations, Tsinghua University

On June 12, 2018, the United States of America and the Democratic People' s Republic of Korea (DPRK) successfully completed their first historical summit in Singapore, which is a great event and a good event with historical significance. The Korean Peninsula is likely to say farewell to the vicious circle of the DPRK' s nuclear and missile tests and strengthening of joint military exercises by the United States and South Korea. The most important thing in the future is how to consolidate the outcomes of the DPRK–ROK summit and DPRK–U.S. summit, implement the DPRK–ROK Panmunjom Declaration and the DPRK–U.S. Joint Declaration concretely, and realize the complete denuclearization of the Korean Peninsula and the establishment of a permanent peace and security mechanism.

I. The real cause of the profound changes in Northeast Asia in 2018

Up to now, the sharp antagonism between the DPRK and the United States & South Korea is caused by the historical factors of the Korean War and the ideological factor, but the decision–makers on both sides firmly believe that their own national security can be ensured only if they have the military means to destroy or deter the counterpart. This traditional military strategic theory and realism of power politics thinking will inevitably lead to escalation between the DPRK nuclear crisis and the U.S.–ROK military exercises, which is a "dead end" with high–cost to insecurity or unsustainable security situation.

So, at the crossroads of history, what can be done to meet the national security interests of the United States, the North side and the South side of the Peninsula?

This is a major issue that policy–makers of the three countries must reconsider and think twice. National decision–making does not depend on the abstract or specific national interests, but depends on the national decision–makers' awareness and judgment of national interests. In order to get out of the "dead end", the relevant parties to the DPRK nuclear issue needs to get free from the "dead end" confined to traditional military theory and realistic political thinking, and to establish a sustainable security concept together, and to put forward new ideas and new measures to solve the issue on the above basis. Without this, neither the complete denuclearization of the Korean Peninsula nor the lasting peace and stability in Northeast Asia will be achieved. The reckless idea of giving priority to the DPRK nuclear issue settlement at the risk of a war or the so–called "Libyan model" is neither realistic nor acceptable to any responsible government.

Old traditional thinking has led some people falling into misunderstanding of "sanction effect", convinced that Kim Jong–un's return to the track of denuclearization is the result of "maximum pressure". However, this logical thinking will inevitably lead to continuing sanctions against the DPRK, to the lack of constructive option and even to a counter–productive policy option. In fact, the theory of effective sanctions is only a part of the "public opinion war" against the DPRK, not a scientific study by the United States. Scientific research is based on a large amount of facts to discover the intrinsic laws of the development and change of things, rather than verifying one's own prejudices of subjective imagination.

Looking back at the 26–year history of the DPRK nuclear issue since the early 1990s, we can find a regular phenomenon: as long as the United States and South Korea implement a reconciliatory and inclusive "Sunshine policy" towards the DPRK, the process of denuclearization can start on the Korean Peninsula; as long as either the United States or South Korea implements a hostile and repressive "North Wind Policy", the DPRK will take advantage of the opportunity to conduct a nuclear test and launch a missile test. In the early post–Cold War period, U.S. President Bill Clinton and South Korean President Roh Tae Woo simultaneously adopted a "Sunshine policy" toward the DPRK, which led to an important step towards the denuclearization of the Korean Peninsula. However, it is regrettable that the Bush Administration overthrew the Clinton's policy in 2001 and implemented the "North Wind Policy" towards the DPRK, which led to the setback of the "Sunshine policy" pursued by the administrations of Kim Dae–jung and Roh Moo–hyun. For more than 20 years since then down to 2018, the U.S. and South Korean policies toward the DPRK have been out of sync, which resulted in the DPRK's opportunity to accelerate its nuclear development. In the year 2018, the leaders of the United States and South Korea finally unified their steps and began adopting the "Sunshine policy" towards the DPRK synchronously. This is what the leaders of the DPRK and all peace–loving peoples of the Peninsula are looking forward to.

Despite some attempts to implement the "North Wind Policy" against the DPRK, advocate continuous sanctions against the DPRK and routine joint military exercises targeted at the DPRK, under the new situation these practices are not only in violation of Article 15 of the UN Security Council Resolution 1718 on sanctions against the DPRK, and also in violation of the DPRK–ROK Panmunjom Declaration affirmed by the U.S.–DPRK Joint Statement, and which should be viewed as acts putting the clock back. Since 2018, DPRK leader Kim Jong–un at the three summits with China, South Korea and the United States has made a clear commitment to complete denuclearization of the Korean Peninsula, and has taken the initiative to abandon the nuclear test site, and the missile test site, and announced that the DPRK will focus on economic development. These positive changes should be affirmed.

In view of this, the logical starting point of the virtuous circle of the situation on the Korean Peninsula should be that the United States and South Korea should stop their joint military exercises against the DPRK in due course, and the UN Security Council should discuss how to lift or reduce sanctions against the DPRK. In 2019, if the Korean Peninsula can achieve the "two complete stops" and the United Nations begins to lift sanctions, the "Six–party talks" on the DPRK' s nuclear issue will hopefully resume, and concretely discuss how the DPRK should phase out its nuclear weapons program and how to give economic assistance to the DPRK. China, the United States, the DPRK and the ROK signing a permanent peace agreement to replace the armistice agreement for the Korean Peninsula will also be expected in the near future.

II. Northeast Asian security urgently needs establishment of a sustainable security concept

One of the important factors contributing to the success of the DPRK–U.S. summit is the simultaneous important changes in the security concepts of Kim Jong–un and Trump. It will be recalled that on September 19, 2017, Trump, in his speech delivered at the general debate of the United Nations General Assembly, said that North Korea' s nuclear weapons and ballistic missiles are a threat to the world, if the United States is forced to defend itself or protect its allies, then there is no alternative to complete destruction of North Korea. In response to Trump' s "complete destruction of North Korea" remarks, Kim Jong-un angrily responded that the DPRK will take resolute action to fight back. Until May this year, such attacks were still going on between senior U.S. and DPRK officials, and nearly interrupted the Kim Jong-un-Trump meeting.

However, on June 12 this year, Kim Jong-un at his first meeting with Trump in Singapore said from the bottom of his heart that it' s not easy to be there, history has dragged them back, and past prejudices and practices had prevented them from moving forward, but they have overcome all of these problems, so they are there on that day. Upon this, Trump stretched out his thumbs to express his appreciation.

Of course, not everyone would reflect on the "prejudices and practices of the past," especially in the United States, where the inertia thinking of the traditional realism of power politics in the "establishment camp" is still in domination. Therefore, it is expected that the Joint Statement reached by Trump and Kim Jong-un will be questioned and attacked in the United States, and there is still uncertainty as to whether the United States will come around in the future after administration reshuffle.

Fortunately, in May 2014, Chinese President Xi Jinping, at CICA Summit held in Shanghai, for the first time put forward a common, comprehensive, cooperative and sustainable concept of Asian security. Since then, Xi Jinping has been advocating and emphasizing this new security concept on many important international occasions.

In September 2015, Xi Jinping pointed out in an important speech to the United Nations General Assembly that we should abandon all forms of Cold War thinking, and establish a new concept of common, comprehensive, cooperative and sustainable security... We should promote international cooperation in both the economic and social fields, coordinate responses to traditional and non-traditional security threats, and prevent the scourge of war from emerging. This is the first time that Chinese leaders formally put forward the concept of sustainable security in the United Nations, thus making this new concept of security globally significant.

On September 3, 2017, Xi Jinping attended the opening ceremony of the BRICS Business Forum and delivered a keynote speech reiterating that we should promote a common, comprehensive, cooperative and sustainable security concept, constructively participate in the process of solving geopolitical hot issues, and play its due role. On May 22, 2018, during the Shanghai Cooperation Organization (SCO) Qingdao Summit, Xi Jinping emphasized that we should continue to uphold the concept of common, comprehensive, cooperative and sustainable security, and promote the security governance model of applying comprehensive measures, and treating both the symptoms and root causes.

I think Xi' s Chinese voice will also have an important impact on the security concept of the DPRK and the U.S. leaders. He creatively proposes that the concept of sustainable security could form a security governance model of treating both the symptoms and root causes in dealing with international hot issues. I believe that the sustainable security concept is a new theoretical thinking of international security and national security, which can be constantly enriched and developed in the practice of international security. Its basic definition is that countries, regions and even the whole world ensure the state of peace and security for a long time at a lower cost. The sustainable security includes traditional security and non–traditional security, domestic aspect and international aspect. Sustainable security is to maintain the sustainability of peace and security. Sustainable security strives, through peaceful cooperation of the international community, to get various countries to ensure a higher level of security at a lower cost, and safeguard humankind security.

The value goal pursued by sustainable security is the sustainability of security at low cost and high level, and the maximization of the balance between national security interests and international security interests. Sustainable security is characterized by a global vision, which is not only a security strategy for an individual country, but also a common security strategy for the international community concerning the future and destiny of mankind. The principles of sustainable security strategy are attaching importance to comprehensive security, advocating cooperative security, pursuing common security and striving for lasting security.

Sustainable security is people–oriented, emphasizing unity between the safe environment and ecological environment of state survival, which requires that disputes between sovereign states should not be resort to war, is especially opposed to the use of nuclear weapons or other weapons of mass destruction, to nuclear proliferation, to arms race, and to acquiring one–sided security interests of a country or a group of countries at the cost of destroying social, cultural, economic and ecological environments. Sustainable security measures should be preventive, comprehensive and coordinative.

Sustainable security includes both lasting peace and political power security. Maintaining peace on the Korean Peninsula is only the lowest goal, and what the Korean Peninsula needs more is the sense of political power security, mutual trust between leaders and the people sense of stability in a peaceful situation. Therefore, sustainable security has more practical importance and guiding significance for the future of the Korean Peninsula and Northeast Asia.

In today' s world, the security threats facing various countries are getting increasingly diversified. Traditional security factors and non–traditional security factors are intertwined and it is difficult for any country to respond to the challenges of the above–mentioned threats alone. So it is necessary for various countries to strengthen cooperation in social, cultural, religious, economic, political aspects and others, and comprehensive governance so as to eliminate the root causes of security threats. If the sustainable security concept can be recognized by leaders of the United States, the DPRK and the ROK, it will surely play an important role in consolidating the outcomes of the DPRK–ROK summit and the U.S.–DPRK summit.

The sustainable security concept involves the top–level strategic design of denuclearization, peace and security for the Korean Peninsula. In order to prevent the war chaos like that in the Middle East and Europe from happening in East Asia, it becomes more and more important to restart the Six–Party Talks and to jointly build a security cooperation mechanism in Northeast Asia under the guidance of the sustainable security concept. Otherwise, even if a multilateral security mechanism similar to that of Europe is established in Northeast Asia in the future, it is still difficult to ensure the sustainability of Northeast Asian security.

III. New factors and new directions for Northeast Asia to build sustainable security

First, currently new factors in favor of security in Northeast Asia are increasing.

--The 2018 U.S.–DPRK summit and the ROK–DPRK summit created a new history of the Korean Peninsula, in which China, Singapore and other countries play an important role and are widely appreciated by the international community.

--The countries in the region have no NATO–like military bloc led by the United States, and have not launched local wars or military interventions in the Post–Cold War era either.

--Except for small number of religious extremists, ethnic separatists and international terrorists, the vast majority of Muslims and other religious believers in the region have lived in harmony for a long time with neither new nor old hatred caused by large–scale religious conflicts.

--The region attaches great importance to economic development, employment and people' s livelihood. Governments of various countries have effectively maintained their social management and order without disorder and losing control.

--Although the reunification of the two sides across the Taiwan Straits and two sides of the Korean Peninsula has not yet been achieved, plus some territorial disputes and territorial sea disputes in the region, yet almost all parties concerned agree to deal with them peacefully.

-- The security and prosperity of the region are benefited from China' s reform and opening up and peaceful development, and diplomacy of neighborliness and partnership. With the development of China' s economy, the expansion of the market and the improvement of people' s living standards, a large number of Chinese enterprises and tourists go global, directly or interactively driving economic growth of all countries in the world, especially in Northeast Asia.

--The hosting of the Tokyo Winter Olympic Games in 2020 and the Beijing–Zhangjiakou Winter Olympic Games in 2022 will also promote regional security, cooperation and development. China, Japan and South Korea should cooperate with the countries concerned to ensure security for the events. The North side and South side of the Korean Peninsula can also improve their relations with help of an international sport event. Taking this as an opportunity, the ship of sustainable security in Northeast Asia can get out of the dangerous waters and sail far smoothly.

Despite Japan' s persistent urging Trump to impose sanctions on the DPRK previously, but as long as Abe changes his policy toward the DPRK and sticks out his olive branch, Kim Jong–un will not refuse, and it is possible for him to listen to Japan' s views on the issue of "kidnapping" . The crux of the matter is that it would be difficult to achieve results if the posture is technically adjusted only for domestic political convenience. In dealing with the DPRK, only through equal consultation based on the concept of common, comprehensive, cooperative and sustainable security can the desired objective be achieved.

Second, Northeast Asia should move in a new direction for sustainable security

As a top–level design for Northeast Asian security strategy, the countries concerned should have their long–term strategic communication and coordination, but not just stick to immediate interests and gains or losses. In the next 30 years to come, Northeast Asia should strive to establish a community of a shared economic future for sustainable development, a community of a shared peaceful future for sustainable security, a community of a shared social and cultural future for harmony and friendship.

Therefore, we should advocate and adhere to "peaceful multilateralism" , resist "violent multilateralism" and promote common security; advocate "sea–land peaceful cooperation concept" of peaceful cooperation between coastal countries and inland countries, and resist various traditional geopolitical ideas serving war and hegemony. As a big country with both sea and land, China proposes the Belt and Road Initiative, which is to seek peaceful cooperation between maritime countries and land–locked countries. It should naturally include the Korean Peninsula, and also welcome the participation of the United States and Japan as maritime countries.

(1) The establishment of denuclearization and peace mechanism on the Korean Peninsula must be based on common security, respect and guarantee the security of every country in Northeast Asia. President Xi Jinping points out: Security must be universal. We cannot just have the security of one or some countries while leaving the rest insecure, still less should one seek the so–called absolute security of itself at the expense of the security of others. Otherwise, just as a Kazakh proverb aptly puts it, "One who tries to blow out other' s oil lamp will get his beard on fire" . Security must be equal. Every country has the equal right to participate in the security affairs of the region as well as the responsibility of upholding regional security. No country should attempt to dominate regional security affairs or infringe upon the legitimate rights and interests of other countries. Security must be inclusive. We should turn Asia' s diversity and the differences among Asian countries into the energy and driving force for regional security cooperation. We should abide by the basic norms governing international relations such as respecting sovereignty, independence and territorial integrity and non–interference in internal affairs, respect the social systems and development paths chosen by countries on their own, and fully respect and accommodate the legitimate security concerns of all parties. To beef up and entrench a military alliance targeted at a third party is not conducive to maintaining common security. Xi Jinping' s speech at the Shanghai CICA on May 21, 2014 can also be appropriately applied to the situation of the Korean Peninsula.

(2) The establishment of the denuclearization and peace mechanism on the Korean Peninsula must attach importance to comprehensive security, i.e., safeguarding the traditional and non-traditional security of Northeast Asian countries by comprehensive means. Xi Jinping points out: We should take into full account the historical background and reality of Asia' s security issues, adopt a multi–pronged and holistic approach, and enhance regional security governance in a coordinated way. While tackling the immediate security challenges facing the region, we should also make plans for addressing potential security threats, and avoid a fragmented and palliative approach that only treats the symptoms. The security problems in Northeast Asia are extremely complex, with the practical problems and historical problems intertwined. There are not only sensitive hot issues, but also challenges brought by transnational crimes, environmental security, cyber security, energy and resources security, major natural disasters, transnational infectious diseases and so on. The way of thinking that only military superiority can ensure security is outdated. Therefore, the future "Six–Party Talks" or the multilateral security mechanism in Northeast Asia should not only stick to the discussion of denuclearization of the Korean Peninsula, but also play an active and constructive role in promoting the comprehensive security of Northeast Asia and finally find a way out for the complete denuclearization of the Korean Peninsula in mutual trust and win–win situation.

(3) The establishment of the denuclearization and peace mechanism on the Korean Peninsula requires exploration for cooperative security. President Xi Jinping points out: Cooperative security means promoting the security of both individual countries and the region as a whole through dialogue and cooperation. As the proverb goes, "Strength does not come from the muscle of the arms, but from the unison of the heart." We should engage in sincere and in–depth dialogue and communication to increase strategic mutual trust, reduce mutual misgivings, seek common ground while resolving differences and live in harmony with each other. We should bear in mind the common security interests of all countries, and start with low–sensitivity areas to build the awareness of meeting security challenges through cooperation. We should expand the scope and means of cooperation and promote peace and security through cooperation. We should stay committed to resolving disputes through peaceful means, stand against the arbitrary use or threat of force, oppose the provocation and escalation of tensions for selfish interests, and reject the practice of shifting trouble to neighbors and seeking selfish gains at the expense of others. In non–traditional security areas such as preventing infectious diseases, cracking down on drug trafficking, preventing major natural disasters, and improving the ecological environment in Northeast Asia, including the DPRK, security cooperation can be carried out between the countries concerned.

(4) Sustainable security in Northeast Asia depends on developing economy and improving people's livelihood. As President Xi Jinping puts forward, sustainable security means that we need to focus on both development and security so that security would be durable. As a Chinese saying goes, for a tree to grow tall, a strong and solid root is required; for a river to reach far, an unimpeded source is necessary. Development is the foundation of security, and security the precondition for development. The tree of peace does not grow on barren land while the fruit of development is not produced amidst flames of war. For most Asian countries, development means the greatest security and the master key to regional security issues. He advocates that to build an Asian security mansion that could stand the test of wind storms, we need to focus on development, actively improve people' s lives and narrow down the wealth gap so as to cement the foundation of security. We need to advance the process of common development and regional integration, foster sound interactions and synchronized progress of regional economic cooperation and security cooperation, and promote sustainable security through sustainable development.

I am happy to note that after the Wanshou Dialogue on Global Security, ROK President Moon Jae–in visited the DPRK and the two sides reached the Pyongyang Joint Declaration in September. I sincerely hope that the Korean Peninsula complete denuclearization and reconciliation process will see no reversal; the relations among China, the DPRK, and the ROK will be further improved, consolidated and strengthened; and the Korean Peninsula and Northeast Asia will usher in a new era of sustainable security and sustainable development.

The Security Situation in Northeast Asia and its Prospect

Sang Hyun Lee

Senior Research Fellow, the Sejong Institute, KOREA

1. Evaluating the U.S.-DPRK Singapore Summit

Finally, U.S. President Donald Trump and North Korea' s Chairman Kim Jong–un met for a historic summit on June 12, 2018 in Singapore. The summit was indeed a 'historic' in the sense that the leaders of two enemy states met for the first time face–to–face.

The Singapore summit reached on four agreements: establishing new US–DPRK relations; building a lasting and stable peace regime on the Korean Peninsula; reaffirming the April 27, 2018 Panmunjom Declaration, the DPRK commits to work toward complete denuclearization of the Korean Peninsula; recovering POW/MIA remains, including the immediate repatriation of those already identified.

In this statement, there' s no mentioning about the denuclearization time frame, inspection and verification procedures.

This indicates that there will be a series of long and arduous follow–up negotiations between the U.S. and DPRK negotiation teams. In fact, U.S. Secretary of State Mike Pompeo has visited Pyongyang for the third time, apparently with little progress. After his visit, however, we have very conflicting messages. North Korea accused the U.S. of "gangster–like tactics" and increasing the "risk of war," whereas Pompeo said that the two sides had "good–faith, productive conversations which will continue in the days and weeks ahead."

Given North Korea' s reaction after Pompeo' s third visit, denuclearization progress looks quite uncertain. The divergent accounts demonstrated the difficulty in translating the broad goal of denuclearization on the Korean Peninsula that resulted from Trump–Kim summit into specifics that would be acceptable to both sides.

2. Building a Peace Regime on the Korean Peninsula: Issues and Hurdles

From South Korea' s perspective, building a permanent peace regime on the Korean Peninsula is a long–cherished goal even before the nuclear crisis has begun. The Korean War came to a halt on July 27, 1953, when the commander–in–chief, United Nations Command (CINCUNC, a four–star U.S. general), on the one hand, and the supreme commander of the Korean People' s Army and the commander of the Chinese People' s Volunteers, on the other hand, signed the Korean War Armistice Agreement. Since then, the peace on the Korean Peninsula has been based on temporary halt of violence rather than on a peace treaty, meaning all parties involved technically remain at war.

A peace regime on the Korean Peninsula consists of a complete denuclearization and security guarantee toward the DPRK, officially ending the Korean War (terminating the cease–fire treaty), and a permanent peace treaty. North Koreans have consistently claimed that they developed nuclear weapons because of U.S. hostile policy against them. Hence, the key to denuclearization was that the United States had to end its "hostile policy," stopping political, security, and economic confrontation in return for eliminating their nuclear weapons.

The political aspect comprises U.S. recognition of North Korea as a sovereign state through establishing diplomatic relations between North Korea and surrounding countries, including South Korea and the United States; the security/military aspect includes officially ending the state of war on the Korean peninsula by replacing the temporary armistice agreement with a permanent peace treaty, and stop using—or threatening to use—strategic assets against North Korea; the economic aspect includes lifting trade restrictions and sanctions imposed on the North over the decades since the Korean War by both the United States and UN Security Council.

In light of North Korea' s condition for terminating U.S. hostile policy toward them, it can be a meaningful interim steps to consider a declaration to end the Korean War as a part of security guarantee, including US–DPRK non–aggression pledge. Declaration itself is an agreement, not a treaty. Hence it can be a symbolic step moving toward a peace treaty between the U.S. and North Korea.

Taking one step further, a peace regime should be better endorsed by international institutional support, either by a multilateral security consultative mechanism, or an involvement of international financial organizations. And, of course, a peace regime on the Korean peninsula should proceed in parallel with the actual progress in implementing the denuclearization process.

3. Remaining Issues

As peace regime proceeds, the status and role of ROK–U.S. alliance, the USFK, UNC and its future will be a controversial issue between South Korea and the United States. U.S. President Trump already declared that U.S. and South Korea will stop joint military drills, as far as the negotiation continues.

A question is the actual cost associated with dismantling North Korea' s nuclear weapons and facilities. Who will bear the cost of denuclearizing North Korea? Will South Korea, Japan, and China pay the cost as President Trump wishes?

The future ahead is like a complex three–dimensional game. On the inter–Korean dimension, genuine rapprochement and improvement of the relationship should be discussed; on the U.S.–North Korea dimension, both leaders should come up with a detailed plan to exchange CVID and provide a regime security guarantee; on the North Korea–international community dimension, lifting sanctions and verification/monitoring mechanism must be discussed. Progress on these three dimensions should proceed in tandem, roughly in a balanced pace. This will give a better chance to finish North Korea' s nuclear crisis once and for all.

Regional Security Governance in Northeast Asia: Major Opportunities and their Command

Tao Jian

Professor and President of University of International Relations

At the important meeting on June 12 in Singapore, the leaders of the DPRK and the United States, with great courage and unconventional acts, reversed momentum of the deteriorating security situation on the Korean Peninsula and restarted the process of complete denuclearization. Currently, all parties concerned should seize the good opportunity brought about by the improvement of DPRK–U.S. relations and steadily strengthen the security governance in Northeast Asia.

I. New developments of resolving the DPRK nuclear issue and its prospects in the future

For many years, the DPRK nuclear issue has been restricting improvement of the security environment in Northeast Asia, and it is the DPRK–U.S. relations that are the main crux for a difficult solution of the DPRK nuclear issue. The reversal of the U.S.– DPRK relations is bound to lead to a series of positive chain reactions. After the ROK– DPRK leaders' summit, the China–DPRK leaders' summit, and the U.S.–DPRK leaders' summit, the Russia–DPRK leaders' summit and Japan–DPRK leaders' summit can be expected. Led by diplomacy of the top leaders, the regional situation in Northeast Asia will see a new change, and regional security governance will have a new opportunity.

In the editorial for the New Year's Day in 2018, Kim Jong–un threw out the olive branch for the North–South reconciliation. Moon Jae–in who inherited the political line of "progressives", i.e. Kim Dae–jung and Roh Moo–hyun, quickly grasped it. On April 27, the leaders of the DPRK and the ROK had the 3rd summit, signed the Panmunjom Declaration, reached a series of agreements, designed a peace blueprint and a new economic blueprint for the future Peninsula, surpassed "peacekeeping" and moved towards "peace–making". The leaders of both sides have made so great efforts and taken so strong actions to improve relationship between the two sides that they are deeply impressive.

Having achieved the above–mentioned progress, in addition to the flexibility shown by the DPRK and the strong push from South Korea, the firm support from China and the major compromise made by President Trump are all extremely crucial. Since the end of March, Kim Jong–un has paid three consecutive visits to China and held historic meetings with President Xi Jinping and China has become strongly supportive of the changing situation on the Korean Peninsula. From the contents of the U.S.–DPRK Joint Statement, the U.S. compromise is obvious. Since Trump has been in power for more than a year, his many "achievements" have been made in "destruction" aspect, such as withdrawal from the TPP and Iran's nuclear deal, but there is little to be mentioned in "establishment" aspect, especially in terms of constructive contributions to international and regional affairs. The breakthrough of the U.S.–DPRK relations can be regarded as a big credit for propaganda. In particular, the contents of the U.S.–DPRK Joint Statement prove the rationality and foresight of China's previous proposals for "two moratoriums" , namely, moratorium on nuclear test conducted by the DPRK, and moratorium on the large–scale military exercise by the United States and South Korea, and the simultaneous progress of denuclearization and peace mechanisms. China' s proposals can stand tests by history, and are rational and forward looking.

Looking ahead, first, we cannot forget the historical setbacks in dealing with the DPRK nuclear issue. For example, after the 9.19 Joint Statements of the Six–Party Talks and the 2.29 deal between the DPRK and the United States, there emerged a very optimistic atmosphere, which did not last long. In view of this, all parties should not be over–optimistic and be highly vigilant against the uncertainty in the U.S.–DPRK relations and the DPRK nuclear issue.

Second, attention must be paid to details. The devil is in the details. The essence of the DPRK nuclear issue is security. The task of achieving the complete denuclearization of the Peninsula and shifting from a security framework based on the Korean Armistice Agreement so far to a more inclusive and sustainable security framework marked by a peace treaty requires a large amount of detailed negotiations and is far more complex and formidable than expected. The United States tries to occupy the commanding heights from the very beginning, i.e., formulating a package plan, implementing it in stages, achieving a clear goal and enabling the whole process controllable. While the DPRK wants to proceed in stages, to act upon action, to base on synchronous steps, and always maintains its own initiative. It can be predicted that even after the "framework" agreement is finalized, the tit–for–tat bargaining between the two sides will remain continuous and sharp.

II. The security governance of Northeast Asia has both opportunities and challenges

To promote regional security governance needs to nurture mutual trust and build consensus. Whether the security governance of Northeast Asia can be put on the right track depends on whether various parties can seize the opportunity generated by DPRK–U.S. relations improving, restore and establish a comprehensive mutual trust.

Northeast Asia is the place where the interests of major countries such as the United States, Russia, China, Japan and others are converging, and where they compete and play games. Especially in the Korean Peninsula, where there is extreme shortage of mutual trust mechanism and effective security mechanism, "Cold War thinking" is serious, "security dilemma" is prominent.

From the regional perspective, apart from distrust, there is mutual fear among various countries. On December 19, 2017, President Trump issued a new National Security Strategy report, which lists China and Russia as "revisionist countries" in the international system and as major challenges and "competitors to the national security of the United States. Especially on July 6 this year, the Sino–U.S. trade war officially started, and there has been a tendency to accelerate the escalation, an enormous erosion of the hard–won mutual trust between the two countries over the years. The 2017 edition of the White Paper on Defense, published by the Japanese Government, has 34–page literature on China, strongly accuses and wantonly distorts China's conventional military activities and legitimate national defense construction. Under such circumstances, mutual distrust among Northeast Asian countries is as hard as a chain of rings set to settle, and has become the biggest obstacle to the regional security governance in Northeast Asia.

From the practice of security governance, the United States, relying on the U.S.–Japan–South Korea alliance, tries to copy the NATO model and build a mini–version of NATO in Asia, while China and Russia advocate the establishment of a multilateral security system based on equal partnership in Northeast Asia. Since these are two sets of completely different thinking on security governance, thus, the construction of a security system in Northeast Asia has become difficult to take steps. Particularly, as the only superpower in the world, the United States, by playing the role of "offshore balancer", controls the situation in Northeast Asia, uses Sino–Japanese historical different recognition and territorial disputes to check and balance the two sides, uses the Taiwan issue to contain China's rise, uses the DPRK nuclear issue to control the security situation in Northeast Asia, and builds "Americana" . Because of this, the coordination of major countries on regional security issues is difficult to achieve good results. Meanwhile, with growing and declining strength of countries in the region, new contradictions of interests have emerged, and also have brought about new variables and difficulties to solve the inherent contradictions in the region.

Trust is one of the most important factors to form the international order, and any treaty or agreement is based on the mutual trust between countries. One important reason for the European region to have maintained long–term peace and stability after World War II is that the regional countries have developed a relationship of mutual trust, for which Europe has deliberately established a series of confidence–building measures. In contrast, the mutual trust relationship in Northeast Asia is extremely fragile, which must be built as a matter of top priority, starting from building mutual trust in security, gradually transiting to active regional security cooperation and governance mechanisms building, and ultimately realizing "long–term stability" in the region.

The Asian security concept characterized by "common, comprehensive, cooperative and sustainable security" advocated by China provides a basic guidance for cultivating regional trust relations in Northeast Asia. Building a community with a shared future is the ultimate goal of achieving security and stability in Northeast Asia. Despite the difficulties of security governance in Northeast Asia, as long as we have the firm determination to promote peace and stability and resolve for solving the problems for the region, and follow the principle of "win–win cooperation" , promote Northeast Asia security from "distrust" to "trust" , and from "uncertainty" to "certainty" , building a community with a shared future for Northeast Asia can be expected. Only the trust relationship in Northeast Asia based on a community with a shared future can it be really lasting.

III. The security governance in Northeast Asia should adhere to a path and mode of "multilateralism plus bilateralism, and security plus economy"

The changing and developing regional situation urgently requires all parties concerned to participate more actively, equally and constructively in the current task of improving the security governance of Northeast Asia. From the path and mode perspective, we should adhere to "multilateralism plus bilateralism, and security plus economy".

Multilateral cooperation is the main mode for security governance in Northeast Asia. Multilateral cooperation is based on the fact that this model helps to enhance transparency, alleviate conflicts of interests and mutual suspicions between various countries, and enhance mutual trust and collective recognition of the rules of cooperation. The practice of security cooperation in Northeast Asia has proved that the stability of a security order in Northeast Asia can not be maintained by the leadership and voice of a major country alone, which is also an important reason why China pushes forward the Six–Party Talks. When responding to a hard problem, countries in Northeast Asia should discuss them together, on equal footing, with mutual understanding and accommodation, let alone excluding any party concerned.

To achieve regional peace and stability in Northeast Asia must deal with several bilateral relationships. Among them, China and the United States are the key countries for realizing the overall peace and stability in Northeast Asia. If the relations between them are not good, Northeast Asia will inevitably become the forward position and the main area of their trial of strength. Both China and the United States should respect each other's major strategic concerns and core interests in Northeast Asia, build a Sino–U.S. relations framework of "overall stability and balanced development", and expand the space for "inclusive coexistence" and win–win cooperation. Presently, it is particularly important to prevent a rapid decline of Sino–U.S. relations because of the trade conflicts. Only making every effort to avoid the "all–round collision" between them can they prevent the "new cold war danger" from befalling Northeast Asia. In addition, China–Japan relations showed a momentum of improvement in 2017, both sides showed willingness to improve their relations, and their interactions increased. It is not easy to get reduction of security conflicts, so both sides should take good care of them.

Establishment of a security governance mechanism conforms to the common interests of all countries in Northeast Asia. Only through the institutional building of a mechanism can the stability and effectiveness of regional security governance be fundamentally guaranteed. Governance mechanisms should be multi–level and diversified, both legitimate, and flexible and resilient, the key is to allow the participants to obtain sufficient security and comfort. In view of tasks, there should be both specific issues–oriented small multilateral dialogue mechanisms, and high–level powerful institutions to discuss major issues such as security concerns between major powers, and important issues such as security and peace agreements programs. More importantly, all participants in security cooperation should practice a common, comprehensive, cooperative and sustainable security concept, abandon the outdated concept of the Cold War mentality and zero–sum game, and promote regional security governance in an open and inclusive spirit. Only in this way can the process of regional security cooperation and political trust be guaranteed to advance steadily and not stagnate or retrogress due to various reasons.

Northeast Asia is an important economic region in the world, whose main feature is the regional economic complementarity brought about by the diversity and difference of economic development of various countries. Northeast Asia is also the region with the strongest economic complementarity, among which the economic and trade relations between China, Japan and South Korea are extremely close, and the three countries are the main trade and investment partners to each other. The DPRK and Mongolia depend heavily on China, Japan and South Korea for their economic development, while the Russian Far East is the most reliable energy base for Northeast Asian economic development in the coming decades. This feature makes the interdependence of various countries in the region continuously deepen. In the medium term, it is expected that the cooperation mechanism between China, Japan, and South Korea may give impetus to the "3+3" cooperation mechanism with Russia, the DPRK and Mongolia. Functionalist theory points out that the "spillover" effect is easy to occur in the process of cooperation, i.e., increasing interests of cooperation in one area will attract participants to extend cooperation to other areas. In Northeast Asia, it is feasible and inevitable for the institutionalization–led economic cooperation first to produce demonstration effects and then "spill over" to the political and security areas.

To sum up, under the conditions that the situation on the Korean Peninsula is turning for the better, all parties concerned should assume an unshakable attitude, actively take actions, activate existing dialogue mechanisms, create new platforms for cooperation, vigorously enhance mutual trust, concurrently develop multilateral & bilateral cooperation and security & economic cooperation, push forward the regional security governance onto a right track, safeguard well the sound situation of regional security and stability and ensure peace and prosperity.

THE NEED FOR A REGIONAL SECURITY REGIME IN NORTHEAST ASIA

Dr. Tytti Erästö

Stockholm International Peace Research Institute, Sweden

Unlike most other regions, Northeast Asia remains largely devoid of mechanisms for political and security dialogue and regional cooperation. The recent convening of summit meetings between the leaders of North and South Korea and the United States and North Korea arguably present opportunities to address this problem.

At the recent US–DPRK summit on 12 June, the leaders of the two countries committed themselves to ambitious goals that have long evaded diplomatic efforts, notably the denuclearization of the Korean peninsula and US security guarantees to North Korea. This development—as well as prior steps that preceded it, such as the Panmunjom declaration in April—signals a significant increase of political will in both Koreas and the United States to tackle the conflict that has been unresolved for over half a century.

While historic, this process is not unprecedented: similar commitments were made in connection with the 1993 US–DPRK Joint Statement, which led to the 1994 Agreed Framework. The Panmunjom declaration should also be seen in the light of North–South joint declarations adopted in June 2000 and October 2007, as well as the 2005 Joint Declaration in connection with the Six–Party Talks.

While the summit has set the stage for a new attempt at diplomacy, many uncertainties remain related to practical implementation and the sustainability of political momentum over time. The personalities of the two leaders have played such a major role in the initial steps towards reconciliation further highlight the vulnerability of the process. These uncertainties stress the need to place the nascent bi– and tri–lateral conflict resolution process on a firmer, multilateral footing that would be less vulnerable to sudden political shifts.

Given the central role of the United States in North Korea' s threat perceptions, denuclearization essentially depends on assurances that neither the current nor future US governments will attack North Korea or seek a regime change in the country. The parties seem to have in principle recognized the need for this basic bargain; the letter signed by the two leaders on 12 June reportedly states that "President Trump committed to provide security guarantees to the DPRK, and Chairman Kim Jong-un reaffirmed his firm and unwavering commitment to complete denuclearization of the Korean Peninsula". [1]This is a major achievement in its own right, but negotiating the details and time-frame can be expected to be a complex and a long process, fraught with potential obstacles.

Arguably, however, the biggest challenge is to establish trust that this bargain will be respected by both sides. In addition to the deep mutual distrust built over the years of enmity and diplomatic failures (including the fact that North Korea broke its previous denuclearization commitments), the credibility problem is currently accentuated by President Trump' s demonstrated readiness to walk away from international agreements, including the 2015 Iran nuclear deal. Indeed, the big question now concerns the sustainability of the recent positive developments.

Both regional and extra-regional actors should support the precarious trust-building process between North Korea and the United States, first, by stepping in when necessary to defuse any tensions that might arise in the course of US-DPRK negotiations—in a similar manner as South Korean mediation helped the parties get back to the diplomatic track after President Trump' s May decision to cancel the US-DPRK summit.

If the political momentum for dialogue lasts, there is also an important role for other countries to play in the actual negotiations. For example, the question of denuclearization is inherently linked with the process of concluding a treaty ending the Korean War, even though the sequencing of these two objectives remains a major point of controversy. As far as negotiation of a peace treaty becomes tied to denuclearization, this would require both South Korean and Chinese involvement in the negotiations (China being one of the signatories of the 1953 armistice agreement).

As for other actors, they should provide support for the denuclearization and peace-building process on the Korean peninsula, and – in the case of Japan –

[1] "Trump and Kim's joint statement" Reuters 12 June 2018 https://www.reuters.com/article/us-northkorea-usa-agreement-text/trump-and-kims-joint-statement-idUSKBN1J80IU

establish diplomatic relations with the North Korean government. The long-term goal, however, should be more ambitious, namely the creation of a regional security mechanism that would allow the countries in North-East Asia to reduce tensions and address disputes according to mutually agreed principles, or a code of conduct. The groundwork for such a mechanism could be laid in parallel with the talks on denuclearization—possibly based on the precedent set by the Six Party Talks. This might also help to include other regional actors in the process, increasing their sense of ownership and ensuring that their perspectives are taken into account.

Here it should be stressed that the nuclear issue—which now seems like the main source of tensions in Northeast Asia—is a symptom of a protracted conflict between North Korea, on the one hand, and the United States and its regional allies, on the other. This conflict has persisted over half a century in the absence of any regional security mechanisms—apart from bilateral and exclusive military alliances, which have further contributed to the problem.

The recent inter-Korean diplomacy and the US-DPRK summit thus stress the need, and simultaneously provide an opportunity for, the creation of an alternative security mechanism. While ad hoc arrangements towards that end might be the most practicable in the immediate future, the ultimate goal should be the development of a regional security regime based on inclusiveness and the principle of cooperative security.

To be sure, such a regime does not necessarily mean a cohesive community with shared institutions and strategic values—which would arguably be unrealistic in the Northeast Asian context. Rather, a regional security regime means an agreement among regional actors "that they will adhere to a set of norms regarding their relations with each other, and that they will settle their disputes in a certain way—most importantly, without recourse to or the threat of violence." [1]

While the post-war European experience with the Helsinki process—including a region-wide conference leading to the endorsement of a non-binding document outlining shared principles and, subsequently, the institutionalization of the conference into an organization—provides one model, regional security regimes come in different shapes and can also be highly informal in nature.

A collective recognition among regional actors that the status quo is too precarious could create the political will needed to lay the groundwork for such

[1] Towards a Regional Security Regime for the Middle East: Issues and Options, SIPRI Middle East Expert Group report 2011 https://www.sipri.org/sites/default/files/files/misc/SIPRI2011Jones.pdf

a regime. In fact, its creation would not have to start from scratch; the already-existing regional processes and organizations—specifically, the ASEAN Regional Forum, ARF; the Shanghai Cooperation Organization, SCO; and the Northeast Asia Peace and Cooperation Initiative, NAPCI, and possibly the Ulaanbaatar Dialogue on Northeast Asia Security—provide useful elements for a security regime.

Finally, the countries in the region could also begin to explore the idea of a Northeast Asian Nuclear Weapons Free Zone (NWFZ), comprised of the two Koreas and Japan.[1] A treaty establishing such a zone—which would include negative security assurances by China, Russia and the United States—could add a significant amount of credibility to US security guarantees to North Korea by tying them into a multilateral treaty framework. At the same time, the establishment of NWFZ would contribute to the development of a regional security regime by introducing shared norms and reciprocal commitments related to one of the hardest security issues.

[1] Chung-in Moon, "Time may be right for a Northeast Asia nuclear-weapon-free zone" Bulletin of the Atomic Scientists 15 August 2016 https://thebulletin.org/north-koreas-nuclear-weapons-what-now/time-may-be-right-northeast-asia-nuclear-weapon-free-zone

Security Cooperation in North East Asia: Mongolian Perspective

Galsanjamts Sereeter

Professor, the Mongolian Institute for Geopolitical Studies

Dear Chairman,

Dear Colleagues,

First of all, thank you for the opportunity to participate in this important international event. Thank you to all previous presenters for sharing their valuable assessments and opinions on current security situation and its prospects.

Let me briefly introduce Mongolia' s perception of this situation and its efforts to contribute to development of security cooperation in North East Asia.

Security of Mongolia and security in NEA.

Mongolia has two neighbors - PRC and RF which are the biggest territories on the earth. Today Mongolia has very favorable external security environment because those two neighbors protect us from the outside threat. And there is no threat from neighbors due to reason of absence of any border or territorial disputes between our countries. I think it is very good reason to be happy, isn' t it?

But if look at the recent history of Mongolia you can find that current happiness had a lot of circumflexions. Until the end WWII Mongolia' s independence was recognized by only SU. Soviet troops were stationed on Mongolian soil four times. Big brother security umbrella was directed against Beijing. From the today' s stand it is clear that concentration huge amount foreign military forces, especially with nukes might become a target for preventive or responsive strike.

Drastic changes in the environment surrounding Mongolia and their further development trends since the end of Cold War made it imperative to Mongolia to consider its future and security within the framework of the Asia–Pacific Region, particularly North East Asia.

It is beyond Mongolia' s capacity to prevent all potential threats by relying solely on its own resources; therefore, since 1990s, Mongolia has been pursuing policy of integration step–by–step to international security cooperation in NEA as a single way to provide its national security.

Mongolia has refused to accept direct foreign military assistance, and it has stated that in times of peace it will not join any military bloc or alliance, station any foreign troops in its territory or allow their transit through its territory as well as declared its territory as a nuclear weapon–free–zone. That could be considered as our contribution to the global and regional security processes.

Changes in Mongolia's foreign policy in connection with security cooperation between NEA countries

After the collapse of the USSR and Eastern European countries at the end of 1980s, our country faced an inevitable task to renew its perception of external security environment of Mongolia, and, first of all, principally change its foreign policy in order to solve a problem how to relate with the two our great neighbors and how to provide the national security by its own means.

In order to find right solution of this problem, the country chose to develop beforehand a balanced, comprehensive cooperation with the two neighbors as the main direction of our foreign policy. Based on this principally new course, Mongolia concluded new Treaty on Friendly Relations and Cooperation with Russian Federation and with People' s Republic of China in early 1990s.

Besides, Mongolia set up a new foreign policy direction of developing active cooperation with the USA and other influential countries in North East Asia. Proper, rational and far–sighted implementation of this policy, called as a Third Neighbor Policy, was vital, in our mind, for the future security of the country.

Comprehensive cooperation with Russia and China in security field as Mongolia's contribution to strengthening security in North East Asia

As I mentioned before, friendly relations and cooperation with its two neighbors are the core of Mongolia' s policy towards development security cooperation with North East Asian countries. It should be mentioned here, that in its essence our Third Neighbor Policy never had intention to prefer any other country over the two our neighbors. And from the beginning these two nations showed their understanding and respect to our policy.

During the last 25 years, our good neighborly relations have been developing and deepening fruitfully being vitally important for our development and security.

Therefore, Mongolia has brought these friendly relations to a new level of trilateral cooperation expressing our interest to be a reliable bridge in progressing cooperation between the two great nations.

In September 2014, a very first summit meeting between the state leaders of our three countries took place in Dushanbe, Tajikistan, setting up a new basis for friendly relations and cooperation between them.

The trilateral cooperation has been proceeding successfully. Just recently, presidents of the three countries met fourth time during the Tsingtao SCO summit and exchanged views on number of topics concerning further development of trilateral cooperation.

The main point is that the two our neighbors, instead of competing to gain dominant position in Mongolia, have accepted Mongolia' s initiative to expand our trilateral cooperation.

We in Mongolia expect that cooperation of Russia and China in development of Mongolian infrastructure would be also profitable for them too, i.e. transiting rail and auto roads, oil and gas pipeline structures through the territory of Mongolia would be very cost effective.

Recently, there are a lot of talks about possible upgrading of Mongolia' s observer status in SCO to a full member status in near future. Some argue that a SCO membership would become a question about its decisive role in providing economic development, security and geopolitical balance to Mongolia.

Participation of Mongolia in international peacekeeping and antiterrorism activity

Active participation of Mongolia in international peacekeeping and fight against terrorism is expression of its sincere desire, as of the other small nations, to make own possible contribution to common efforts towards providing international and regional peace and stability.

Successful participation of Mongolian military in peace keeping missions under the UN mandate not only brings us respect from international community, but also provides us with possibility to bring up our Armed Forces capability closer to international standard. Participation of Mongolian Armed Forces in international peace keeping is now an integral part of our efforts for peace in the North East Asia.

Mongolia's policy towards a non-nuclear world

The Government of Mongolia put nuclear free issue to level of national state policy and rightfully declared the territory of the country as a NWFZ from the UN podium in 1992.

The unique single state NWFZ of Mongolia, in difference from other traditional NWFZs had no legal and internationally binding background. As a result of the numerous negotiations and meetings the five nuclear powers in 2012 recognized

NWFS of our country and agreed to issue a joint declaration in due regard. Consequently, in September of the same year, their Permanent Representatives at UN signed the above–mentioned Declaration and pronounced the fact to the world community.

The main content of this Declaration is that the five nuclear powers recognize the Law of Mongolian Nuclear Weapon Free Status adopted in 2002 and pronounced to hold united position against any acts negatively affecting such independent status of the country.

The world community has been greatly recognizing and supporting the idea of NWFZ set by a single state that was initiated by Mongolia. This was a success of Mongolia' s national security policy.

Korean Peninsula: Mongolia's stand

Having friendly relations with both Koreas, Mongolia has been striving to make its possible contribution to easing tension on Korean Peninsula. Mongolia constantly expresses its interests in developing Six Party Talks into a North East Asian security dialogue mechanism and in such case to be a part of this mechanism in possible form.

Mongolian state and government leadership officially pronounced that it is against isolation of North Korea on international arena. In order to solve the problem realistically, instead of forceful, rushed attempt to change the situation, it would be more rational to involve North Korea into international cooperation gradually, and make this a part of policy aimed at resolving its nuclear program.

Therefore, the government and people of Mongolia are very satisfied with results of the recent USA–DPRK summit.

We also consider that our experience of restless efforts for 20 years for international recognition of self–declaration of Mongolia as nuclear weapon free zone, and consequent recognition of such a status by the P5–Permanent members of the Security Council and official issuance of the UN declaration in due regard, could be taken as an important example that a small nation, like Mongolia, may warrantee its security without implementing a nuclear program or deploying nuclear weapon on its soil. That is an important message for nations of NEA, particularly on Korean Peninsula.

In conclusion, we consider that PRC peace oriented foreign policy based on its intensive economic development has a good impact on international security, including NEA region. The government of Mongolia puts a lot of hope on Chinese foreign policy aiming creation of stable and effective mechanism for security cooperation in North East Asia.

The strategy of joint development, peace and harmony with neighboring countries declared by the Government of PRC was well received in our country. We are sure that implementation of this great endeavor aimed at peace and stability would meet with common interests of NEA countries, including Mongolia.

Session III:
Security Mechanism Building in the Asia Pacific Region

Building a Comprehensive Cooperative Security Partnership in Asia Pacific Region

Malik Qasim Mustafa

Senior Research Fellow, Institute of Strategic Studies, Islamabad.

Ladies & gentlemen, first of all, I would like to express my gratitude to the Chinese People' s Association for Peace and Disarmament (CPAPD) for organising "Wanshou Dialogue on Global Security" and providing me an opportunity to be a part of it.

Ladies & gentlemen, as we all know that in the 21st century the diversity and stability of the Asia–Pacific region is challenged by a wide spectrum of traditional and non–traditional security threats, which broadly includes: nuclear proliferation and territorial disputes; terrorism and transnational crimes; growing geo–political and military competition; emergence of new players and formation of defence alliances; slow peace process in troubled parts; naval build–ups and maritime challenges and humanitarian emergencies and environmental challenges. As a result, achieving all the goals of comprehensive security, sustainable development and a sustainable peace have become difficult for the developing and weaker nations of the Asia–Pacific region.

Initially, after the end of the Cold War, the Asia–Pacific communities focused more on rapid economic development, but they did not adequately address growing security challenges. By each passing day, these challenges are becoming more complex and extreme in their nature. These existing and emerging challenges are also making it difficult for the available instruments, institutions and mechanisms to deal with them effectively, and to ensure a lasting peace. Here question arise that what the Asia–Pacific communities require or they should do to deal with current and future security challenges? Although several bilateral, quadrilateral and multilateral measures, initiatives and dialogues have been initiated, the growing security complexities require that the Asia–Pacific nations should modify their old security structure and build a new comprehensive multilateral long–term cooperative security partnership, with shared responsibilities and prospects, like the Chinese concept of shared destiny and economic prosperity under its Belt and Road Initiative (BRI), with the China–Pakistan Economic Corridor (CPEC) as it flagship game–changer regional economic integrity project.

Key players from the Asia–Pacific region, including China, have already expressed their willingness and desire to revisit the existing security architecture. Most recently, in June 2018, at the 17th Shangri La Dialogue (SLD), China highlighted that the important task, currently faced by the Asia–Pacific region is to re–examine the concept of international security, re–evaluate the regional security architecture and focus on fundamentally resolving security issues. [1]China strongly advocates a common, comprehensive, cooperative and sustainable security concept. [2] It has already expressed its willingness to pursue security through dialogue and cooperation in its 2017 white paper on Asia–Pacific security. [3]The Chinese advocacy for the "establishment of a regional framework for security and cooperation" was already stated by Xi Jinping, in his May 2014 speech at the 4th Summit of the Conference on Interaction and Confidence Building Measures in Asia (CICA) held in Shanghai and underlined again in the white paper on China's military strategy, published in May 2015. [4]A key component of the Chinese security policy was also released at the 2016 Xiangshan Forum that the new security architecture should be held together by partnership not by any formal alliance system. [5]It believes that win–win cooperation would serve as the base for the formation of new international relations, which would be built by all, shared by all and safeguarded by all. [6]

Pakistan, like China, also firmly believes that to achieve a lasting peace, development and prosperity, there is a need to address key internal and external

[1] Wang Lili and Chen Yao, "Chinese Military Experts Expound 'China Plan' at Shangri–La Dialogue," China Military, June 4, 2018, http://eng.chinamil.com.cn/view/2018–06/04/content_8051700.htm

[2] Ibid.

[3] Ministry of Foreign Affairs of the People's Republic of China, "China's Policies on Asia–Pacific Security Cooperation," January 11, 2017, http://www.fmprc.gov.cn/mfa_eng/zxxx_662805/t1429771.shtml

[4] "At the 2016 Xiangshan Forum, China Outlines a Vision for Regional Security Governance," Diplomat, October 15, 2016, https://thediplomat.com/2016/10/at–the–2016–xiangshan–forum–china–outlines–a–vision–for–regional–security–governance/

[5] Ibid.

[6] "China's Security Concept Contributes to Asia's Long– term Security, Development," Xinhua, June 2, 2018, http://www.xinhuanet.com/english/2018–06/02/c_137225923.htm

security challenges through cooperation and partnership as a shared future. Pakistan, despite its all internal and external security challenges, is making its every effort to ensure peace and prosperity at bilateral, regional and international levels. It respects international norms, institutions and mechanisms and is a part of several bilateral, regional and international initiatives. Pakistan strongly believes that in order to mitigate existing and emerging challenges to security, the international community, particularly developing nations, require collaborative and comprehensive partnership strategy, active diplomacy and dialogue and effective tools and mechanisms. Pakistan has always expressed its willingness to extend its support and cooperation with the international community. Pakistan' s involvement in Afghan peace process, its invitation to regional states to be a part of a shared destiny under the CPEC and sharing of its success stories of operation Zarb–e–Azb and National Action Plan (NAP) to combat terrorism and extremism are some recent examples. Pakistan has also been able to secure commitments and partnerships from regional countries to fight the menace of terrorism. A recent formation of Pakistan, China, Tajikistan and Afghanistan Quadrilateral Cooperation and Coordination Mechanism (QCCM) is also another example.

Building a Comprehensive Cooperative Security Partnership

Ladies & gentlemen, here a question arises that how a long–term comprehensive cooperative security partnership could be built for the Asia–Pacific region? (Back in 2016, I was also a part of the 2016 Xiangshan Forum and this forum addressed wide ranging traditional and non–traditional security issues being faced by the Asia–Pacific communities.) I firmly believe that "Wanshou Dialogue on Global Security" is going to promote the very idea of the formation of a new comprehensive cooperative security partnership in the Asia–Pacific region. Since the commencement of this dialogue we all are not only discussing global security related challenges, particularly to the Asia–Pacific region, but we have been also assessing their likely impact. We have been trying to revise the existing security architecture and the very concept of ensuring a lasting peace in the region. All these deliberations point towards the need to draw new comprehensive mechanisms and tools to deal with emerging and future security challenges. In order to build a long–term comprehensive cooperative security partnership mechanism in the Asia–Pacific region, following recommendations should be considered;

◎ There is a realisation of "Our People, Our Community, Our Vision," but a broader approach for a comprehensive human security and development is missing. Therefore, a comprehensive security partnership should be developed around a common understanding and a common vision that human security and development will lead to a lasting peace.

◎ The Asia–Pacific communities should develop this common vision based on the Principles of Humanity; strengthen their political will; enhance their trust; reduce their traditional hostilities; allocate more resources and work for a comprehensive security partnership in the region.

◎ A greater degree of coordination and active cooperation of all regional communities, at all levels, is prerequisite for developing such a comprehensive security partnership mechanism in the Asia–Pacific region. And it should be aimed at taking effective and credible collective efforts on the basis of consensus.

◎ To achieve the objectives of an all–inclusive security, new security mechanisms and tools should be devised from local, national, sub–regional and regional perspectives, as states alone cannot counter major internal and external security challenges. This approach can only effectively work when there is continuity and coordination between all policies at all levels. It will also help to identify right security related tools, which could further replicated at other communities.

◎ For a comprehensive security approach, there is a need to reinforce a genuine and practical regional partnership framework. A true understanding of the existing and emerging challenge and to fight for common security challenges, states require a genuine and practical regional cooperation. Such partnership should be aimed at reducing social, economic and political vulnerabilities of a particular territory, area, or group. In this regard the role of regional organisations can be reinforced to provide a shared platform to address security challenges. Existing regional organisations can be tasked with the responsibilities of a joint human development task force; a joint coordination and capacity building platform; a joint legal coordination mechanism and a joint venue to link with other regional and global organisations.

◎ There is a need to develop sub–regional and regional dialogue mechanisms to identify security challenges and their understanding. The Wanshou Dialogue is such an example. This can be completed by establishing joint regional coordination centres and through an integrated network of all national level centres, which contains rapid assessment and analysis of the immediate security challenge and peace related needs.

◎ There is a need to improve bilateral relations to build trust for increased cooperation and to achieve comprehensive security objectives.

◎ Bilateral traditional hostilities and trans–boundary irritants like terrorism have gained enough strength to disrupt peace prospects among states. Therefore, a move towards resolution of deep rooted issues is necessary to remove mistrust. Both multilateral and bilateral approaches are necessary to build trust among adversaries to promote a lasting peace.

◎ A need to enhance human and institutional capacity at all levels. A comprehensive capacity–building approach should be aimed at developing rights tools to ensure security and lasting peace. This requires a top to bottom approach for capacity–building at local level and a bottom to top approach to bridge human security and human development and peace.

A single and isolated approach and effort cannot ensure a comprehensive regional security. A sincere and holistic national and regional approach will help to form peaceful and prosper communities across the region. A consolidated and well coordinated approach, in continuity with local and national human security policies can help to deal with existing and emerging security challenges. It is now a time for a genuine and practical commitment at all levels to secure mankind' s prosperity and peace.

Pakistan is committed to the principles of justice, fairness, non–discrimination, and equal security for all. It has always followed internationally recognised norms of interstate relations, i.e. respect for sovereignty, non–interference; non–aggression and peaceful settlement of disputes. Pakistan is ready to utilise its national resources for regional and international cooperation for sustainable development and sustainable peace.

Two Initiatives and One Regional Order: The Integration of Japan's FOIP and China's BRI

Yuichi Hosoya

Professor of International Politics
Keio University, Japan

We Are in Crisis

The rapid rise of Chinese power has been transforming regional balance of power in the Asia–Pacific. It brings both opportunities and challenges to Japan. China has been Japan' s largest trading partner since 2009. China has become the second largest economy in 2010. China is expected to play a more responsible role in this region to bring both peace and prosperity in cooperation with other powers, especially since American President Donald Trump has shown its "America First" policy in the areas of trade and security.

As the closest ally to the U.S. in the Asia–Pacific region, Japan faces serious challenges. Prime Minister Shinzo Abe has met with President Trump more frequent than any other leaders, and has persuaded him to play a responsible role in international affairs as the single remaining superpower. However, Prime Minister Abe is showing just a limited success in it. President Trump becomes more critical than before on the trade deficit with Japan, and has prepared a series of unilateral actions that could easily damage both mutual trust and friendly cooperation.

Under these circumstances, it would be naturally that both Japan and China consider that regional cooperation would become more vital than before. With the vacuum of American leadership in presenting its vision of regional order in the Asia–Pacific, Japan and China seem to consider it more necessary than before to create a more stable and more prosperous regional order based on their own initiatives.

Japan's New Diplomatic Initiative

(1) "The Confluence of Two Oceans"

The origins of Japan's FOIP strategy go back to August 2016, when Prime Minister Abe talked on the importance of linking two Oceans in his speech at the Tokyo International Conference on African Development (TICAD IV) held in Kenya on August 27, 2016.

He stated that "Japan bears the responsibility of fostering the confluence of the Pacific and Indian Oceans and of Asia and Africa into a place that values freedom, the rule of law, and the market economy, free from force or coercion, and making it prosperous. … The population in Asia living in democracies is more numerous than that of any other region on Earth. Asia has enjoyed growth on the basis of the democracy, rule of law, and market economy that has taken root there." [1]

Prime Minister Abe launched this concept of "the confluence of two oceans" when he visited India at the end of his first administration on August 22, 2007. He said to Indian Members of Parliament that "Now, as this new "broader Asia" takes shape at the confluence of the two seas of the Indian and Pacific Oceans, I feel that it is imperative that the democratic nations located at opposite edges of these seas deepen the friendship among their citizens at every possible level."

Abe could not deepen his concept in 2007, as he was forced to resign from his post due to his illness within five days after he made this historic speech in India. This concept was regarded as the creation of a coalition between Japan and India which was aiming at counterbalancing rapidly rising China. Therefore, this concept could not have a strong appeal to other Asian countries which rather liked to create a closer and friendlier relationship with China.

(2) Connecting Economic Growth in this Region

Japan's new initiative with the name of the "Free and Open Indo-Pacific strategy" differs considerably from Abe's original idea of a coalition of "democratic nations" in the Indo-Pacific region. First, this new strategy is open to any countries in this region including China and Russia. Second, this strategy came out of the idea of linking rapidly growing economies in this region including Africa, the Middle East Asia and North America.

Likewise, Foreign Minister Taro Kono stated in his speech at Columbia

[1] Address by Prime Minister Shinzo Abet the Opening Session of the Sixth Tokyo International Conference on African Development (TICAD VI), August 27, 2016, Nairobi, Keny. https://www.mofa.go.jp/afr/af2/page4e_000496.html

University that "Japan has been promoting the "Free and Open Indo–Pacific Strategy." The Indo–Pacific Ocean links rapidly growing Africa, the Middle East, Asia, and North America. … Japan also intends to pursue economic prosperity through the reinforcement of connectivity by improving infrastructures, such as sea ports and railways and roads." [1]

The "reinforcement of connectivity" is the essence of Japan' s FOIP, as we all can benefit from it. Northeast Asian countries will soon face a serious problem concerning with population change and an aging society. Therefore, it would be essential that Northeast Asian countries together with some of the Southeast Asian countries can help countries in the other regions to benefit from rapid economic growth. Foreign Minister Kono, thus, said in his speech at the National Diet on January 22, 2018 that "The Indo–Pacific region, which extends from the Asia–Pacific through the Indian Ocean to the Middle East and Africa, is the core of global development where more than half of the global population resides." [2]

There are several overlapping aims in the two regional initiatives, namely Japan' s FOIP and China' s BRI. Therefore, it would be valuable to understand how these two initiatives can benefit from each other.

(3)The Initiatives

Abe's Support for China's BRI

Since Prime Minister Abe' s first summit meeting with China' s President Xi Jinping in November 2014, the second and the third largest economies in the world have been expanding the areas of cooperation and reducing tensions particularly in the field of security. This should be a natural result as Japan cannot sustain its economic growth without deeper and more stable cooperation with China. China can benefit from better relationship with Japan since its foreign direct investments in China have been a source of China' s rapid economic growth. Thus, Prime Minister Abe began to show his willingness to collaborate with China' s BRI in June 2017. He underscored the importance of connecting Japan' s economic growth with China' s BRI. In the Editorial of The Japan Times, it was correctly written that "Reversing his position, Prime Minister Shinzo Abe has indicated that Japan is ready to cooperate with China' s 'One Belt, One Road' (OBOR) initiative for cross–continental infrastructure development under certain conditions.

[1] Speech by Foreign Minister Taro Kono at Columbia University, "Diplomacy in Creeping Crises" , September 21, 2017. https://www.mofa.go.jp/na/na1/us/page3e_000749.html

[2] Foreign Minister Taro Kono, Foreign Policy Speech to the 196th Session of the Diet, January 22, 2018. https://www.mofa.go.jp/fp/unp_a/page3e_000816.html

He is also now willing to consider Japan joining the China–initiated Asian Infrastructure Investment Bank (AIIB) — of which Japan, along with the United States, sat out when it was set up in 2015 — once doubts about its governance and operation are cleared." [1]

Japan-China Summit Meeting

This position was confirmed at the Japan–China summit meeting of July 8, 2017, when Prime Minister Abe and President Xi agreed that "Japan and China will discuss how to contribute to the stability and prosperity of the region and the world, including the One Belt, One Road initiative". [2]

Furthermore, at the summit meeting between Prime Minister Abe and China's Prime Minister Li Keqiang on November 13, 2017, at Manila, "Both sides shared the view that they will discuss approaches for Japan and China to contribute to the stability and prosperity of the region and the world, including 'the Belt and Road Initiatives' ". [3]

These are a clear sign of Japan's renewed attitude towards China's BRI. One of the reasons for changing Japan's stance would be that Prime Minister Abe considers it necessary to assist the BRI mainly for creating a better Sino–Japanese relation in the era of President Trump.

Conclusion

Both Japanese and Chinese governments have ameliorated tensions between the two in the last several years. Prime Minister Li Keqiang's visit to Japan from May 8 to May 11 was one of the highlights that we see in the recent cooperation between the two governments.

At the summit meeting on May 9, Prime Minister Abe "congratulated Premier Li on his reappointment, and expressed his gratitude that Premier Li chose Japan as the destination for his first foreign visit after his reappointment". Then, Abe continued that "he wished to make the 40th anniversary of the conclusion of the Treaty of Peace and Friendship between Japan and China a year that would be a

[1] "The Editorial: Japan and 'One Belt, One Road' ", The Japan Times, June 24, 2017.

[2] MOFA, "Japan–China Summit Meeting", July 8, 2017. https://www.mofa.go.jp/a_o/c_m1/cn/page4e_000636.html

[3] MOFA, "Japan–China Summit Meeting", November 13, 2017. https://www.mofa.go.jp/a_o/c_m1/cn/press3e_000119.html

new start for Japan–China relations" . [1]

Abe' s statement was cordiale one and he showed his good will to create a more friendly relationship between two leading nations in this region. Prime Minister Abe also remarked that "Japan and China share great responsibility for the peace and prosperity of the region and the international community. Improvement and development of the relations between the two countries will also lead to meeting the expectations of other countries. I would like to work together with Premier Li." [2]

Prime Minister Li responded to Abe' s kind message by stating that "Over the past few years, our two countries experienced a detour with wind and rain, but the wind and clouds have passed away and the sky has cleared up when I participated in today's welcome ceremony." [3]

Prime Minister Li continued that "When we met at an international conference, we discussed about our hopes for improving relations and the necessity of moving closer to each other. Subsequently, we maintained the momentum toward improvement, and the relations between our two countries have got back on normal track through my official visit. Going forward, we should aim to achieve new development for stable and sound development over the long term." [4]

During this summit meeting in Tokyo, two sides signed two agreements and eight memorandums which cover a variety of areas. In fact, there still exist many disagreements, and one or two summit meetings cannot easily fulfill the gap. Furthermore, more serious problem is that there can be seen only slight improvements in the public opinion in each country on the mutual public images. The Sino–Japanese relationship has largely been conducted and developed largely by political dialogues and official negotiations. We see the clear limit in it. Having said this, Japan and China, the number three and the number two economies, should take more responsibility to created more stable and more prosperous regional order with deeper understanding on each other' s good will.

---

[1] MOFA, "Premier of the State Council of China Li Keqiang Visits Japan Japan–China Summit Meeting and Banquet" , May 9, 2018.

[2] Ibid.

[3] Ibid.

[4] Ibid.

South Asia & the Indian Ocean's Contribution to Asia-Pacific Security: Opportunities and Challenges

Antoine Levesques

Research Fellow for South Asia
The International Institute for Strategic Studies (IISS)

Security in South Asia is growingly shaped by wider Asia-Pacific trends. Across the Asia–Pacific, the policy primacy of the 'Indo–Pacific' notion of inter– and cross–regional relations is irreversible. The administration of US president Donald Trump encouraged and accelerated this trend in 2017–2018. Simultaneously and for the first time ever in 2018, governments of South Asia, now led by India, all recognise the policy–relevance and coherence of another canvas for cooperation: 'Southern Asia' (South Asia plus China).Thirdly, security across India, Pakistan, Afghanistan, Bangladesh, Nepal, Bhutan, Myanmar, Sri Lanka and the Maldives is ever strongly shaped by China' s Belt and Road Initiative (BRI). Implications for China: China' s structural relevance to security policymaking in and about South Asia is unprecedented and yet to peak. China is only one of several resident and non–resident powers, whose collective will and ability to bring their security interests to overlap – or not – across Asia, growingly shapes security perceptions inside South Asia. South Asian nations are aware that as proximate neighbours of China, they happen to be as much a focus point than a way point, for China' s otherwise global foreign policy outlook.

Current and emerging security problems in South Asia remain over-determined by intra-regional rather than extra-regional factors. India and Pakistan' s behaviours as nuclear weapon states remain overwhelmingly self–referential, though China growingly shapes India' s nuclear mindset. China may also play a greater, unprecedented role if India–Pakistan spilled into another bilateral crisis. In Afghanistan, stability will be primarily shaped by US and Pakistani policies. But China has supported these bilaterally and jointly (e.g.

Quadrilateral Coordination Group). Non–traditional security worries in the Indian Ocean, starting with piracy, increasingly call on littoral and regional states to step up, as net security providers (including but not limited to China) diversify or reprioritise their security footprints in the region. Management and crisis prevention with India on their disputed border (as well as, in time, in the Indian Ocean) provide China with its strongest, most overt role in shaping a discrete South Asian security outcome. Implications for China: China (like many other countries) is right to already eschew the temptation of one–size–fits–all policies across South Asia. It does well to examine the detailed, parochial security perceptions and dilemmas of national policymakers through 'geopolitical due diligence'. This raises an as–yet unaddressed question of whether the Belt and Road Initiative requires a degree of regionalisation (e.g. considering the China–Pakistan Economic Corridor as "BRI with Pakistani characteristics"). China, primarily as UN Security Council permanent member, may benefit from deepening its existing 'South Asian Dialogues' with other top–table powers.

South Asian nations will generally remain strategically introverted but will not want to miss out on an emerging security architecture: South Asian nations' prosperity is ever more dependent on Asia's wider economic fortunes, given how little South Asia is economically integrated; yet security concerns on their borders (e.g. India with Pakistan and China; Pakistan with India and Afghanistan; Afghanistan with Pakistan) will continue to focus most policy–planning and –making 'awake time', crisis management and 'fire–fighting' capacity; and even much of the regional statecraft. India, under Prime Minister Modi (and regardless of who is India's next Prime Minister from May 2019) is the regional exception. India is incrementally growing its capacity to set and hold its strategic gaze beyond Pakistan and South Asia only, in pursuit of wider Asian prosperity and security goals. Implications for China: South Asian nations' willingness and capacity to spare national resources for 'burden sharing' or assuming a 'responsible behaviour' (as part of any regional emerging security architecture) will remain overall limited and highly case–, context– and stakeholder–dependent, especially in the pursuit of regional security east of Malacca. South Asian capitals will intensify their cost–benefit analyses of introversion and how to balance the influence of major powers, if US–China ties further strain, owing to trade tensions escalation from February 2019. India can be expected to assign itself greater 'responsibilities' to safeguard 'free', 'open' and 'inclusive' commons, foremost in the Indian Ocean region. But India will own up to these notions on its very own terms, including at the now–institutionalised "Quad" series of meetings with US,

Japanese and Australian officials. So, all South Asian nations are more likely than not to continue participating a bit in many 'clubs' or groupings (including the Shanghai Cooperation Organisation), rather than put most of their strategic equities in one only.

Conclusion: China will play a key role in shaping the future of South Asian security and how South Asia is able and willing to help shape – or let itself be shaped by – a wider, changing, but persistently piecemeal and disjointed 'Indo-Pacific' security architecture for cooperation and competition. In 2019 and beyond, how China identifies and seizes on relevant opportunities and challenges will overly depend on how it coherently prioritises its approaches to South Asia, as a global major power that has 'strategically arrived', a permanent member of the UN Security Council, an immediate neighbour, and a development lender of first or last resort. In April 2019, China's second Belt and Road Forum will explicitly address matters of shared prosperity. Yet the security perceptions the Forum will inevitably inform could shape policymaking in South Asian capitals to an even greater extent than the 2017 inaugural summit did. Only weeks later, in June, South Asian ministers will re–join their regional colleagues to uniquely and openly discuss these security perceptions with top–table powers at the 18th Asia security summit, the IISS Shangri–La Dialogue. The tone of that conversation will be set by the Keynote address of President Emmanuel Macron of France, a resident country of the Indian Ocean with growing interests in security and cooperation across Asia.

No Conflict: the Bottom Line of the Indo-Pacific Strategy

Lamba Arvinder

President, Institute of Peace and Conflict Studies, Retired Lieutenant General
India

The Indo–Pacific region has become the centre of 21st–century geopolitics, wherein the regional and external powers are actively competing and collaborating with one another to counter and expand their own and others’ influences.

Evolution of the Concept of Asia Pacific

The concept of Asia Pacific dates backs to 1960s, as a mean of linking East Asia to the wider Pacific region duly promoted by countries like United States, Japan and Australia. "Asia Pacific" highlights the Asian dimension in a way that "Pacific region" does not. However, from a political perspective the United States cannot portray itself as an Asian power but its extensive involvement in the Pacific justifies describing it as part of Asia Pacific.

Power Rivalries and Contestations

During the post Cold War era, the international relations in Asia Pacific witnessed new international roles of China, Japan and the United States. The significant developments during the era were the Cold War conflicts in the 1950s and 1960s, Southeast Asia's decolonization, Sino–Soviet conflict, direct confrontation between United States and China in the context of the Korean War (1950–1953), Sino–American rapprochement, the emergence of Southeast Asian regionalism and postcolonial conflicts in Southeast Asia.

The end of the Cold War once again witnessed US main contest in Asia Pacific with China. Asia Pacific encompassed a broad range of political systems from liberal democracies to Communist and authoritarian countries.

Failure of Existing Mechanisms

“Regional institutions in the Asia– Pacific are not as robust as those that have evolved in Europe," says Rudd. "Because the Asia–Pacific region looms as being the strategic cockpit of the 21st century, we need more robust institutions than those we have at present."

It was felt that there needs to be an agreeable and sustainable power mechanism and structure to keep this region safe from conflict.

US identification of India as the most credible partner for stability in this region has been stark and forthright. To recall, the US State Department under Condoleezza Rice, during the George W Bush administration, declared its policy goal "to help India become a major world power in the 21st century." Rex Tillerson' s recent remarks have added immense clarity to the future direction and drivers of this region.

What makes Indo–Pacific an active regional construct is the competitive and convergent security interests of actors such as Australia, China, India, Japan and the United States - who are the central actors in the region.

The Architecture and Mechanism of Power in This Region

The Indo–Pacific idea connecting the Pacific and Indian oceans now make a single geopolitical space and a new map of Asia, has witnessed significant changes in foreign and security policies and strategic partnerships ,

The increasing importance of Indo–Pacific is evident in the strategic equations, most importantly, China' s "Maritime Silk Road" , India' s "Act East Policy" , United States' "Rebalance/Pivot to Asia" and Japan' s idea of "Confluence of the Two Seas" – all aimed at playing a proactive role in the Indo–Pacific region.

There cannot be a perfect model that meets all requirements of regional and external countries, but there is an urgent need for all powers to evolve a comprehensive, converging and objective system that is mutually acceptable and can enable prevent disputes, allow freedom of seas and ensure peace and stability in the critical region.

The Indo–Pacific Region must be free from conflict. For that, the US, India, Japan, Australia and China can work to evolve such a control mechanism and structure.

Epilogue

The current world is in a period of major development, change and adjustment. The trend of global multi–polarity, economic globalization, social informationzation, and cultural diversity are developing in–depth, mutual connectivity and interdependence among various countries become increasingly deepened, the relative international forces are becoming more balanced, the megatrend of peaceful development is irreversible. Meanwhile, the world is confronting more prominent instability and uncertainty, the smog such as the Cold War thinking, power politics, unilateralism, trade protectionism, etc. still remains; while risks such as regional turbulence, terrorism, cyber security, climate change, the displaced people flooding, etc, emerge one after another, the global economic growth is lack of driver, the gap between the rich and poor gets wider, and the mankind faces many common challenges. To study and make judgment on the changing international security situation is very important to promote global security governance and effectively respond to various problems and challenges.

As the largest national non–governmental peace organization in China, the Chinese People's Association for Peace and Disarmament (CPAPD), actively further develops its unique advantages, and strives to create a distinctive brand on the study of security issues, has decided to hold the first Wanshou Dialogue on Global Security, focusing on the high–end and specialty distinction, inviting well–known experts on security studies from the mainstream think tanks in the world to share exchanges and discussions on international and regional security situations, to grasp their characters as well as the drivers for and the changing trend of their profound and complex changes, proposing ideas and suggestions for responding to challenges, and gathering consensus and contributing wisdom to maintain world peace and security, and to achieve development and prosperity of various countries. The Wanshou Dialogue on Global Security is planned to be held annually, the theme of which is determined by the changes of international and regional security situation as well as the concerns of the international community.

The first thematic symposium entitled Wanshou Dialogue on Global Security was successfully held in Beijing from June 20 to 21, 2018. More than 50 experts and scholars from 19 countries, including the United States, the United Kingdom, France, Germany, Russia, Japan, the Republic of Korea, Canada, Australia, Sweden, India, Pakistan, Vietnam, the Philippines, Indonesia, Malaysia, Thailand, Sri Lanka, Mongolia as well as from the host country' s institutions such as the Chinese Academy of Social Sciences, the National Defense University, China' s Institutes of Contemporary International Relations, China' s Institute of International Studies, Tsinghua University, the Renmin University of China and the University of International Relations participated in the seminar. The seminar is themed with Asia–Pacific Security, with three topics of China–U.S. Relations and Asia–Pacific Security, the Security Situation and Prospects in Northeast Asia, and the Building of the Asia–Pacific Security Mechanism. Song Tao, Minister of the International Department of the CPC Central Committee (IDCPC), attended the symposium and delivered a keynote speech. Former State Councilor Dai Bingguo had in–depth exchanges with some foreign participants. Fu Ying, Vice Chair of the Foreign Affairs Committee of the 13th National People's Congress, attended the seminar evening party, delivered a special speech and exchanged views with some foreign participants. The participants from home and abroad had deep discussions on the theme and the three topics.

The participants spoke highly of the First Wanshou Dialogue on Global Security, hope to see this platform to be run still better, gather more global well–known think tanks experts to carry out in–depth interactions and exchanges on international and regional security issues, search for the greatest common divider on the security issues, explore rational options in conformity with the long–term interests of various countries, enable the rational voices to influence and even guide the public opinions and government decision–making, and contribute wisdom and force to achieve global and regional peace and security.

In order to show the results of the Wanshou Dialogue on Global Security, the CPAPD edited some of the speeches and papers presented to the seminar and compiled them into a book to be published for exchanges and reference.

CPAPD Secretary–general An Yuejun and Deputy Secretary–general Tao Tao conduct the planning and command the selections, Chen Xiangyuan and Hou Hongyu conduct the editing and compiling, Lin Li, Yang lei, Song Yiming, Shen Fang, Lin Yongfeng, Sun Bowen, Wang Qing, Niu Na, Wang Shan, Feng Wei, Wang Ruijuan and Wu Kesheng do some editing and translating work.

Because of limited capability and lacking relevant work experience, the selection may have impropriates which we sincerely hope relevant experts indicate to the Editorial Group.

Editorial Group
November 2018.